WITHDRAWN

5/21/80

The French Revolution in San Domingo

BY

T. LOTHROP STODDARD

A.M., PH.D. (HARV.)

F
1923
.S87
1970

NEGRO UNIVERSITIES PRESS
WESTPORT, CONNECTICUT

Originally published in 1914
by Houghton Mifflin Company, Boston

Reprinted in 1970 by Negro Universities Press
A Division of Greenwood Press, Inc.
Westport, Connecticut

Library of Congress Catalogue Card Number 74-111588

SBN 8371-4614-3

Printed in the United States of America

TO MY MOTHER

PREFACE

THE world-wide struggle between the primary races of mankind — the "conflict of color," as it has been happily termed — bids fair to be the fundamental problem of the twentieth century, and great communities like the United States of America, the South African Confederation, and Australasia regard the "color question" as perhaps the gravest problem of the future. To our age, therefore, the French Revolution in San Domingo — the first great shock between the ideals of white supremacy and race equality, which erased the finest of European colonies from the map of the white world and initiated that most noted attempt at negro self-government, the black republic of Haiti — cannot but be of peculiar interest.

Strangely enough, the real story of this tremendous racial and social cataclysm has never been told, and it is to fill this gap in the history of modern times that this book has been written. For, be it noted, in this field, the race question, important though it be, is not the sole noteworthy element. San Domingo in 1789 was the most striking example of French colonial genius, and the struggle of the colony's formative ideals with the new political, economic, and social conceptions of the French Revolution is of great importance to the history of European colonization. The attempt to apply the Revolutionary ideals to an environment so radically different from that of France yields a most valuable side-light to the study of the French Revolution itself, while the attempt made under the Consulate to restore French authority and economic prosperity to San Domingo is one of the most illuminating episodes in the career of the master-figure of the age — Napoleon Bonaparte.

The keynote to the history of the French Revolution in San Domingo is a great tragedy, — the tragedy of the annihilation of the white population. The period opens in 1789 with a resident white population of nearly 40,000 souls, at the very pinnacle of material prosperity and possessed of a complex social organization, jealously guarding its supremacy and race identity in face of a large caste of half-breeds whose only bond of interest with their white superiors was a common exploitation of some half-million negro slaves. The period closes sixteen years later with the complete annihilation of the last remnants of the white population, the subordination of the mulatto caste to the negroes, and the destruction of the island's economic prosperity.

In this grim tragedy the chief figure is that of the black leader Toussaint Louverture. Unfortunately it seems improbable that the mists enveloping his personality will ever be cleared away. Extremely little first-class material exists, and practically everything written about him is of such doubtful value that his figure seems destined to remain forever shrouded in the haze of legend and tradition.

Excluding my five opening chapters of an introductory nature, describing the condition of San Domingo in 1789, the body of the work falls under two main heads. The

PREFACE

first of these is the downfall of white supremacy, brought about by internal dissensions, by the revolt of the mulattoes and negroes, and by the vigorous determination of Revolutionary France to destroy the colonial ideals of slavery and the color line. This culminates in the general collapse of white authority in the year 1793. The second main heading of the book is the progress of black supremacy, personified in the career of Toussaint Louverture. After seven years of constant struggle this supremacy becomes absolute; the English invaders are expelled, the mulattoes crushed, the Spanish portion of the island overrun, and French authority reduced to a vain shadow. By the year 1800, Toussaint Louverture is absolute master of San Domingo. But his power is short-lived. France is now under the First Consul Bonaparte, and the peace with England in 1801 frees his hands for the restoration of San Domingo to France. Under the shock of Leclerc's expedition Toussaint's power collapses, and though the complete conquest of San Domingo is delayed by yellow fever and Napoleon's restoration of slavery, the French triumph is averted only by the renewal of the struggle between France and England in 1803. The English war is, however, fatal to the French cause. Within a year the island is completely lost, and shortly afterward the last French colonists are exterminated by the negro leader Dessalines. White San Domingo has become only 'a memory, and the black State of Haiti makes its appearance in the world's history.

Of the source-materials for the present work, by far the richest collections are those preserved in the French archives, a full description of which may be found in the

PREFACE

appended bibliography. It is almost certain that no archival material remains in San Domingo itself. Toussaint's papers were captured by the French in 1802, and but few documents can have survived the century of civil strife which sums up Haiti's turbulent history. The printed material on San Domingo is extensive. From the earliest times the island attracted attention, the first writers on San Domingo being learned ecclesiastics. As early as 1733 the Jesuit Charlevoix published a four-volume history of the island, based upon still earlier unpublished writings. After the Seven Years' War (1763), San Domingo was by far the most important French colony, and the lively interest displayed by French thought on political and economic questions resulted in a considerable number of writings concerning the island. This growing literature was soon swelled by the humanitarian antislavery agitation which began to be noticeable after 1770. The outbreak of the French Revolution saw a flood of books, pamphlets, and brochures of every description and shade of opinion upon colonial questions in general and San Domingo in particular, and the intensity of output continues till the year 1793, when it sharply declines owing to the repressive influence of the Terror. The revived interest in colonial affairs under Bonaparte and the prospects of a restoration of white authority in San Domingo called forth a large number of writings from exiled colonists, while Leclerc's expedition resulted in several accounts by officers and civilians. The years following the Bourbon restoration in 1814 saw a series of writings by exiled colonists similar to that following the establishment of the Consulate in 1799, noted above; for France

PREFACE

had not renounced her claims on San Domingo and many persons hoped that the Bourbons would follow Napoleon's example after the Peace of Amiens, now that the general pacification of 1815 had again given the French fleets the freedom of the sea. When this hope was seen to be a vain one, however, interest in San Domingo died away. The few writings on the island during the years preceding the final abolition of slavery in the French colonies in 1848 are of little value. Of late years the subject has been touched upon by modern writers on the Old Régime and on Napoleon, while some twenty-five years ago an American writer (Mills) wrote a scholarly treatise directly on the first two years of the French Revolution in San Domingo, though he did not utilize any of the unpublished archival material. Critical notices upon all the important books in this field may be found in the appended bibliography.

In closing I desire to express my profound appreciation to all those who have so kindly assisted me in my work; especially, to Professor A. C. Coolidge, of Harvard University, the inspirer of the present volume; to Professors R. M. Johnston and R. B. Merriman, of Harvard University, for their suggestions on certain parts of the book; and to Messrs. Waldo G. Leland and Abel Doysié, of the Carnegie Bureau for Historical Research, for their assistance in my French archival researches. I desire also to express my appreciation of the privileges extended me by the Library of Harvard University, which so greatly facilitated my examination of printed material.

T. LOTHROP STODDARD.

BOSTON, June 20, 1914.

CONTENTS

I. INTRODUCTION AND EARLY HISTORY 1
Approach to San Domingo. Area. Spanish Conquest. The Buccaneers. Their Impress on San Domingo.

II. NATURAL FEATURES, POPULATION, AND GOVERNMENT 6
Contrast of French and Spanish San Domingo. French San Domingo: — The North, — The West, — The South. Population. Climate. Government. Confusion of Powers. Character. The Judiciary. Economic Situation of San Domingo. Trade with France. The "Pacte Coloniale." Its Results.

III. THE WHITES 19
Complex Structure of the White Population. Europeans and Creoles. Sterility. The Official Caste. The Nobility. The Clergy. Irreligion. The Middle Class. The "Petits Blancs." The Creoles. Wealth and Luxury. Consequences. Town Life. Country Life. The "Legend" of San Domingo.

IV. THE MULATTOES AND THE COLOR LINE . . 37
The "Free People of Color." Mulattoes and Free Negroes. Concubinage. Increase of Mulattoes. The Color Line. Its Necessity. The "Law of Reversion." Abhorrence of Miscegenation. Punishment of Renegades. Indelibility of Color. Status of the Mulattoes. The Mulatto Character.

V. THE SLAVES 50
Slavery. The Slave Population. Its Sterility. Slave Imports. The Slave Trade. Preponderance of Foreign-Born Negroes. Variety of Types. The African Negro. The Creole Negro. General Character. Religion. Condition. Work. Discipline. Legal Status. Actual Status. "Marronage." The Maroon Negroes. Negro Revolts. Macandal.

VI. THE EVE OF THE REVOLUTION IN SAN DOMINGO 68
States-General. Discontent in San Domingo. The Idea of Colonial Representation. Beginning of the Movement. In

France, — in San Domingo. Propaganda in France. The Authorities in San Domingo. Colonial Opposition to Representation. Fear of the States-General, — and of the Anti-Slavery Movement in France. Election of Deputies to the States-General. The Government Falls into Impotence. Colonial Propaganda in the French Elections. The "Club Massiac." The Struggle in the States-General. Fatal Results of Colonial Representation. Possibility that San Domingo might have Escaped the Revolution.

VII. FIRST STAGE OF THE COLONIAL STRUGGLE IN FRANCE 82
Rapid Progress of the Revolution. Alarm of the Colonists. Plan of a Colonial Assembly. The Mulatto Agitation in France. The Colonial Committee. Its Report, — and Decree of March 8, 1790. The "Instructions" of March 28. "Article 4."

VIII. THE FIRST TROUBLES IN SAN DOMINGO . . 90
Latent Unrest at San Domingo. Effect of the "14th of July." The Poor Whites enter Politics. Flight of Barbé-Marbois. The Provincial Assemblies, — they call a Colonial Assembly. Mulatto Unrest. Negro Unrest. White Reprisals. Results. The Mulatto Rising of March, 1790. Effects. Possibility of a Government-Planter-Mulatto Alliance, — which is not Realized.

IX. THE ASSEMBLY OF SAINT–MARC 100
Character of the Colonial Assembly. It draws up a Constitution. Its Nature. Tension between Government and Assembly. Peynier's Referendum. Beginning of Hostilities. The Chevalier Mauduit. The "Pompons Blancs." The Mutiny of the Léopard. Mauduit's *coup d'état*. Vincent's Expedition. The Fall of Saint-Marc. The Assembly leaves for France. The "Treaty of Léogane." Unsettled State of the Colony, — the West, — the South, — the North. Lack of Union against the Revolution. Ogé's Rebellion. Its Meaning. Its Results. It fails to heal White Disunion. Overthrow of Royalism in the West. Realignment of Parties.

X. THE DECREE OF MAY 15, 1791 115
Relative Security of the Colonial System till 1790. Attitude of French Conservatives, — and of the Colonists. Its Effect

CONTENTS

on the National Assembly. The Tide Changes with 1791. Report of the Grand Committee. The Great Debate on the Colonies. The Rewbell Amendment. It becomes the Decree of May 15, 1791. Its Results. Its Arrival in San Domingo. Its Reception. The new Colonial Assembly.

XI. THE NEGRO INSURRECTION IN THE NORTH . 128

Its Outbreak. Premonitory Symptoms since 1789. White Disregard. First Negro Successes. Causes of White Inactivity: — Mental Shock, — Disaffection within Le Cap. Bravery of the Country Whites. Terrible Nature of the Struggle. Negro Leaders and Tactics. Primary Cause of the Insurrection. Contributory Responsibility of the French Radicals, — of the Royalists, — of the Colonists.

XII. THE MULATTO INSURRECTION IN THE WEST . 142

The Mulattoes resolve to Strike. The Royalists of the West. The Alliance of Royalists and Mulattoes. The Confederation of La-Croix-des-Bouquets. The Concordat of September. Its real Significance. Renewal of the Troubles. Arrival of the Decree of September 24, 1791. Its Effects. The Burning of Port-au-Prince. Race War in the West, — and South.

XIII. THE FIRST CIVIL COMMISSIONERS . . . 153

Character of the Commission, — and of the Commissioners. Their Arrival at San Domingo. Their Negotiations with the Negro Rebels. Their Failure. Its Results. Breach between Commissioners and Assembly. The Commissioners and the West. Saint-Leger in the West. He returns to France. Crisis at Le Cap. The March Riots. Mirbeck sails for France. Roume remains, — to combat a Royalist Reaction.

XIV. THE LAW OF APRIL 4, 1792 166

Jacobin Hostility to the Decree of the 24th September. Jacobin Power in the "Législatif." Appeals from San Domingo. The Jacobins prevent the Sending of Aid. Effect on San Domingo. The Jacobin Assault on the Colonial System. The Report of January 10, 1792. The Approach of Jacobin Victory. The Law of April 4, 1792. Effect on San Domingo. The "Council of Peace and Union." Policy of Roume. His Journey to the West. Blanchelande in the South.

CONTENTS

XV. THE SECOND CIVIL COMMISSIONERS . . . 181
Coercive Nature of the Law of the 4th of April. The Second Civil Commission, and Commissioners, Polverel, Ailhaud, Sonthonax. Opinions on their Character. Was there a Jacobin Plot? The Commissioners' Instructions. Their Arrival at San Domingo. Their First Measures. Effect of the "Tenth of August" on San Domingo. The Royalist Conspiracy. The October Riots.

XVI. SONTHONAX'S RULE IN THE NORTH . . . 194
Arrival of Rochambeau. Plans against the Color Line. The "Affaire Théron." Polverel's Voyage to the West. Sonthonax's Rule at Le Cap. Remonstrances of Polverel. The December Riots. Results. Increasing Difficulties. Foreign War. First Moves toward Emancipation.

XVII. POLVEREL'S GOVERNMENT OF THE WEST . 206
Polverel at Saint-Marc, — and at Port-au-Prince. His Alliance with the Town Whites. The Desertion of Ailhaud. Polverel in the South. The Break-Up of Western Royalism on the Color Line. Hyacinthe's Maroon Rising. The Revolt of Port-au-Prince. Sonthonax in the West. Fall of Port-au-Prince. Rigaud's Defeat.

XVIII. THE DESTRUCTION OF LE CAP 215
Unrest at Le Cap. The Arrival of Galbaud. Alarm of the Commissioners. They Return to Le Cap. The Revolt of the Fleet. The Destruction of Le Cap. Attitude of the Commissioners.

XIX. EMANCIPATION 222
Exodus of the White Population, — and of the White Troops. Advance of the Spaniards. State of Le Cap. Sonthonax's New Policy. His Emancipation Proclamation. Its Extension to the West and South. Its Effects. Sonthonax's Perilous Situation. His Flight to the West.

XX. THE ENGLISH INTERVENTION 231
White Desire for English Aid. The Grande Anse calls in the English, — and receives a British Garrison. Surrender of the Môle-Saint-Nicolas. Defection of the West. Hopeless Condition of the North. Attitude of the Commissioners. Defection

CONTENTS   xvii

of the Mulattoes. The Convention Decrees the Commissioners in a State of Accusation. It is Disregarded. Anti-Colonial Feeling in France. The Convention abolishes Slavery. Effect on San Domingo. The Commissioners leave for France.

XXI. THE ADVENT OF TOUSSAINT LOUVERTURE . 246

His Early Life. His First Acts. Toussaint in Spanish Service. He changes Sides. Campaign against the English (1794). The Campaign of 1795. Rivalry of the Colored Castes. Rigaud's Rule in the South. Toussaint's Policy in the West. Rigaud's Policy in the North. The Mulatto Troubles at Le Cap. The Rising of the 30th Ventôse. Its Results.

XXII. THE THIRD CIVIL COMMISSIONERS . . . 258

The Third Civil Commission, — and Commissioners. Their First Acts. Sonthonax's Policy. Its Results in the North, — and South. Policy of Sonthonax and Toussaint. Toussaint expels Sonthonax. His Fears of its Effect on France. His Attitude.

XXIII. THE MISSION OF GENERAL HÉDOUVILLE . 269

Reasons for his Mission. Toussaint's English Policy. Hédouville's Policy. His Clash with Toussaint over the English Evacuation. The Expulsion of Hédouville.

XXIV. THE WAR BETWEEN THE CASTES . . . 276

Toussaint's Difficulties. He gains over Roume. The Conference between Toussaint and Rigaud. The War between the Castes. The Siege of Jacmel. The Conquest of the South. The "Bloody Assize" of Dessalines. The Ruin of the West.

XXV. THE TRIUMPH OF TOUSSAINT LOUVERTURE . 283

Toussaint's Projects against Santo Domingo. Opposition of Roume. It is Broken. Bonaparte's Commission. The Resistance of Santo Domingo. Its Conquest by Toussaint. Condition of French San Domingo. Toussaint's Reconstruction of San Domingo. His Favor to the Whites. Moyse's Rebellion. Toussaint's Constitution.

XXVI. THE ADVENT OF BONAPARTE 296

The Colonies at the 18th Brumaire. Napoleon's Constitutional Changes. Conflicting Views on the Future Colonial

xviii   CONTENTS

Policy of France. First Abortive Expedition for San Domingo. Further Tentative Measures. The English Peace frees Napoleon's Hands. Leclerc's Instructions.

XXVII. THE COMING OF LECLERC 308

Leclerc's Arrival at San Domingo. Toussaint's Attitude. His Position. Leclerc's Plan. Fall of Le Cap, — and Port-au-Prince. Surrender of the South, — and of Santo Domingo. Dessalines's Failure at Léogane. Leclerc's Negotiations with Toussaint. Capture of Port-de-Paix. Leclerc's Campaign. Toussaint's Defeat at Couleuvres. Dessalines's Defence of the West. His Failure at Port-au-Prince. Humbert's Defeat at Port-de-Paix. Capitulation of Maurepas. Siege of the Crête-à-Pierrot. Effect of its Capture. Submission of the Black Generals. Necessity for Leclerc's Policy of Conciliation.

XXVIII. THE COMING OF THE YELLOW FEVER . 326

Yellow Fever. Toussaint's Arrest. Its Effects. Toussaint's End. The Disarmament. Napoleon's Reactionary Policy. Leclerc's Alarm. The Reaction at Guadeloupe. Its Effect on San Domingo. Loyalty of the Black Generals. Leclerc's Despair. Ravages of the Fever. The Death of Leclerc.

XXIX. THE LAST PHASE 344

Defection of the Mulattoes. Their Attack on Le Cap. Defection of the Black Generals. Improvement under Rochambeau. Terrible Nature of the Struggle. The English War. The Loss of San Domingo. The Extermination of the Whites. The End of "San Domingo."

NOTES 351

BIBLIOGRAPHY 393

The French Revolution in
San Domingo

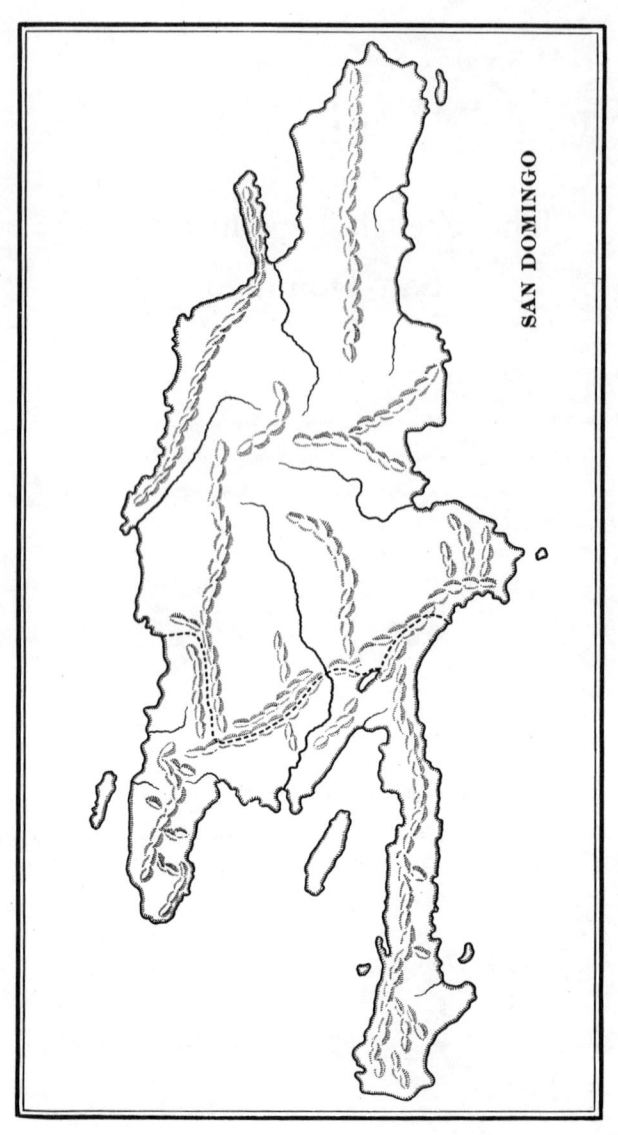

The French Revolution in San Domingo

I

INTRODUCTION AND EARLY HISTORY

THE European voyager who, on a morning of early 1789, raised the eastern cape of the island of San Domingo and sailed along its northern shore, had before his eyes substantially the panorama of to-day: a wall of high green hills, clothed with forests and backed by glimpses of mountain-peaks far in the hazy distance. No sign of man broke upon the lonely coast, for this was the decayed and neglected colony of Spanish Santo Domingo.

But when he had crossed the wide bay-mouth of Mancenille and again neared the land, the scene was changed as by an enchanter's wand. There lay before him a noble plain, teeming and throbbing with human life to its very background of lofty mountains; a vast checkerboard of bright green sugar-cane, upon which rose white columns of tall chimneys and tree-embowered plantation mansions. Where a mountain spur neared the sea, its slopes were belted with coffee-plantations almost to its wooded crest. When the sudden tropic night fell, the long coast sparkled with lights, while ever and anon a sudden flame from some boiling-house stack lit up the countryside with its glare.¹ For this was the French portion of the island, — "La Partie Française de Saint-Domingue."

Sailing next morning past the guns of Fort Picolet, the city of Cap Français came into view nestling under the craggy "Morne du Cap." ² This, the Metropolis of San Domingo, was a fine, stone-built town of twenty thousand souls. Over a hundred ships lay at anchor or beside its broad quays, while three thousand sailors swarmed upon its water-front or made merry in its many taverns.³ Into its warehouses poured ceaselessly the tribute of the great North Plain, — the produce of nearly three thousand plantations and the labor of two hundred thousand slaves.⁴ Here glowed most brightly the strange, hectic life of those eighteenth-century West Indies; — those island-factories, producing sugar and consuming slaves.

This magnificent colony, which supplied not only France but the half of Europe, was not very large. As a glance at the map will show, it was little more than two long peninsulas to north and south, connected by a strip of territory in places not more than twenty miles wide. By far the greater portion of the island remained in the possession of its original masters the Spaniards.

Columbus, its discoverer, had named it Hispaniola, and it had been the earliest centre of Spanish colonization. But a brief period of brutal exploitation had exhausted its mineral wealth and annihilated its numerous Indian population. The discoveries of Mexico and Peru rapidly drained away the restless *conquistadores*, and the island sank almost into oblivion. The few colonists who remained turned loose their cattle on the lonely land, and in time

INTRODUCTION AND EARLY HISTORY

troops of swine rooted in its virgin forests and herds of wild cattle grazed upon its silent plains.[5]

It was early in the seventeenth century that bands of interlopers began to settle upon those northern and western coasts which were to form the French portion of San Domingo.[6] These people were by no means predominantly French. The English were nearly as numerous, and there were other minor elements.[7] They found the western end of the island entirely deserted, for the Spaniards had always confined their settlements to the east, the regions of mineral wealth. Many of these men ranged the woods after the herds of wild cattle, whence their name "buccaneers";[8] others settled upon the little island of Tortuga, off the north coast, from which they sallied forth to prey upon Spanish commerce.[9]

For nearly forty years these nests of hunters and pirates pursued a bloody and tumultuous history. Three times the Spaniards descended upon Tortuga and laid it waste, while throughout this period the French and English elements strove for supremacy. The struggle was long and doubtful. As late as 1657 an Englishman ruled Tortuga, and not until 1663 were the French firmly established.[10]

Henceforth these regions might be considered French; but their early history had set upon them an indelible stamp which was to differentiate San Domingo from all the other colonies of France. Not French adventurers alone, but men of other nations as well, had settled the land and wrested it from the Spaniard; neither crown nor chartered company had brought them thither, but their own adventurous wills. Hence, the basic spirit of this young society was Liberty: Liberty in all its phases,

4   FRENCH REVOLUTION IN SAN DOMINGO

— political, legal, social, religious, moral, — the very antithesis to that ordered despotism of the Grand Monarque which ruled contemporary France[11]

Royal Governors now sat at Tortuga, men of ability and natural force, — but they could do little to increase the power of the Crown. The wild buccaneer spirit flamed up at the least sign of encroachment; indeed, this very temper was needed to protect the infant colony from its foreign enemies. For the Spaniard continued to threaten till the Peace of Ryswick,[12] while the English made continual descents up to the general peace of 1714.[13] Thus, after nearly a century of existence, San Domingo still essentially retained its lawless independence.[14]

At the death of Louis XIV, San Domingo was, it is true, no longer the pirate nest of an earlier time. The Governors had done their best to attach their unruly subjects to the land, had brought in wives, and had encouraged agricultural immigrants. There were distinct beginnings of farming and trade.[15] The long peace which prevailed until almost the middle of the eighteenth century saw the rapid growth of San Domingo in wealth and population.[16]

But the old spirit lived on. All the West Indies received unruly elements, but San Domingo seems to have been particularly marked in this respect. A Governor of Martinique complains of the number of persons leaving that island for San Domingo, "where they may give themselves up to hunting and disorder, and where licentious liberty is complete." [17] The Governors needed all their tact and coolness to prevent continual outbreaks. "In a word, insolence and mutiny were everywhere." [18]

Attempts to infringe upon commercial liberty were

INTRODUCTION AND EARLY HISTORY

answered by serious rebellions in 1670 and 1723, and the proposed chartered company régime had to be dropped. And it was very evident that these risings were but symptoms of the basic spirit of the colony. "These people have risen not only against the Company but against the King's authority," writes the Governor in 1723. "They demand tax exemption, free trade with all nations, and a republican liberty." [19] It is no mere academic interest which thus emphasizes the origin and early spirit of San Domingo. For, despite the marvellous economic and social transformation of the later eighteenth century, the old ideas lived on. In 1789, the colonists had not forgotten their early history. They claimed that San Domingo had "given itself to the King of France" upon certain conditions; [20] they considered the island no mere subject colony, but a "Franco-American Province," bound to France through the Crown: [21] a species of personal union somewhat like that of France and Navarre. On the day when the French people should destroy the Crown and claim for itself the right to break conditions which the Crown had always respected and which the colonists considered vital to their existence (the color line and slavery), it is easy to realize the moral sanction given to projects for resistance and rebellion.

II

NATURAL FEATURES, POPULATION, AND GOVERNMENT

IN 1789 French San Domingo was the gem of the West Indies, and the spectacle of its marvellous prosperity was perhaps enhanced by contrast with its Spanish neighbor. A short journey away from the fierce energy of the west coast across the border mountain wall brought one to a land where it was always afternoon: the same soil and a better climate had here produced only a deepening lethargy. Santo Domingo, the capital, was a handsome, picturesque old town, with many stately landmarks of its early prosperity, but elsewhere all was decay and solitude.[1] The total population was barely 125,000. These were mostly ranchers and herdsmen, for there was almost no agriculture and only some fourteen thousand slaves. Of the free population about half were rated white, though the color line seems to have been pretty loosely drawn.

French San Domingo was divided into three provinces, — the North, the West, and the South; this order corresponding to date of settlement and relative importance. The North Province was the oldest, richest, and most densely populated. Its glory was the incomparable "Plaine du Nord": its chief city, Cap Français (colloquially known as "Le Cap"), was the metropolis of the colony.[3] The North Province was shut off from the rest of the island by a difficult mountain-chain running east and west,

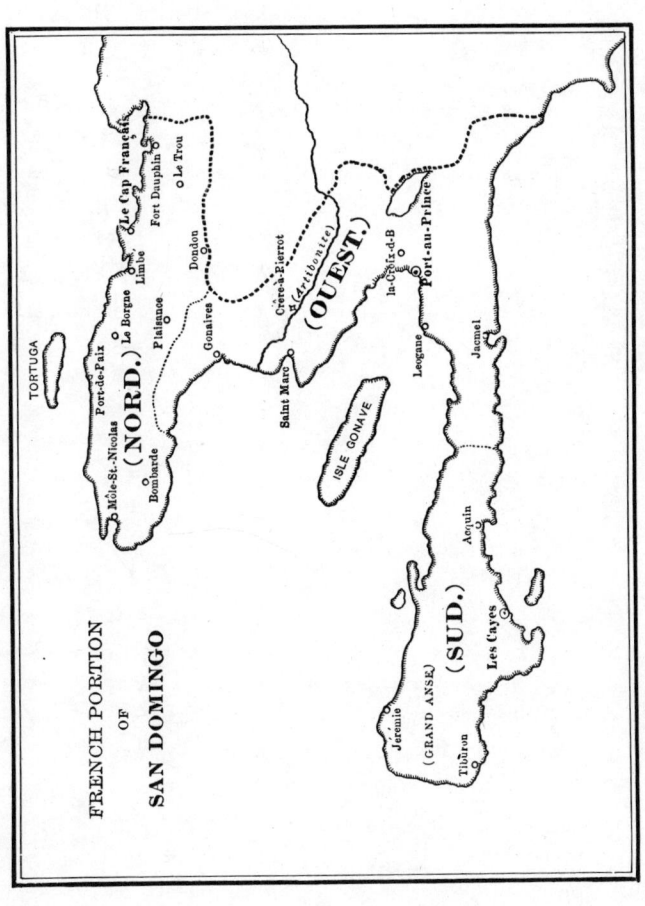

POPULATION AND GOVERNMENT

which continued out into the sea as a high peninsula tipped by the strong fortress of the Môle-Saint-Nicolas, the "Gibraltar of the Antilles." Although the North was so largely mountainous, the valleys were of great fertility and the lower hill-slopes eminently suited to coffee-planting. Only about the Môle was there a dry and sterile region unfit for agriculture.[4]

The West Province embraced the central portion of the colony, and much of the southern part as well. A glance at the map will show its extraordinary irregularity of outline, pressed close to the sea as it was by the sinuous mountain wall of the Spanish border. It must be noted that much of the long southern peninsula, which was the colony's most striking geographical feature, fell within its jurisdiction.

Although nearly twice the size of the North, the West Province was not so well favored by nature. The mountain ranges to north and east cut off the rainfall, and made its climate hot and unhealthful; precipitation came mostly from violent thunderstorms which were often more a damage than a benefit. Its prosperity in 1789 was largely due to elaborate irrigation, which made possible the regular cultivation of its plains. These were three in number: the wide, inland valley of the Artibonite in the upper portion of the Province, the small but rich plain of Léogane at the base of the southern peninsula, and the great plain of Cul-de-Sac, in rear of the city of Port-au-Prince.[5]

Port-au-Prince, although dating only from the middle of the eighteenth century, was a thriving town of some eight thousand inhabitants. The produce of the Cul-de-Sac made it a busy port, while its selection as the colonial

8 FRENCH REVOLUTION IN SAN DOMINGO

capital gave it added importance. Its appearance, however, was far inferior to that of Le Cap, for the prevalence of earthquakes made it a town of low wooden houses, which European visitors slightingly compared to a Tartar camp.[6]

The South Province was in all respects the least important. Its small area was entirely confined to the long southern peninsula, in reality little more than a mountain ridge sloping precipitately to the sea. Still largely undeveloped, the South's rather primitive economic and social conditions recalled the earlier times. It was, however, not devoid of possibilities, for there were many fertile valleys, and a real plain behind its busy little capital, Les Cayes.[7] One thing should be especially noted; — a narrow strip of sea alone separated the South Province from the English island of Jamaica, and a close intercourse had always existed in defiance of the laws against contraband trade.[8] In the storms of the Revolution this was to have important consequences.

The population of San Domingo was divided into three castes: the whites, the "free colored" (including both mulattoes and negroes), and the slaves. It is impossible to discover their numbers for the year 1789 with any great accuracy. The last official census was taken in 1788, and it seems to have been far from accurate. No official returns for the slave population can be trusted, since the planters made false reports to avoid the head-tax on their human chattels.

The official returns for 1788 give slightly under 28,000 whites, 22,000 free colored, and some 405,000 slaves.[9] For the year 1789 we have no official returns, but we do

POPULATION AND GOVERNMENT

possess two estimates from experts worthy of every consideration. The Intendant Barbé-Marbois, an exceedingly careful man whose official position ensured him accurate information, estimates the whites at 35,500, the free colored at 26,600, and the slaves at 400,000.[10] The deeply learned Moreau de Saint-Méry gives as his figures, 39,000 whites, 27,500 free colored, and 452,000 slaves.[11]

The climate of San Domingo was very bad, — possibly the worst of the West Indies. Official correspondence almost always mentions the writers' failing health, while the history of military operations in the island is one long tragedy of disease, from the decimation of the Anglo-Spanish expeditions in the wars of Louis XIV down to the final catastrophic annihilation of Napoleon's great army in 1803.

The writers on San Domingo unite in a general condemnation. "In this climate," writes an intelligent traveller about the year 1785, "the European must be always on his guard. The sun is a danger, the evening-cool a menace, the rain not less fatal." [12] Good health could be preserved only by abstemious living and the most careful precautions.[13] Hilliard d'Auberteuil's is the only voice raised in its favor,[14] but he is obviously making a polemical point,[15] — and his words called forth protests of amazement and indignation. "To-day," writes a colonist, "is the 30th of January; it is four o'clock in the afternoon; — and I am obliged to prop up Monsieur d'Auberteuil's book because I am sweating such great drops. What has caused this? — the climate or Monsieur d'Auberteuil's assertions? We will let him settle the question." [16]

The hot months from April to September were the most

unhealthful; they were the time of malaria and yellow fever. But the cooler rainy season was also scourged by intestinal troubles.[17] The only healthful spots were the barren island of Tortuga, and the dry and sterile district of the Môle-Saint-Nicolas.

Although the storms of the Revolution were to prove that the population of San Domingo had neither forgotten its early history nor lost its turbulent character, the profound transformations of the preceding half-century had greatly altered the spirit of government. Increase in wealth and closer connections with France had enabled the Bourbon Monarchy to tighten its grip upon the island.

"The government of the colony vested ultimately in the Minister of Marine, representing the King." [18] His edicts were laws, and he appointed the high officials.[19] But Paris was distant a six-weeks voyage, and the local heads of government were in practice the supreme authority. "Heads," be it remarked; for the local power was twofold, — the Governor and the Intendant. No parallel should be drawn with their fellows of contemporary France, for the Governor of San Domingo was the stronger factor.[20]

Theoretically each was assigned a special sphere, with a middle ground of joint activity. The Governor was the titular representative of the Crown, the military chief, and the medium of external relations. The Intendant, whose office dated only from the beginning of the eighteenth century,[21] headed the civil administration and the judiciary.[22]

But this division of powers remained largely a theory. To begin with, the respective spheres had never been permanently delimited. "The powers of the Governors were not fixed definitely by law, but were described in the commission given to each appointee and varied from time to time. To a Governor possessing a greater degree of the King's confidence, especial power would be given." [23] That large range of duties in which joint action was prescribed was another fruitful source of ambiguity. And, to these inherent difficulties, there was added the personal element. The Governor was always an old soldier or sailor; the Intendant always a bureaucrat. To place members of the "Noblesse d'Épée" and the "Noblesse de Robe" upon a remote island with interlaced authority was to court the usual result, — chronic rivalries and usurpations, which extended down through every grade of the administrations.[24] For each stood at the head of a numerous official hierarchy which naturally espoused the cause of its superior.[25] All eighteenth-century writers are loud in their censure of the endless confusion and scandal. "This hybrid civil and military administration called a government," exclaims Hilliard d'Aubertcuil in 1776, "has degenerated into a frightful mixture of tyranny and anarchy." [26]

In these struggles the Governor generally came off victorious. He was not only master of the regular military forces, but also head of the elaborate militia and *gendarmerie* system demanded by the island's strategic position and immense slave population.[27] His local commandants sometimes usurped both civil and judicial authority, and governed their districts under virtual martial law.[28] But the Intendant always opposed an annoying obstructionism, continuously invoked the intervention of the

12 FRENCH REVOLUTION IN SAN DOMINGO

Minister of Marine, and courted the favor of certain elements of the colonial population.[29]

As might have been expected, such a régime had a harsh and arbitrary character.[30] Its incumbents, however, boldly defended its necessity. "Yes," writes a Governor in 1761, "authority is in the hands of the military power: but this is the natural consequence of the colony's origin and present condition. Eight thousand whites capable of bearing arms are dispersed along three hundred leagues of coast. Nearly two hundred thousand blacks, their slaves and potential enemies, are about them day and night. Furthermore, these are men not bound to the land by ties of birth, loyalty, and blood, but drawn by self-interest from many regions." [31]

Nevertheless, though arbitrary and severe, the Government of San Domingo was by no means so black as painted by the democratic theorists of the time. Such a population, with arms in its hands and the backing of past tradition, would not have submitted to a very grinding tyranny. A native planter like Venault de Charmilly describes the force of public opinion, favored as it was by the internecine struggles of authority itself.[32]

But though there might be a dispute as to this Government's tyranny, there could be none whatever as to its costliness.[33] Bad finance was the besetting sin of the Old Régime, but nowhere was its disorder, wastefulness, and graft seen to better advantage than at San Domingo. In the year 1785 the Abbé Raynal had protested strongly against an expenditure of three million livres.[34] The official report of December, 1789, itemizes an expenditure of nearly five millions.[35] Taking Barbé-Marbois's census figures, this

POPULATION AND GOVERNMENT

would mean a yearly burden on the colonists of nearly one hundred and forty livres per head. The wealth of San Domingo, it is true, enabled it to carry the burden; but taxation was keenly felt, especially the hated poll-tax on slaves.[36]

The mere presence of antiquated methods, red tape, and the lack of a well-audited budget produced much leakage.[37] But there was a great deal of downright graft besides. A conservative observer like the Baron de Wimpffen speaks scornfully of the venality of the Governors,[38] and official peculation seems to have been as brazen as it was serious.[39]

Nevertheless, with all its faults, the Government was not without its good side. "Especially since the middle of the eighteenth century it had done much to better the economic situation of the island, had organized a good police, clarified justice, and improved taxation." [40]

But all this had been done in the spirit of the contemporary maxim, "Everything for the people, and nothing by the people." The official world was a caste of Europeans, in which the colonists had no part.[41] There was not even the humblest form of municipal self-government,[42] and the reforming era of Choiseul had given San Domingo only a couple of chambers of commerce.[43] It was this complete lack of political education which was to weigh so heavily in the Revolution.[44]

Until well past the middle of the eighteenth century, San Domingo had possessed a native judiciary. If we are to believe the colonists, it was endowed with every virtue,[45] but the testimony of officials and travellers leaves a different impression. In 1711, a royal officer is greatly scandalized at the procedure of a magistrate who pronounced judgment between pipe-puffs, the while a district attorney allowed litigants to curse one another at pleasure.[46] And, although time seems to have lent more dignity, the conduct of the legal class remained unedifying. In 1750, a registrar, formerly the proprietor of a gambling-house, installed a faro layout amid his official records to while away his idle moments.[47]

Nevertheless, though crude and unlearned in the law, this colonial judiciary seems to have given cheap and speedy justice in accordance with local conditions.[48] Not so the trained European lawyers who replaced them. Their procedure was as tedious at San Domingo as in the Parliament de Paris, and their pedantic application of French precedents to radically diverse cases was a constant source of injustice and irritation.[49] "The erudition of these gentlemen," exclaims Raynal, "has well taught us that the Coutume de Paris and the Institutes of Justinian were drawn up under a latitude very remote from that of San Domingo." [50] This impatience at the slowness and pedantry of the courts caused executive encroachment, and royal officers often usurped judicial functions, especially as they were thus striking at henchmen of the hated Intendant.[51] The cost of this latter-day justice seems to have been very great. De Wimpffen states that the Provincial Court at Jacmel had a budget of over four hundred thousand livres a year.[52]

In 1789, San Domingo "had attained a height of prosperity not surpassed in the history of European colonies. The greatest part of its soil was covered by plantations on a gigantic scale which supplied half Europe with

POPULATION AND GOVERNMENT 15

sugar, coffee, and cotton." [53] And the degree of this prosperity was increasing by leaps and bounds. Since 1786, "the planters had doubled their products, and a large amount of French capital had poured into the island for investment — a hundred millions from Bordeaux alone. The returns were already splendid and still greater were expected." [54]

San Domingo had undergone the economic transformation of the other islands. In the seventeenth century its products had been tobacco, cocoa, and indigo. These had been grown by many small proprietors of modest fortune, with the aid of white indentured servants and a few slaves.[55]

But the coming of sugar changed all this. The production of sugar is as much an industrial as it is an agricultural operation; it requires broad acres, a costly plant, and large working capital. The small holders quickly vanished before huge plantations worked by great gangs of slaves.[56] In 1789, the number of sugar-plantations was close upon eight hundred.[57]

However, sugar was by no means San Domingo's only product. Its cultivation was necessarily restricted to the plains and broader valleys, but French thrift had utilized everything except the mountain crests.[58] It is true that tobacco and cocoa had practically gone and that indigo was fast going, but other staples had come to take their place. First among these stood coffee, whose three thousand plantations covered every mountainside; while the cotton acreage was advancing year by year. The less favored districts were given up to pasture which fed some two hundred and fifty thousand cattle and swine.[59]

Such a colony was patently the most precious over-seas possession of France. The imports from her American colonies for the year 1789 totalled two hundred and eighteen million livres,[60] fully three fourths of which came from San Domingo.[61] Furthermore, of these imports France reëxported nearly two thirds, mostly after economic transformations which supported many branches of her industrial system.[62] In supplying the wants of the island, both the industry and the agriculture of France were interested. The fifty million livres of exports to San Domingo included everything from foodstuffs to tobacco-pipes; — "in a word, every object indispensable to civilized life." [63] Lastly, to all these profits there must be added the rich returns from the slave trade,[64] and San Domingo's predominant share in maintaining the fleet of a thousand ships and fifteen thousand sailors trading with the colonies.[65]

The splendid position of San Domingo might seem to have meant contented colonists; — in reality, they were hot with discontent: though prosperous, they well knew that they might have been more prosperous still. For they saw themselves the victims of that tyrannous economic system known as the "Pacte Coloniale." [66]

Normand has well summarized the principles of this system under five rules: (1) the colony must send its products only to the mother country; (2) the colony must buy only from the mother country; (3) the colony must establish no manufactures; (4) the mother country agreed to buy its tropical products only from the colony; (5) the carrying-trade with the colony must be the monopoly of the mother country's merchant marine.[67]

It is clear that only the fourth rule favored the colony; — the others sacrificed it to the mother country in the most ruthless fashion. Yet at the time, no principle was more generally established than the "Pacte Coloniale": all nations held it to be the keystone of colonial policy, and Colbert's dictum, "Colonies are founded by and for the mother country," [68] was considered an axiom. Even the intellect of a Chatham could contend that the colonies should not be allowed to make a nail or a horse-shoe. "The mother country saw in her colonists only a special kind of subjects, predestined to receive her products at an excessively high price and to yield theirs at a value abnormally lowered by the absolute lack of foreign markets and consequent competition." [69] They were "in every respect victims of monopoly." [70]

But, although the system of France was no stricter than her neighbors', it bore with especial hardship on her colonies. The reason for this was that the French merchant marine, although granted the monopoly of the carrying-trade, was quite inadequate to the supplying of the colonies.[71] Indeed, it showed no real desire to do so, and strove to keep up famine prices by this artificial scarcity.[72] The bitter gibes of De Wimpffen show the deep indignation felt at this conduct.[73]

And if the French colonies were kept short in normal times, how was it during the long wars of the eighteenth century, when the superior English fleets swept the French flag from the sea? For, be it understood, this was no mere question of annoyance or of loss, but a matter of downright life and death. Not one of these over-specialized islands produced enough tropical foods to feed its negroes, while the whites lived almost entirely upon imported provisions.[74] Were no grain-ships to enter their harbors, the colonists would die like Midas in his treasure-chamber. As a matter of fact, great numbers of slaves at San Domingo died of hunger during the Seven Years' War.[75]

Of course this preposterous state of things wrought its own cure. Smuggling had always existed at San Domingo; smuggling of the most flagrant character and with a backing of public approval which made its suppression impossible. A regular traffic existed with the English and Spanish islands, and with the North American continent.[76] Indeed, the Governors themselves openly permitted trading in times of especial scarcity.[77]

The growing enlightenment of the eighteenth century had led the French Government to attempt to remedy the situation, though in hesitating fashion. In 1767, Choiseul established a port of entry for foreign trade at the Môle-Saint-Nicolas, although legalizing only a small list of the most necessary foodstuffs.[78] In 1784, further concessions were made by the opening of the chief ports (Le Cap, Port-au-Prince, and Les Cayes), and by an extension of the legal list.[79] Finally, the Anglo-French commercial treaty of 1786 and the Franco-American convention of 1787 broke a wide breach in the "Pacte Coloniale." [80]

But, after all, the old system still existed in principle, and in 1789 the measures taken were either too partial or too recent to have produced much effect. In 1788, the foreign imports were only 7,000,000 livres, the exports only 3,700,000; [81] — not very much by comparison with the French trade. At the outbreak of the Revolution colonial discontent was bitter and unassuaged.[82]

III

THE WHITES

THOUGH small in number, the white population of San Domingo [1] was in structure extraordinarily complex. Its lines of cleavage were both many and transverse. This handful of Europeans formed in one sense the Microcosm of contemporary France, since all French classes were there represented;[2] yet in spirit the two societies were by no means the same, for in San Domingo, class relations had been much modified by a tropical environment.

To form a correct idea of this colonial society is by no means easy. Its observers often differ in their impressions and in their judgments. Still, the main lines seem to be fairly clear. Differences of opinion arise usually on details; on fundamentals, the bulk of both private and official testimony is in agreement.

The most obvious line of demarcation was one of birth. The antagonism between native- and foreign-born — or, in the language of the time, between "Creoles" and "Europeans" [3] — seems to have greatly impressed observers. "The first thing that strikes every traveller," says De Wimpffen, "is that in spite of the conformity of origin, color, and interests, the whites from Europe and the white Creoles form two classes, which, by their mutual pretensions, are so widely sundered that necessity alone can bring them together. The former, with more breeding, more politeness, and more knowledge of the world, affect over the latter a superiority which is far from contributing to unite them."[4] The number of shady characters among the Europeans did not promote good feeling.[5] Hilliard d'Auberteuil is particularly severe in his criticism of the European population and advocates radical restriction of immigration to protect the Creoles, whom he regards as by far the sounder element.[6] Of late years, however, the quality of the new arrivals would seem to have been improving.[7]

Yet even within its own ranks, the European class suffered from disunion: "This element, although generally energetic, hardy, and enterprising, at bottom lacked cohesion."[8] Environment and interest had succeeded in producing only the most superficial "consciousness of kind." The Abbé Raynal brings this out very well. "There is here," he says, "no national consciousness; because each one brings his own with him, — his native prejudices, education and vices. At the same time, while all these people retain their peculiar manners and customs, they yet take on what I may call the 'habits of the colonies.' This distinction is important, and should not be overlooked. Ordinarily, we seek for the character of a people in its national point of view; but, in San Domingo, there is no real 'people,' — only a mass of individuals, with common interests but isolated viewpoints. Even the Creole is not always an American; he is a Gascon or Provençal, if he has chanced to learn his father's dialect or imbibe his principles."[9]

Another point to be noted is that the white population of San Domingo was predominantly foreign-born; certainly over one half,[10] possibly even three fourths,[11] were of European birth. For this state of things there were several reasons. In the first place, the presence of an immense slave population had made a class of native white laborers impossible;[12] the "poor whites" of 1789 were in great part a vicious rabble of adventurers.[13]

And even among those townsmen and planters who composed the middle and upper strata of society, there were few marriages and fewer children. The causes of this sterility are not far to seek. To begin with, San Domingo had always lacked white women. In the buccaneer days their number had been extremely small, and the quality of those then sent from France had made these a doubtful blessing.[14] Although the large white immigration of the later eighteenth century had brought about more normal conditions, the numerical disparity of the sexes was still very great. In 1789, there were 24,700 white males to 10,800 females.[15] Then, again, the climate was very hard on the children of Europeans; "it took at least two generations before the race could strike root in this new land."[16] As among Anglo-Indians to-day, children were sent to Europe to escape the climate as well as to get an education.[17] Lastly, this was a population of fortune-hunters, not settlers, and the return to France was ever in men's minds. Absorbed in their affairs, with few ties of sympathy or social life, and possessed of luxurious or dissipated habits,[18] these men could have but little inclination to married life and the rearing of families.[19]

There was one element in this strange society which occupied a decidedly anomalous position. This was the official class. Although composed almost exclusively of Europeans, it stood as much aloof from its compatriots as from the Creole population, — a veritable caste apart.[20] The officials "had all that cool assumption of superiority and that disdain for those around them which so commonly mark the man of the metropolis when in the provinces." [21] Naturally, they were disliked, — a fact of importance for the Revolution.

The nobility had played a vital pioneer rôle in the other French islands,[22] but this had not been true of buccaneer San Domingo. However, from the first the Royal Governors had been men of birth, and the aristocratic element had steadily grown in importance.[23] In 1789, the colony possessed some of the oldest blood of France.[24] The nobility was one of the best elements of the island's population. Very many were settled as resident planters, and had become a genuine squirearchy. They officered the militia and the *maréchaussée*,[25] and were the stanchest supporters of law and order.[26] The relations of this island aristocracy with the French nobility were very close, and were becoming closer through frequent intermarriage.[27] "Sire," said a San Domingo deputation to Louis XVI, "your court has become Creole by alliances." [28] From these marriages there had grown up an intermediate class of absentee nobles. These men owned great plantations in San Domingo, but rarely visited their estates and were in no way a blessing to the colony. They were, however, to play an important part in the early days of the Revolution.[29]

The clergy of San Domingo were inferior to those of the other French islands: [30] their character seems to have been consistently bad from the first. "Most of the priests here are as debauched as the rest of the inhabitants," says an official memoir of 1681.[31] A century later, things were no better. "A succession of bad and ignorant priests," says the Abbé Raynal in 1785, "has destroyed both respect for the cloth and the practice of religion in almost every parish of the colony. An atrocious greed has become the habitual vice of most of the parish priests." [32] The sacraments were turned into so many instruments of extortion, while the churches were "falling into ruin." [33] The Baron de Wimpffen is even more severe. "The clergy of San Domingo," he writes in 1790, "seem to have voluntarily renounced the advantages which a system of conduct procures them elsewhere. Tranquil in their parsonage-houses, they spend in peace an income sufficiently large to enable them to live comfortably. Mass is celebrated one way or another in churches where none go to hear it — so that to avoid reproach of preaching in the desert, they do not preach at all. . . . Meanwhile, the conjectures, which public scandal delights to indulge on the children with which the female mulatto of Monsieur the Rector may have peopled the parsonage-house, keep their course; and, as this increase of family is, for His Reverence, as well as for the rest of the colonists, a sensible increase of fortune, you may easily comprehend that few will have the candor to suppose he is indebted for them solely to the good-will of his parishioners." [34] His opinion of the monks is equally unfavorable. "I am persuaded, sir," he writes, "that there are to be found amongst them men of real merit: at the same time, truth obliges me to avow they are not numerous; because the superior clergy, who nominate to the vacant benefices, have contracted the pernicious habit of sending none thither but such intriguing and suspicious characters as they wish to be rid of. To speak my mind fully on the subject, nothing, generally speaking, can be more irregular than the regular clergy of San Domingo." [35]

With such pastors, it is not surprising that the flocks lacked religious zeal. "It is incredible," writes the Governor in 1743, "what indifference these people have for spiritual things." [36] The sacraments were ignored, and parents left their children unchristened or mockingly baptized them in a punch-bowl.[37] The pious Father Labat is greatly scandalized both at the appearance of the churches and the temper of the people. He found the main church of Le Cap in a state of positive dilapidation, while the congregation "acted as if at a play-house. They talked, laughed, and joked; especially those in the balcony, who drowned out my voice, and mingled the name of God with their discourse in a perfectly intolerable fashion." [38]

The middle class at San Domingo was made up entirely of merchants and small shopkeepers. It was thus a strictly town population — a true *bourgeoisie*. No rural middle class could exist upon a countryside cut up into large, self-sufficing economic units like the plantations. The greater merchants, as the trusted factors of French commercial houses, were men of standing, but the small-fry contained many persons with a shady business past.[39] The middle class was almost exclusively European; the Creoles disliked town life, and lived in the country.[40]

The lower ranks of the white population of San Domingo were known as the "petits blancs." [41] This term may be best translated "poor whites," although it must be borne in mind that these people were in many ways dissimilar to the "white trash" of the Southern States, since the town-dwelling element was a heterogeneous rabble of foreign birth.

This absence of a normal white working-class was the inevitable consequence of a slave population outnumbering the whites tenfold. It might have been otherwise. In the early days San Domingo had possessed a class of small landholders and farm-laborers,[42] while the French Government had made real efforts to build up a white population by the system of indenture-men, or *engagés*.[43] In spite of their poor quality and bad treatment, these *engagés* had done fairly well, and it seems practically certain that if slavery had been excluded, San Domingo would have become the home of an acclimated white people.[44] But it was not to be. Slavery became the very basis of society — and wrought its logical consequences.

Among the poor whites of 1789 there ran a strong line of demarcation between those of the country and those of the town. All that was sound in the poor white population was to be found in the rural element. In the first place, these men earned an honest living. On every large plantation there was a small corps of whites, — overseers, technical experts, and mechanics.[45] In all, these must have numbered several thousands.[46] Then, the scattering small truck-farmers and ranchmen were usually classed as "poor whites" rather than "planters," while in the less tropical region of the Môle were certain agricultural colonies of Acadians and Germans.[47]

The poor whites of the towns, however, were nothing but a vicious rabble of adventurers, drawn to San Domingo by the luxury and dissipâtion of urban life. They were the scum of France, and of Europe as well, for very many were foreigners. Italians and Maltese predominated among the foreign element,[48] though there were representatives of many nations.[49] Even in ordinary times this mass of crooks and criminals needed careful police watching,[50] but with the revolution it became a downright peril. For it promptly caught up the patter of Jacobinism, and seized every chance of riot and plunder.[51] Furthermore, the brutality of these men to the negroes and mulattoes did much to envenom the race question.[52]

The garrison troops and the sailors in the ports were also not unimportant elements of white San Domingo. The island was permanently assigned two royal infantry regiments[53] and a strong detachment of artillery, in all about three thousand men.[54] The number of sailors of the royal navy and merchant marine in the ports of San Domingo must have always averaged several thousand. The presence of these men did much to determine the character of the port towns.[55]

But the native-born element of the population must not be disregarded. The Creole whites differed in many respects from those of European birth. In the first place, they were a rural, landowning population: a large proportion of the planters, with their dependents, were Creoles, and most of the small farmers and ranchmen as well. Both in mind and body the Creoles showed the influence of their tropical environment. Physically they were tall and slender, well-featured though pale, and with a proud nonchalance of bearing.[56] In character they were generous, warm-hearted, and brave, with a lively intelligence and an ardent imagination; at the same time they were reckless, frivolous, passionate, and often cruel, while their indolence usually hindered the development of their talents.[57]

The two main causes of the Creole's special nature were climate and slavery. It was the burning climate of San Domingo which gave him his mercurial temperament, — his intense crises of reckless passion or feverish energy, followed by reactions into languorous apathy.[58] But even more important was the influence of African slavery. He certainly owed most of his bad qualities to this evil institution, which seems to have degraded the master even more than the slave. Vaissière comments upon this very well. "Lost as they were among their immense herds of slaves, the colonists suffered two fatal consequences: by contact with these primitive beings, they necessarily absorbed much of these people's nature, defects, and vices; from a life spent almost wholly among inferiors, their own characters naturally degenerated."[59]

This fatal influence weighed upon the Creole from the very moment of his birth. A royal officer laments those Creole children "corrupted in the cradle by the negresses' milk and vices."[60] And everything contributed to stimulate the Creole child's wilfulness and vanity. That slave nurse, who dared give him no direct command;[61] those slave playmates, "condemned to flatter his lightest whim";[62] those parents, proverbial for over-fond indulgence;[63] — all these combined to make of him a pampered little tyrant, unable to endure the slightest opposition.[64] Most writers on San Domingo quote the classic story of the Creole child who, told there was no egg, demanded two.[65] Add a precocious knowledge, gained by constant observation of the indecencies and cruelties of plantation life,[66] and the conduct of the future man when exposed to the temptations of unrestrained authority is easy to foresee.[67]

Much of the evil might have been remedied by a sound education. But to the Creole even this was denied. "What, then," exclaims De Wimpffen, "is the inhabitant of San Domingo? That which every man must be who is born under a burning atmosphere, with a vicious education and a feeble government. He is born neither corrupt nor virtuous, neither citizen nor slave, but his character will form itself the instant education and government, in concert with nature, shall occupy themselves with the care of giving him morals. At present, we ought to set the higher value upon his good qualities, as his education has hitherto been calculated to give him none but bad ones.[68] . . . To tell you what should be done to ensure the children of San Domingo a good education, would be to tell you precisely everything that is not done at present." [69]

Many children, it is true, were sent to France for their education. But they there learned little to fit them for a colonial existence, and generally returned fine ladies and gentlemen to whom the monotony and loneliness of plantation life were unendurable.[70]

In the Creole women, the type characteristics came out most strongly. Piquantly beautiful, their languorous grace charmed all observers. Their love was passionate in the extreme, their jealous hate often terrible in its consequences.[71] An American woman, who saw them in the days of their adversity, is favorably impressed. "The Creole ladies," writes Miss Hassal in 1802, "have an air of voluptuous languor, which renders them extremely interesting. Their eyes, their teeth, and their hair are remarkably beautiful, and they have acquired from the habit of commanding their slaves an air of dignity which adds to their charms. Almost too indolent to pronounce their words, they speak with a drawling accent which is very agreeable. But since they have been roused by the pressure of misfortune, many have displayed talents and found resources in the energy of their own minds, which it would have been supposed impossible for them to possess." [72]

Even more than her brothers, the Creole girl suffered from the blight of slavery and the lack of education. Too often, she lived in the most complete indolence; passing her days, like an Eastern odalisque, amid the chatter and singing of her slave girls.[73] She had few friends, for social life was confined to infrequent balls, to which she gave herself with the greatest *abandon*.[74]

In 1789, San Domingo rightfully enjoyed a widespread reputation for wealth and luxury. Its prosperity really dates from the long peace after 1714, but from then on progress was rapid.[75] Increase in wealth, however, quickly destroyed the simplicity of buccaneer days.[76] "At first," says an official memoir of 1718 on the state of the North Province, "the inhabitants of this quarter were adventurers, used to all kinds of labor; they walked barefoot in the sun without a thought of danger, so hardened were they by continual exposure. But since the late peace [77] has made as many fortunes as there are inhabitants, their manner of life is entirely changed. Instead of a bit of wild boar and bananas, on which they used to make merry after having had to hunt the beast in the woods, their tables are now laden with well-served delicacies. The best burgundy and champagne are not too dear for them, — they must have them at any price. They no longer dare go out before sundown for fear of the heat, and even then only in a carriage with comfortable springs." [78]

With such rapid progress in wealth, it is no surprise to find that at the outbreak of the Revolution there were many persons possessed of large fortunes. From three plantations in San Domingo, Alexandre de Beauharnais drew a revenue of forty thousand livres,[79] and many a great planter had an income of over one hundred thousand a year.[80] These figures, however, by no means represent net cash values. The hardships of the "Pacte Coloniale,"[81] the scarcity of ready money,[82] and the universal extravagance combined to devour these princely revenues; and some of the greatest proprietors were deeply in debt.[83]

A prodigal luxury was, indeed, the most striking feature of life. "Everything at San Domingo," writes Moreau de Saint-Méry, "takes on a character of opulence which astonishes the European."[84] People dined "'à la créole' — that is to say, with profusion,"[85] and their tables were served by such numbers of waiting-men as cut off the very air.[86] A numerous troop of domestics was the surest way to show one's wealth and self-importance.[87] "That crowd of slaves which hangs upon the master's lightest word or sign," says Moreau de Saint-Méry, "lends him an air of grandeur. It is beneath the dignity of a rich man to have less than four times as many servants as he needs. The women have an especial gift for surrounding themselves with a useless retinue." [88]

However, about all this magnificence one peculiarity must soon have struck the attentive observer, — its "personal" character. These costly feasts were very likely served between bare walls, while the guest, who bore upon his person ten thousand livres in lace and jewels, probably dwelt in a house unfurnished and unadorned.[89] But the trend of conversation would soon give the key to the riddle, — the table-talk must have inevitably turned upon the delights of Paris and the prospect of approaching trips to France.[90]

Except among the Creoles, few persons cared to prolong their stay beyond a lucky turn of fortune. "The pleasures of San Domingo," exclaims a colonist, "are easily counted. A blue sky, and no cold weather: I can name no others." [91]

The consequences of all this were obvious. "A man," says Moreau de Saint-Méry, "regards himself as camping upon a property worth several millions. His air is that of a life-tenant already old, his extravagance is in servants and good-cheer, — and you would think him to be living in an 'hôtel garni.'" [92] "In a San Domingan town," says Raynal, "you never see a man seated by the domestic hearth and talking with interest about his borough, his parish, or the home of his fathers; you see only inns and travellers. Everything will confirm my statement. Enter these people's houses, — they are neither comfortable nor adorned. 'We have no time' — 'it's too much trouble' — that is what they tell you." [93]

In fine: "All wish to be gone, every one is in a hurry; — these people have the air of merchants at a fair." [94]

With such a general passion for money-making in the shortest possible time, a high code of business ethics could not prevail, and it is no surprise to learn that many of the fortunes made at San Domingo were amassed by very shady practices.[95]

Of course, in such a society, there was much high living. Drunkenness had always been a common failing at San Domingo. "There are many heads here, used up by drink," writes a Governor in 1710,[96] and his words would have equally well applied to 1789. Rum was cheap, — and full advantage was taken of the fact. "The people here," writes an Intendant, "drink this sort of liquor (which is of uncommon strength) as naturally and as copiously as we do wine." [97] The number of taverns was very great.[98] Gambling was also common to all ranks of society;[99] while the fame of the mulatto girls of Le Cap had spread far and wide through the West Indies.[100]

Such were the port towns of San Domingo, — crude, but full of life. Those rich merchants and ladies, decked in gay clothes and jewels; those gangs of sailors on shore-leave; those chattering crowds of negresses with their vivid turbans; those mulatto courtesans, gorgeous in towering headdresses and flaming scarves, — all these must have made a brilliant picture of peculiar interest.[101]

The life of the countryside, though it differed in many respects from that of the towns, was in essence the same: the same material crudity was there, the same intellectual poverty and mental isolation. The planter's house, though large and spacious, was generally bare and comfortless; it was always devoid of taste.[102] "Taste, sir," exclaims De Wimpffen, "is still Creolian at San Domingo. And unfortunately, the Creolian is not the right taste. It smells too much of the Boucan."[103] Even the richest plantations had about them an air of shiftless neglect. In a journey through the West Province, De Wimpffen is greatly surprised at its aspect. "What you will have some difficulty, sir, to believe of a country so rich as this," he writes, "is, that of the two kinds of plantations which we passed, one showed us only the picture of indolence in the last stage of wretchedness; and the other, that of the negligence and disorder of poverty, contrasted with the pretensions of opulence directed by the most execrable taste. Thus, you would sometimes meet an elegant carriage drawn by horses or mules of different colors or sizes, with ropes for traces, covered with the most filthy of housings, and driven by a postilion bedaubed with gold — and barefoot."[104]

The chief drawbacks to plantation life were monotony and loneliness. The strict regimen imposed by the climate [105] and the unvarying cycle of tropic agriculture [106] made the planter's existence one of deadening routine. Furthermore, he was practically cut off from the world. His nearest neighbor was sometimes miles away, and he lived as on an island, — alone with his family or mulatto housekeeper, surrounded by a horde of negro slaves. "The loneliness of the plantations" is a recurrent phrase in letters from San Domingo.[107]

And that distant neighbor? With him our planter was probably upon the worst of terms. Isolation had ended by giving both of them the hermit's abnormal craving to be alone, and "imperceptibly they had at last become by nature what they had been at first merely through necessity." [108]

All observers note these unsocial and quarrelsome tendencies among the planters.[109] "In the spot where I reside," writes De Wimpffen, "the neighbors hardly know one another. Pretensions, either ill-founded or ridiculous; jealousies of each other's fortune, more ridiculous still; disputes about boundaries . . . and finally trespasses committed by the negroes or the cattle — occasion such a misunderstanding, or such a coolness, that all reciprocal communication is out of the question. Consequently, as nothing is so savage as the recluse who is not so by choice, you must not be surprised that each owl rests in his hole, and that so little sociability reigns among men who have few or no sociable qualities." [110] Indeed, the famous "Creole hospitality" of former days was become little more than a memory.[111]

Such was San Domingo: assuredly the place to find fortune, but scarcely the choice for a home. And yet, curiously enough, there has grown up the "legend" of San Domingo. All the popular writers have painted this lost colony of France as a cross between Paradise and Eldorado.[112]

This legend seems to have been first built up by the "memories" of those refugees who, scattered through France, North America, and the West Indies, filled two continents with their lamentations. It was but natural that these impoverished exiles should have looked back with longing to their better days, and should have promptly idealized their lost homes. It is interesting to

THE WHITES 35

find the legend already well formed by the opening of the nineteenth century.[113]

And of course, human sentiment also favored. The dramatic shock of this immense catastrophe, by which a land at the very pinnacle of wealth and prosperity was suddenly blotted out and as much lost to white civilization as though sunk like Atlantis beneath the waves, lent an aureole of mystery and poetic charm.

But the foundations of the legend had been laid long before. The returning colonist had always loved to dazzle the French public, and many a man had ruined himself by a scale of living suited only to the purses of the wealthiest planters. De Wimpffen overwhelms this failing with his scorn. "Do not," he writes, "suffer yourself to be imposed on by the puerile and ridiculous pomp which certain planters display in their transient residence at Paris or in the maritime towns. I am in the secret of these quacks. This coach in which His West Indian Worship so awkwardly parades, that wardrobe of the Marquis de Mascarille, these jewels which sparkle on his tawny fingers, are the profit of many crops and the price of no small number of his slaves. Yet a little while, and hard necessity will send the clownish niggard back, half-civilized and wholly stripped (like the daw in the fable) of his borrowed plumes, to begin again with an aching heart those labors which scarce produced in ten years as much as he spent in ten months, with no other advantage than having raised a laugh at his expense from the *chevaliers d'industrie* who stripped him of his wealth, and the prostitutes who shared with them in the spoils. I never met a West Indian in France who did not enumerate to me, with more emphasis than accuracy, the charms of a residence in San Domingo: since I have been here, I have not found a single one who has not cursed both San Domingo and the obstacles eternally reviving, which, from one year to another, prolong his stay in this abode of the damned." [114]

De Wimpffen is, at times, a little hard on San Domingo. The returned colonist was probably moved not merely by vain-glorious pride, but also by the joyous intoxication of the man just back from the wilds with plenty of money in his pocket. Still, the result was the same; and the "Creole" became to France what the "Nabob" was to England, — the archetype of the wealthy man.

IV

THE MULATTOES AND THE COLOR LINE

MIDWAY between the white and slave populations of San Domingo stood a caste known as the "free people of color." [1] Numbering some twenty-seven thousand,[2] and possessing a considerable share of the island's wealth, it was a factor of the utmost importance.

Although certain of these people were full-blooded negroes, by far the greater number were mulattoes [3] of various shades.[4] The mulattoes looked upon the free negroes with unconcealed dislike, but this never caused an open breach within the caste; the free black fully shared the mulatto's contempt for the slave, and refused to make common cause with his blood-brother. For this reason the free negroes never played an independent rôle, and the "free people of color" may be treated as the caste of the mulattoes.[5]

The scarcity of white women had made illicit relations between the colonists and their negresses inevitable from the first. The Government disapproved, but its efforts availed little to check this concubinage,[6] and "scions of the great names of France — a Vaudreuil, a Chateauneuf, the last of the Boucicaults — might be seen passing their lives between a negress and a bowl of rum."[7] The negro women made no resistance. They lacked the European ideal of chastity,[8] and they had strong reasons for welcoming their masters' favor. "The negresses," says an

38 FRENCH REVOLUTION IN SAN DOMINGO

official memoir of 1722, "are proud of having children by white men. Also, they cherish the hope that the fathers will free them or buy their liberty." [9]

Later on, when mulatto women had become sufficiently numerous, the wealthier whites took them as their concubines. So general became this custom that the census of 1774 showed five thousand out of seven thousand free colored women living as white men's mistresses,[10] while mulattresses also formed the courtesan class of the port towns.[11] Other influences besides that of sex contributed to bring about this state of things: the planter or merchant regarded his mulattress as a necessity, both to manage his complex household and to warn him of plots among his slaves.[12]

Given such conditions, however, it can be no surprise that mulattoes appeared early and increased rapidly in numbers. The exact rate of this increase cannot, it is true, be known, for the census counted only the free mulattoes, not those who remained in slavery. But even these partial figures are significant enough. The census of 1681 shows 210 mulattoes in San Domingo.[13] By the year 1700, the numbers of the free colored had risen to some 500 individuals; and this figure progressively rose to 1500 in 1715; 3000 in 1745; 6000 in 1770; 12,000 in 1780; and 27,000 in 1789.[14] Of course, in this series, allowance must be made for free negroes. Also, of the mulatto element many were the children of mulatto parents. Still, from the habits of the mulattresses, it is clear that a large proportion of their children must have had white fathers.

Although marriage between the races was never pro-

MULATTOES AND THE COLOR LINE

hibited by law,[15] the number of such unions was always extremely small. Now and then a wealthy mulattress did succeed in obtaining a white husband, but this was an exceptional event.[16] Hilliard d'Auberteuil, writing in 1776, states that there were only three hundred such cases in the colony.[17] For few white men there were bold enough, or reckless enough, to cross the color line.

White San Domingo was obviously much divided against itself, but there was something upon which it was at one. Creole or European, poor white or planter, smuggler or governor, — all remembered that they were white; all were determined that the white race should keep white and should rule San Domingo.

Yet, in numbers, the white stock was but a handful scattered amid the masses of the black; and beside it there stood a growing mixed caste, part of which was white to the casual eye.

To safeguard the ideal which they held most at heart, the colonists felt there was but one way, and they ran a racial dead line, so straight and clear that there could be no crossing. To this the Home Government made no demur, for the Old Régime shared the colonial ideal to the full and backed it with all the force of authority.

The color line is the key to the Revolution in San Domingo. When the Men of 1789 questioned it, the colonists warned them that no change would be tolerated. When the conquerors of the Old Régime laid hands upon this social fabric, white San Domingo rose in furious rebellion; and this small handful, though threatened with annihilation by its race enemies at home, defied the whole power of regenerated France. When they had been beaten in the horrible struggle that ensued, these men refused to surrender, abjured France, and gave themselves to the foreigner. In their grim devotion to an ideal, the colonial whites passed the bounds of politics: the religious fanaticism of the Vendée was no fiercer than the racial fanaticism of San Domingo.

From the very earliest days the colonists had been brought to realize one apparent fact, — the fact of that greater assimilative power of the black blood later formulated as the "Law of Reversion." Once let the black principle enter a stock, and it seemed impossible ever to breed it out again: the moment fresh infusions of pure white blood ceased, the mulatto apparently began to revert to the negro. The learned Jesuit Father Labat notes this early in the eighteenth century,[18] and Moreau de Saint-Méry writes to the same effect.[19]

Elaborate scientific experiments were made by slave-owners with an enquiring turn of mind, — and the law apparently held good in the most extreme cases.[20] On a plantation of one of the smaller French West Indies there were married two mulattoes, neither of whose ancestry had suffered an infusion of black blood for six generations. "These young people were of remarkable beauty. Their hair was extremely blond, their features retained no negroid trace, and their skin was so white that they might have been taken for albinos, had it not been for the supple vigor of their limbs and the unusual brightness of their minds. Well — their children were unmistakably colored, and their grandchildren of an extremely dark shade.[21]

"After an experiment such as this, a man might well

MULATTOES AND THE COLOR LINE 41

ask how many successive marriages with whites were necessary to really destroy in a family all trace of negro blood, and it is easy to understand why pure white families always refused to marry with persons having the smallest drop of the black. For, once permit this first marriage, and it needed only a second to turn a white family into mulattoes. And — from mulatto to negro, the way was short; it needed only one or two steps of the same kind.[22]

"The instinctive horror of the European for mixed marriages is thus easy to understand, and the reason becomes plain why, in San Domingo, law and custom united to devise every possible means of preventing this confounding of the bloods." [23]

The feeling against miscegenation was present from the earliest times, and it was shared by both the Government and the Church. "I do not think," writes an Intendant in 1681, "that marriages of whites to mulattresses, or of mulattoes to white women, would be good for the colony. Indeed, by what I have already seen, I am only too well convinced of the bad results of such marriages, which have caused much scandal and disorder. It is true that the debauchery of the Spaniards and Portuguese has brought them to alliances with such an impure stock; but I can also say that their colonies are abodes of abomination, vice, and filth, and that from these unions there has sprung a people so wretched and so weak that an hundred of our buccaneers can put to rout a thousand of that *canaille*." [24]

In his official report of 1722, the Superior of Missions is perhaps even more emphatic. According to this high ecclesiastic the increasing numbers of mulattoes, illegitimate or not, is exposing the colonies "to the terrible punishment of those famous cities of abomination, which were destroyed by the fire of Heaven." To him, the mingling of the races is "a criminal coupling of men and women of different species, whence comes a fruit which is one of Nature's monsters." [25]

And the Home Government shared this attitude. In certain of the French colonies [26] mixed marriages were forbidden, and although they were never formally prohibited in San Domingo, the disapproval of the royal authority was made perfectly clear. A ministerial letter of 1741 commends an Intendant who had prevented such a union. "His Majesty's pleasure," it runs, "is not to permit the mixing of the bloods; your prevention of the marriage in question is therefore approved." [27]

On the white renegade who married a woman with the least trace of negro blood, law and opinion joined in imposing a legal and social ostracism which made of him a veritable outcast. He could hold no public office, no position of trust or confidence.[28] His wife's wealth could do but little to relieve his miserable condition. "Everything around these men," says Hilliard d'Auberteuil, "calls forth regret. Everything which consoles others plunges them in sadness. Their life is one long agony." [29] The status of the white renegade is well defined by the legal commentator Desalles. "The white who marries a colored woman," he writes in 1786, "descends from his rank of white, and becomes the equal of the freedman. In equity, he ought to be put lower; for he who, through weakness, is untrue to himself, is still more likely to be

MULATTOES AND THE COLOR LINE 43

untrue to the laws of human society." [30] Like the political traitor, the white renegade suffered "corruption of blood." His children followed the mother, and became merely free mulattoes.[31]

Nevertheless, these measures were largely of a preventive character. But, if mulattoes possessed of wealth and almost imperceptible in color were not to slip across the line, positive measures appeared to be called for. It was therefore thought necessary to mark down the members of this caste through all its generations.[32] This was possible through a careful system of birth and marriage records, and every disputed case involved lengthy genealogical researches. The elaborate care exercised to prevent a mulatto from changing his legal identity is best shown by the minute classification of his color. Moreau de Saint-Méry enumerates over sixty recognized combinations.[33]

On the necessity for this indelibility of color, the Home Government was as strict as colonial opinion. "The negroes," writes the Minister of Marine in 1766, "were brought to the colonies as slaves, and slavery has imprinted an indelible mark upon all their posterity whether of mixed blood or otherwise. Consequently, their descendants can never enter the white class. For, once reputed whites, they could, like whites, lay claim to every honor and office; — a state of things absolutely contrary to the constitution of the colonies." [34] And a ministerial letter of 1771 states that nothing can destroy that difference "which Nature herself has created between white and black, and which policy has ever been careful to uphold as a barrier which the mulattoes and their posterity may never overcome." [35]

The color line was valued not only as the sole means of preserving the purity of the white blood, but also as the best moral restraint upon the slaves. "This law is hard," says an official paper, "but it is both wise and necessary in a land of fifteen slaves to one white. Between the races we cannot dig too deep a gulf. Upon the negro we cannot impress too much respect for those he serves. This distinction, rigorously upheld even after enfranchisement, is the surest way to maintain subordination; for the slave must thus see that his color is ordained to servitude, and that nothing can make him his master's equal. The colonial authorities should be ever zealous in severely enforcing both this distinction and this respect." [36]

A planter expresses colonial opinion very well. "It was by means of this unalterable superiority of the white race," says Carteau, "that, until the Revolution, nearly 600,000 blacks, continually armed,[37] obeyed without a murmur a handful of masters. Especially, as this superiority was not purely ideal. The negroes themselves recognized it by daily comparing the activity, energy, knowledge, and initiative of the whites with the degree of those same qualities in themselves and in the mulattoes." [38]

On the eve of the Revolution, the growing pressure of that section of French public opinion which favored the mulattoes led the Home Government to waver slightly in its attitude. In 1788, the Minister of Marine asked the Governor whether it might not be feasible to forbid research into the origin of persons whose appearance was entirely white. But the Colonial Government answered that this would be positively dangerous. "The colonial prejudice toward mulatto families," came the reply,

MULATTOES AND THE COLOR LINE 45

"cannot be overcome. Any attempt to coerce public opinion on this point would endanger the King's authority." [39] In the light of what was so soon to follow, this reads like a prophecy.

From the theory of the color line, the actual status of the free mulattoes in 1789 can be easily imagined. The discriminations against them were both many and severe. They were forbidden to hold any public office or to engage in the learned professions; they were declared incapable of acquiring a patent of nobility or of receiving the higher decorations, such as the Cross of Saint-Louis; they were hindered by sumptuary laws from adopting European dress and habits; they were assigned special places in theatres, inns, churches, and public conveyances.[40]

Many of these measures were of quite recent date, for, as time passed, the mulatto status had become more and more rigidly defined. This has been sometimes held as the result of growing race feeling; but such a theory mistakes the effect for the cause. In the early days, the mulattoes had been too few to even dream of effecting any change in their situation. But, with the course of time, things had become different. The mulattoes had grown very numerous; they were often wealthy and possessed of a European education; many of them appeared white. Such persons devised every possible means to escape from their present condition, and strove desperately to evade the laws which bound them to their caste.[41] It was this increasing pressure upon the color line which called forth the sharper legislation of the later eighteenth century. Of course feeling steadily rose on both sides, and race hatred was very intense in 1789.

There was one field, however, in which the mulattoes had never been restrained, — the acquirement and holding of property.[42] How large a share in the wealth of the colony was held by them is difficult to say. In 1789, the mulatto leader Raymond claimed that his caste was possessed of one third the landed property and one fourth of the slaves.[43] On the other hand, Gouy d'Arcy, one of San Domingo's deputies to the States-General, writes that the mulattoes owned one tenth of the land and fifty thousand slaves.[44] Gouy d'Arcy's statement is probably nearer the truth, for he was then attempting to prove the generosity of the white planters in endowing their natural children, whereas Raymond is trying to show the general importance of his caste.

The bitter feeling between the races exposed the mulattoes to much ill-treatment. For this, the poor whites were mainly responsible. The wealth which many of the mulattoes possessed filled the needy adventurers of the towns with envious fury, and spurred them on to insult and injury.[45] In the latter part of the eighteenth century, the authorities seem to have protected the mulattoes against the grosser forms of outrage,[46] but there was a wide field which existing law could not reach.

This persecution, however, had very serious consequences. To the mulatto's general feeling of social oppression there was added a sharp sense of personal injury, a burning thirst for vengeance, of ominous import for the days to come.[47] This danger had not passed unnoticed by attentive observers. At the very beginning of

MULATTOES AND THE COLOR LINE 47

the eighteenth century, a high ecclesiastic had predicted that the mulattoes would become a future menace to the colony.[48] "Be on your guard," says an official memoir of somewhat later date; "these people are but waiting their chance to take a terrible revenge."[49] The council of Port-au-Prince is positively prophetic. "These are dangerous people," says its memoir to the Home Government. "In a time of trial or of revolution, they will be the first to throw off a yoke which galls them the more that they have become rich, have whites in their pay, and have lost much of their respect for our kind."[50] With the first signs of the coming storm, the thousands of mulattoes, trained to arms in the militia and the *maréchaussée*, were to become a menace to be greatly feared.[51]

The mulatto's character was not of a high order. How much his failings were due to his nature, how much to his environment, it is difficult to say. Undoubtedly, his position under the Old Régime was both hard and degrading. Nevertheless, many mulattoes were men of considerable wealth, who had received a European education, and who had lived for years in France, where they not only suffered little social discrimination, but were greeted with sympathy and consideration by an increasingly large section of society. And yet, when the Revolution had given them complete equality and when circumstances had made them masters of much of the island, they failed to rise to their opportunities. The mulatto caste produced no man of striking talents or eminent ability. There is no mulatto Toussaint Louverture.

The most detailed analysis of the mulatto character is in Moreau de Saint-Méry. "The mulattoes," he says, "are well made and of a quick intelligence, but they share to the full the negro's indolence and love of repose. Experience has shown that these men would be capable of succeeding in all the mechanical and liberal arts, were it not that their great desire is to do nothing. The mulatto journeyman works when pressed by want, then idles till the same thing happens again. Undoubtedly, there are exceptions. We all know mulattoes who are really industrious. But the ease with which these may be counted proves the general rule. The mulatto loves pleasure. It is his only master, but a despotic one. To dance, ride, and sacrifice to voluptuous pleasure, — behold his three passions. He equals the white creole in the first, he far surpasses him in the last." [52]

The mulattoes always had the reputation of being generous and hospitable people, and the women were especially noted for kind-heartedness, and for extreme compassion towards poverty and suffering. But their moral natures were weak. The mulatto women were very vain, frightfully extravagant, and extremely licentious.[53] Their moral standing in the later eighteenth century has been already noted,[54] and it seems to have been the same from the earliest days. "Most of the mulattresses," says a Governor in 1681, "are not only prostitutes themselves, but the procuresses of others' prostitution." [55]

From the controversial writings of the Revolution, it might almost be thought that the mulattoes were, *ipso facto*, freedmen. The reason for this is that both sides were interested in diverting attention from the slaves of mixed blood. The mulattoes wished to make out that they had little in common with the slave class, while the

MULATTOES AND THE COLOR LINE 49

colonists desired to prove a generous dislike of leaving their own blood in servitude.[56]

But a study of earlier writers and of official correspondence proves that mulatto enfranchisement was by no means a matter of course, and that the number of such slaves was very large.[57] As careful a modern writer as Roloff estimates them to have made up ten per cent of the entire slave population,[58] — that is, a figure of from forty to forty-five thousand.

This is a matter of some practical importance. Surprise has sometimes been expressed that, in the struggle between the mulattoes and the negroes which took place after the collapse of white authority, the mulattoes should have held out so long. This is far easier to explain if we consider that, as far as the mulattoes were concerned, it was a war of colors, not of castes, and that all, regardless of origin, had united against black domination.

The lack of union between the free negroes and their slave brethren has been already noted.[59] This was not the case with the mulattoes. The mulatto slave felt himself the superior of the free black. "There is not a negro who dares buy a half-breed or quadroon," says Moreau de Saint-Méry. "Should he do so, the slave would prefer death to such a dishonor;"[60] — a striking testimony to the prestige of white blood in colonial San Domingo.

V

THE SLAVES

AFRICAN slavery was the curse of San Domingo. From the very beginning, this dark shadow lay athwart its path, and perverted both its social and economic history. Present even in buccaneer days, with the opening years of the eighteenth century the evil institution became a basic principle and wrought its most fatal consequences. "Negroes, and food for the negroes; that is the one rule for the Colonies." [1] This maxim sums up the eighteenth-century ideal.

Under the régime of slavery, San Domingo prospered, it is true; but only for the moment, and at the cost of its whole social and economic future. Socially, it was a land based upon brute force and a racial dead line. Economically, it became a field of feverish exploitation, whose end must be complete exhaustion. Negro slavery touched this young society, just quickening with lusty life, and made it an abortion.[2]

In 1789, the slave population of San Domingo was enormous; — certainly 450,000,[3] very possibly half a million.[4] And it had been increasing with ever-growing rapidity. The census of 1681 gives the slave population as but 2000,[5] and that of 1687 as only about 3400.[6] Later census figures are unreliable, owing to fraudulent returns,[7] but we possess certain official memoirs drawn up for the information of Ministers of Marine, which are probably near the truth. In one of these, the number of slaves by the year 1701 is estimated at 20,000,[8] and another memoir reckons 230,000 slaves by the year 1754.[9]

But rapid as was this increase, it was due to immigration, not to births; the slave population of San Domingo never reproduced itself, and always showed a tendency to die out. The annual excess of deaths was fully two and one half per cent, — over 11,000 persons, reckoning on the conservative basis of 450,000.[10] When we consider that by the year 1789, nearly a million negroes had been introduced into San Domingo during the course of its history,[11] this matter appears still more important.

The continual dying-out of the slave population in a favorable climate excited much comment at the time, and many reasons for it were given. In 1764, a Governor attributes it to improper food, undue labor imposed upon pregnant women, and a very high infant mortality.[12] The general opinion seems to have been that the negroes were worked too hard,[13] and Hilliard d'Auberteuil asserts that this was often deliberately done, as many masters considered it cheaper to buy slaves than to breed them.[14] A colonial writer lays much of the trouble to immorality among the negroes, and to the ensuing ravages of venereal disease.[15]

Modern writers have advanced further reasons. Peytraud, perhaps the ablest student on the subject, thinks that much stress should be laid on the great nervous strain imposed by the sudden change from the careless indolence of savage existence to a life of continuous labor.[16] His contention seems to be sound. It was apparently this more than anything else which killed off the enslaved Indian population; if the negro, less nervous and more robust, survived, it was only after a costly process of natural selection.

Leroy-Beaulieu holds that, by some fundamental law of nature, slavery hinders man's reproduction, as captivity does that of wild animals.[17] Certainly the sterility of the slave population was not confined to San Domingo; it was common to the other West India islands without distinction of nationality.[18] Wallon pithily sums up the matter. "Slavery," he says, "like Saturn, devours its own children." [19]

It is obvious that to cover an annual deficit of two and one-half per cent,[20] and to provide a steady increase as well, the yearly importation of negroes must have been progressively large. The statistics, however, are both insufficient and faulty, while no record was kept of the smuggled negroes, whose number is put at fully three thousand a year.[21] The official figure for 1764 is ten thousand and that of 1766 is thirteen thousand.[22] An official memoir on the state of French commerce in 1785 gives the number of negroes exported to San Domingo from the West Coast of Africa as thirty-four thousand, not including three or four thousand from Mozambique.[23] Another memoir estimates the importation of negroes for the year 1787 at over forty thousand.[24] This is probably the approximate figure for 1789.

These great importations were effected by means of the slave trade.[25] At the outbreak of the Revolution, this was a great and highly organized industry.[26] In 1787, there were ninety-two ships exclusively employed in supplying the French colonies with negroes,[27] and in 1788 the number had risen to one hundred and five.[28] The traffic was enormously lucrative, and was considered as the great source of prosperity by the French maritime towns.[29]

The slaves were obtained from a chain of "factories," stretching from the Senegal clear around the Cape of Good Hope to Mozambique. The Senegal region had been the earliest slaving centre, but as time went on this moved steadily down the coast. In 1789, the trade centred on the Congo and Angola coasts, while the Mozambique branch was a late development.[30] At every stage of the traffic the slaves were exposed to great hardships, and the crowded slave-ships often became veritable death-traps. The horrors of the "middle passage" have left an evil memory. The average death-rate during the voyage was from seven to eight per cent.[31]

One of the most important considerations for the history of the Revolution in San Domingo is the fact that a majority of the negro population was African-born. Hilliard d'Auberteuil writes that in 1775 the Africans outnumbered the Creole negroes by ten thousand,[32] while Moreau de Saint-Méry states that in 1789 this proportion had increased to almost two thirds.[33] It is therefore essential to know something of this majority, born, not under the influence of white supremacy, but in African savagery.

As might have been expected from the extent of the slave coast, the negroes of San Domingo were of very mixed origin.[34] The first slaves had naturally come from the Senegal region. They were all of a relatively high type. The pure negro races of this region (Bambara,

54 FRENCH REVOLUTION IN SAN DOMINGO

Mandingo, etc.) rank well up in the scale of negro ethnology, while much of this section of Africa is inhabited by races which are not straight negroes at all. Such are the Fulah, a copper-colored people of doubtful origin, and the "Black Moors" and Joloffs, who have much Fulah, Berber, and Arab blood.

As time went on, however, the new arrivals became of a steadily lower type. The slaving centre gradually shifted to the Guinea Coast, and the Guinea negro was a being far inferior to the black of the Senegal. In 1789, the slavers were bringing mostly Congo and Angola negroes, many of these being among the lowest of the black race. Such were the cannibal Mondongo, who sawed their teeth into sharp points, while the Angola negroes smelled so horribly that the air was "tainted for a quarter of an hour after they had passed." [35] The negroes of Mozambique seem to have been physically weak and to have stood the climate badly. They began to come only on the eve of the Revolution.

But despite diversity of origin, certain general traits appear to have been common to all the various types. Peytraud has ably summed up the opinions of writers who have observed the negro in his African home. "The negro," he writes, "is a grown-up child, living quite in the present and the absolute slave of his passions. Thus his conduct displays the most surprising contradictions. He is trifling, inconsistent, gay; a great lover of pleasure, and passionately fond of dancing, noisy jollification, and striking attire. His natural indolence is unparalleled, — force and cruelty alone can get out of him the hard labor of which he is capable. This, together with an inordinate sensuality, an ineradicable tendency to thieving, and absolute lack of foresight, a boundless superstition favored by a mediocre intelligence, and timidity in face of imaginary terrors combined with great courage before real danger, appear to be the causes of the negro's lack of progress and of his easy reduction to slavery." [36]

Turning now to those who observed the African in San Domingo, we find the most careful analysis in Moreau de Saint-Méry. "The Africans," he says, "usually remain indolent and lazy. They are quarrellers, boasters, liars, and given to thievery. Always addicted to the most absurd superstition, there is nothing more terrifying to them." [37]

The negroes born in the colony appear to have been somewhat superior to those fresh from Africa. As to the degree of this superiority there seems to have been a slight difference of opinion. According to Moreau de Saint-Méry, "The Creole negroes are both physically and mentally above those just brought from Africa. Accustomed from their birth to a civilized environment, their minds are less dull than the Africans'.... Generally speaking, their value exceeds that of the Africans by about one fourth." [38] And he adds that house-servants and artisans were nearly always Creole negroes, on account of their higher intelligence. Another colonial writer is not so optimistic. "As regards the Creole negroes," writes Ducœurjoly, "their up-bringing improves them a little; but they always closely resemble the original type." [39]

One thing seems clear: the differences between native- and foreign-born were so comparatively slight that observations on the negro population as a whole will apply to both classes. A correct estimate is, however, a matter of difficulty. Opinions are very numerous, sometimes irreconcilable, and frequently prejudiced. Even the most conscientious observer could study only a limited number of individuals, whose environment must have varied extremely between a good and a bad master, and whose inconsistencies of conduct must have caused great perplexity. Add to these inherent difficulties the fact that many years before the Revolution the question of slavery had begun to inflame opinions and change observers into partisans, and the obstacles to correct judgment can be easily seen.

Partisan writings vary in the most extraordinary fashion. Antislavery circles pictured the negro as a good type of that "man in a state of nature," that "noble savage," which was one of the favorite ideas of radical thought in the later eighteenth century.[40] The most extreme example of this is probably a certain three-volume romance published in 1789, entitled "Le Nègre comme il y a peu de Blancs," which endowed the negro with all the virtues of the legendary Golden Age. On the other hand, the hotter defenders of slavery portrayed him as a depraved species scarcely to be classed among mankind,[41] while one writer roundly asserts that the negro is not a human being at all, but a superior species of orang-outang.[42]

The bulk of moderate opinion, however, follows fairly closely the estimates previously quoted regarding the African negro.[43] De Wimpffen probably best avoids extremes. "The negro," he says, "just like ourselves, is good or bad, with all the different shades that modify the

THE SLAVES 57

two extremes. His passions are those of uninformed nature: he is libidinous without love, and gluttonous without delicacy. ... He is indolent because he has few of the wants that labor is calculated to satisfy. He loves repose, not for the sake of enjoying it as we do, nor for the opportunity of finding in tranquillity the moral fruition which a state of physical activity had deprived him of; but for the sake of doing nothing. ... Generally speaking, the negroes are neither false nor perfidious; sometimes you will find a knave among them, who was probably in Africa a physician, sorcerer, or priest. Such a man is extremely dangerous. ... Whether it be that they have false or confused ideas on the nature of 'meum' and 'tuum' I know not, — but so it is, that the greatest part of the negroes are thieves. Like all men whose religion is confined to a few superstitious practices, they have no idea of a conventional morality. Whatever good qualities the negro has, he derives from nature." [44]

Those of the negroes who came from the Senegal country had a dim idea of Mohammedanism.[45] The great majority, however, were adherents of that fetishism which appears to be the native African religion, and though they quickly acquired a veneer of Christianity, the hold of this old religion never seems to have been broken.[46] The cult of "Vaudoux" flourished in spite of every effort to stamp it out,[47] and is powerful in Haiti to-day.[48] The fact that the negroes possessed a religion and a priesthood of their own was to be of the greatest importance in the coming uprising against white rule.

The negro's happiness or misery depended entirely upon the character of his master. This is proved by the amount of contradictory testimony from careful observers. We are given pictures of really happy life — and glimpses of a perfectly intolerable existence. In general, the good seems to have outweighed the bad.[49] The negro's surroundings were, it is true, of the simplest character. His "quarters" were primitive in the extreme, his creature comforts few. But then he had known nothing better in his African home, and the climate required little in the way of shelter or of clothing.[50] On Sundays and feast days he was free from labor, and he was allowed to keep the profits of his garden-patch and hen-yard. That these earnings were not negligible is shown by the quality of his holiday attire, which seems to have greatly struck observers.[51]

Yet, after all, the great central fact in the negro's life was work. The house-servants and artisans seem to have had a fairly easy time,[52] but the mass of the slave population led a life of hard and unremitting toil. From dawn to dark the field-gangs pursued their monotonous round of labor, exposed to the burning tropic sun, spurred on by the whips of the black "commanders" under the overseer's eagle eye.[53]

The fundamental principle of San Domingo's economic life was forced labor. "The refractory slave could not be discharged like the free workman — he must be coerced." [54] And it was evident that this coercion must be severe: to extract continuous labor from such essentially indolent beings as the negroes, an iron discipline was necessary. "To manage those immense herds of men and to keep them in order," says Vaissière, "there was needed a master with a hand of iron. This becomes doubly clear when we consider the enormous disproportion which everywhere prevailed between blacks and whites. Here were isolated plantations where two or three whites were surrounded by two or three hundred slaves. The slightest weakness might engender a revolt which could never be put down. Thus, this system of perpetual coercion was not only the one way to extract from the negro continuous labor, — it was also the sole means of repressing his bent towards crime and of guarding against his plots." [55]

All persons well acquainted with colonial conditions affirmed this necessity. "I arrived at Martinique," writes a Governor of that island to the Minister of Marine, "filled with all the European prejudices against harsh treatment of the negroes. But I have quickly become convinced that there must be a discipline not only severe, but severe in the extreme." [56]

The great enforcer of this discipline was the lash. "The whip," exclaims a French antislavery writer, "is the symbol of labor in the Antilles." [57] And this was perfectly true. Whipping was the chief recognized punishment, though its variations extended all the way from a slight correction to a virtual sentence of death.[58] At the same time many other forms of punishment were inflicted in practice, and cruel or depraved masters were guilty of most horrible excesses.[59]

In the very early days, the negro had no legal protection whatever. As regards the purchaser, the negro was his "thing," and the master might "do as he would with his own." The slave of the seventeenth-century Antilles was thus the *instrumentum vocale* of the old Roman Law.[60]

But this state of things ceased legally after 1685. In

that year, Colbert promulgated the "Black Code," [61] which, though inspired more by economic than humanitarian motives, set distinct bounds to the master's power.[62] The principles of the Black Code were reaffirmed and slightly strengthened by the Edict of 1724, while the Ordinance of 1786 reflects the progress of ideas by its very sharp provisions against neglect and cruelty.[63]

Such was the law; — in theory really humane on the eve of the Revolution; the trouble was that it had never become a fact. There is no doubt that the softening of manners and the increasing enlightenment of self-interest had combined steadily to better the lot of the slave.[64] At the same time he enjoyed little real protection against a cruel or ignorant master.[65] For, however much authority and public opinion might reprobate these excesses, they simply did not dare to punish the guilty for fear of the effect upon the slaves.

The Royal Government recognized this clearly. "If it be necessary to repress abuses of unhumane masters," writes the Minister of Marine to Governor Larnage in 1741, "see that you take great care to do nothing which may impair their authority over the slaves, for this might cause a breaking-down of the necessary bounds of dependence and submission." [66] "It is only by leaving to the masters an almost absolute power," read the instructions given a new Intendant in 1771, "that we can succeed in holding such vast numbers of men in that state of submission necessitated by their preponderance over the whites. If persons abuse their authority, repress them covertly; — but never let the slaves think that their masters can do them wrong." [67]

THE SLAVES 61

Edwards touches the fundamental difficulty. "In countries where slavery is established," he writes, "the leading principle on which government is supported is fear; or a sense of that absolute, coercive necessity which, leaving no choice of action, supersedes all question of right. It is in vain to deny that such actually is, and necessarily must be, the case in all countries where slavery is allowed. Every endeavor, therefore, to extend positive rights to men in this state, as between one class of people and another, is an attempt to reconcile inherent contradictions, and to blend principles together which admit not of combination. The great, and I am afraid the only certain and permanent, security of the enslaved negroes, is the strong circumstance that the interest of the master is blended with, and in truth altogether dependent upon, the preservation, health, strength, and activity of the slave." [68]

In 1788, on the very eve of the Revolution, the illusory character of slave protective legislation was strikingly illustrated by the "Affaire Lejeune." Lejeune, a coffee-planter, had suspected a poisoning conspiracy among his slaves. To discover the guilty parties, he inflicted upon several of his negroes a series of fiendish tortures. Some of the terror-stricken blacks complained to the authorities, an investigation followed, and Lejeune's guilt was proved to the hilt. But this was only the beginning. The case had become the talk of the colony, already stirred as it was by news of the antislavery agitation in France. Governor and Intendant were soon bombarded with letters, petitions, and addresses, begging them to suppress this dangerous scandal. "In a word," writes the

Intendant Barbé-Marbois to the Minister of Marine, "it would appear that the safety of the colony depends upon the acquittal of the Sieur Lejeune." [69] This was, indeed, what actually occurred. The case was appealed to the highest court of the island, which handed down a decree of acquittal, — "thus affirming once again the solidarity of all whites as against their slaves." [70]

Bryan Edwards, as we have seen, states that the base of slave societies is fear.[71] This is true, — and true in its broadest sense. For, if the slave feared the master, the master also feared the slave. In the background of San Domingan life, there lowered a dark shadow, of which men thought much even when they spoke little.

And this was no veiled or distant peril; no year passed in which it failed to give bloody proof of its imminent presence. The mass of the slave population, indeed, might bend or break beneath the yoke, but there was always a minority of untamable spirits who burst their bonds and sought an outlaw's freedom. In a mountainous country like San Domingo this was easy, and soon every tract of forest and jungle came to have its wild denizens.

This state of outlawry was termed "marronage," and the runaways themselves were known as "marrons," — or, in English, "maroons." For like conditions were common to all the West India islands; as Peytraud justly remarks, "Marronage was the endemic social plague of the Antilles." The greatest efforts were made to stamp out this evil, but in spite of a well-organized rural *gendarmerie*, the maroon bands could never be exterminated. The many wide tracts of tangled mountain, covered with

THE SLAVES 63

impenetrable tropical forest, offered the fugitive negroes an almost inaccessible retreat. This was especially true of the high ranges along the Spanish border. Safe in these wild solitudes and secured against hunger by a spontaneous food-supply, the maroon bands would often descend by night upon the plains and valleys to steal cattle, sack plantations, and murder travellers.[72] A colonist, writing in 1772, states that at that very moment the mountain districts back of Port-au-Prince were "desolated by their frequent incursions."[73]

And, as time went on, the numbers of the maroons steadily increased. During the year 1720 alone, over one thousand negroes took to the woods, while in 1751 a high official estimated the refugees in the mountains of the Spanish border at over three thousand.[74] Of course great numbers were recaptured or killed by the *maréchaussée*, while many soon died from the accidents of a wild life; but the stream of recruits never ceased, and, as there were many women among the bands, a native maroon population gradually came into existence. These men, born out of slavery and inured to a savage life, acquired a tribal consciousness which marked them off as a peculiar people. On the eve of the Revolution, the Colonial Government followed the example of the English in Jamaica and the Dutch in Surinam,[75] and recognized the tribal existence of the maroons on the Spanish border by a convention of the year 1784.[76]

The maroon negroes are a not unimportant factor in the struggles of the Revolution. They jealously maintained their identity, rendered important service to the English and Spanish invaders, and fiercely resisted Tous-

64 FRENCH REVOLUTION IN SAN DOMINGO

saint Louverture's efforts to subject them to his authority. They welcomed Napoleon's army, and, together with the free negroes of the Old Régime, they became the most loyal allies of the French.

Even in the best of times, the maroons were a source of trouble. The reason why colonial writers do not devote more attention to the problem is because it was one of those constant factors which had come to be taken as a matter of course. Now and then, however, a significant side-light is thrown upon the question. For instance, when the first rumors reached France of the great negro insurrection of August, 1791, a retired officer of the *maréchaussée* wrote an open letter to one of the daily papers, warning against exaggeration. He thinks that the reports then current may be based upon some acute access of the chronic marronage, and he gives a sketch of his own experiences which portrays a state of genuine guerilla warfare.[77] Of course, as it turned out, rumor had not belied the truth; yet this letter is none the less valuable evidence for conditions under the Old Régime.

And now and then these wild bands found a leader. Then the annoyance became a peril; — it acquired the consistency of a revolt. For the maroons kept in touch with the enslaved negroes, and could always stir many to trouble.

Slave revolts had taken place throughout the colony's history. In 1679, a Spanish negro formed a conspiracy "to massacre all the French."[78] Foiled in this purpose he formed an entrenched camp among the mountains, and was only put down after a regular campaign.[79] And this, at a time when the slave population was only two

THE SLAVES

thousand as against five thousand whites. In 1691, two other black leaders were hunted down and executed for having planned "to massacre all the whites in the district of Port-de-Paix,[80] down to women and children at the breast." [81] In 1704, the negroes about Le Cap conspired "to kill by night all the whites of that quarter." [82] It is true that the hand of Spain was thought to have been in these troubles, but subsequent affairs of a perfectly spontaneous nature prove that foreign instigation was at most only a contributing cause. In 1703, an able leader arose who for seven years spread terror by the sack of plantations and the rape of white women, while scarcely was he killed than a successor appeared who baffled the *maréchaussée* for twelve years.[83] These men, it is true, do not seem to have entertained the idea of a regular insurrection, and the steady increase of settlement after 1714 must have discouraged the prospects of a successful rising; nevertheless, the early decades of the eighteenth century show quite a list of notorious outlaws.[84]

But about 1750 there appeared a man of real ideas and powerful personality who was to become a veritable menace to the colony. This man was the famous Macandal. Macandal was an African, whether from the Senegal or Guinea is uncertain. For more than six years he abstained from active warfare against the whites while strengthening his influence over the negroes. His power was of a religious nature, for he announced that he was the Black Messiah, sent to drive the whites from the island. His magic powers gave him the authority of a veritable Old Man of the Mountain, and the superstitious negroes considered him a god. He had a clear idea of race, and concerning it, gave utterance to the following remarkable prophecy: One day, before a numerous assembly, he exhibited a vase containing three handkerchiefs colored yellow, white, and black, which he drew out in turn. "Behold," said he, "the first people of San Domingo — they were yellow. Behold the present inhabitants — they are white. Behold those who shall one day remain its masters" — and he drew forth the black handkerchief.[85]

At last, about 1758, he thought the moment come for his great stroke. His plan rested on the wholesale use of poison. Poison had always been the chief slave method of obtaining revenge. It assumed the most diverse forms: poisoning of the master, of his children, his cattle, his slaves, — even self-inflicted poisoning, if the party thought himself a chattel of value.[86] But Macandal united poisoning to marronage for a definite end. According to an official memoir, the plot was woven with consummate skill. On a certain day all the water of Le Cap was to be poisoned, and, when the whites were in convulsions, Macandal and his maroon bands were to raise the waiting negroes of the "plaine" and exterminate the colonists. Only by the merest chance was the conspiracy discovered. The terror among the whites was great, and Macandal was relentlessly hunted down and executed. Yet even in death he left behind a legacy of unrest, for he prophesied that he would one day return, more terrible than before. This was believed by many negroes, and the colony was never free from poisonings and disturbances.[87]

The great negro insurrection of 1791 was thus only the coming to pass of what had been awaiting the favor of circumstance since the colony's beginning. Its possibility had long been foreseen. "We have in the negroes most dangerous enemies," writes a Governor in 1685. A century later,[88] a royal officer exclaims, "A slave colony is a town menaced by assault; we are walking on barrels of powder." [89] His words were true; — and sparks from the edicts of Revolutionary France were soon to fall upon those powder-barrels.

Such was San Domingo: materially prosperous, but socially diseased. In closing this sketch of the colony at the outbreak of the Revolution, let us quote the farewell of De Wimpffen: "Will you have, sir, my parting word on this country? It is: the more I know the inhabitants, the more I congratulate myself on quitting it. I came hither with the 'noble' ambition of occupying myself solely in acquiring a fortune; but destined to become a 'master,' and consequently to possess 'slaves,' I saw, in the necessity of living with them, that of studying them with attention, to know them, — and I depart with much less esteem for the one and pity for the other. When a person is what the greater part of the planters are, he is made to have slaves; when he is what the greater part of the slaves are, he is made to have a master! Tout le monde est ici à sa place!" [90]

VI

THE EVE OF THE REVOLUTION IN SAN DOMINGO

On the 19th of November, 1787, Louis XVI promised a calling of the States-General. The phrasing, it is true, was vague, and the date set 1792, but now that the Notables had failed to give relief [1] it was plain that the bankrupt Government of France could never stagger through another four years. For the first time since the far-off year 1614, the French people was about to assemble legally before the throne; there to lay bare its grievances and demand redress.

But redress of grievances was not the hope of France alone; — it was shared by Frenchmen over-seas, and nowhere more ardently than in the chief colony of the empire. San Domingo, as we have seen, was filled with discontent: discontent at the caste of arbitrary soldiers, supercilious bureaucrats, and pedantic lawyers who came from Europe to rule her with such arrogance and waste; [2] discontent at that colonial system which pinched and mulcted her at every turn. [3] That a movement for economic reform and some measure of colonial self-government should speedily arise was inevitable.

The most obvious means of furthering these ends was the sending of representatives to the coming States-General. True, no precedent existed for such a step. But precedent could clearly play little part in the convocation

THE EVE OF THE REVOLUTION 69

of a body which had not met for nearly two hundred years, and San Domingo might claim that her rights were as good as those of great European provinces such as Franche-Comté and Lorraine which had also come under the French Crown since the last States-General in 1614, yet whose admission was certain not to be refused. Of course, San Domingo was not a contiguous province but a remote colony, and no nation had ever admitted colonial representatives to its council board. But then the States-General was no modern legislature like the English Parliament, but a mediæval assembly for the stating of grievances and with no direct power of enforcing redress. Theoretically, there seemed no good reason for denying the Frenchmen of San Domingo this opportunity of laying their complaints before the King.

In the early months of 1788 such a movement began, both in San Domingo itself and among that numerous group of absentee nobles, planters, and merchants then living in France.[4] On July 15, 1788, the French section organized as a regular party styling itself the "Colonial Committee." It was dominated by a group of great absentee nobles, and at Court it had powerful connections and the patronage of the Duke of Orléans. Its adherents numbered about a thousand persons, centring in Paris, but also scattered through the provinces and the commercial towns. Furthermore, the party had the good luck to discover among its members a man of real ability in the person of the Marquis de Gouy d'Arcy, whose stirring pamphlets and clever political tactics were at length to bring it success.[5]

In San Domingo, the party showed equal activity.

Here also the movement was headed by a number of wealthy planters of noble birth, seconded by some of the rich merchants and lawyers, while the semi-official Chamber of Commerce at Le Cap set itself up as the steering-committee of the movement.[6] The fear of government interference restrained the Chamber from too open a propaganda, but in the month of May it drew up a manifesto claiming the rights of San Domingo to representation in the States-General, and circulated among its adherents a petition to the King.[7] Backed by three thousand signatures, this petition was forwarded to the Colonial Committee in Paris.[8] In rather flamboyant language it set forth the signers' griefs and hopes. "Sire," it reads, "you are about to call all France around you. The clarion call is already sounding, and its note carries across the sea. Our hearts are at your feet. We are Frenchmen; we lament that the ocean hinders us from being the first to reach the footsteps of your throne."[9]

This address did much to stimulate the French Committee's propaganda. Within the next few weeks a number of pamphlets appeared, mostly from the clever pen of Gouy d'Arcy; wires were industriously pulled at Versailles; and on September 4 a deputation styling themselves the "Commissioners of San Domingo" appeared before the Minister of Marine, La Luzerne, and presented their petition now swelled to four thousand signatures by the adherents of the party in France. La Luzerne avoided committing himself, but laid the petition before the King, and Louis referred it to the Conseil d'Etat, which advised against colonial representation on grounds of inexpediency.[10]

THE EVE OF THE REVOLUTION 71

However, this check was far from discouraging the Colonial Committee. Fresh pamphlets appeared to win over French public opinion,[11] and the growing weakness displayed by the King's Government emboldened the party to more radical action. By this time whole provinces, like Dauphiné and Brittany, were acting at their own will and pleasure in open defiance of the King's authority,[12] and the lesson was not lost upon the partisans of colonial representation. "The Government," says Boissonnade, "was denying them access to the coming States-General; they resolved to force it. The Government was denying them the right of assembly; they invoked the right of nature." [13] They passed the word to their comrades in San Domingo to elect deputies to the States-General.

In San Domingo what was the strength of that royal authority now to be put to this decisive test? The well-meaning but irresolute Minister of Marine, La Luzerne, had been the island's last Governor,[14] and his successor, the Marquis du Chilleau, had not yet left France. Nevertheless, San Domingo was in good hands. For the last four years the intendantship had been held by the Marquis de Barbé-Marbois. A man of strong character and great ability, he had effected striking financial and administrative reforms, and was the acknowledged head of the Government.[15]

Under better conditions this man might have been a tower of strength against the forces of disorder and revolution. But here, as elsewhere, the wretched Government of Louis XVI deserted its most faithful servants. Faced by the rising storm, he demanded again and again

of the Home Government what attitude he was to assume.
"We administrators," he writes, "can only wait upon
your orders." [16] But the Government had no orders to
give. In December, 1788, arrived the new Governor, Du
Chilleau; yet his instructions contained not a line of positive direction; they simply ventured a pious confidence
"in the prudence of the administrators." [17]

To Barbé-Marbois this was all the more perplexing
since it was becoming evident that in spite of their noisy
propaganda the partisans of colonial representation were
only a minority: fully two thirds of the white population
were showing themselves either indifferent or positively
hostile. The poor whites had nothing to gain from the
aristocratic régime proposed by the Chamber's manifesto, the official caste was in violent opposition to claims
for self-government which would have deprived its members of their berths; finally, a majority even of the
planters expressed lively apprehensions as to the results
of this agitation.[18]

The dissent among the planters is most significant.
The reasons for official opposition are patent, but these
planters were fully alive to colonial abuses, and were
by nature just as susceptible as the adherents of representation to prospects of power and reform. The
reason for their opposition was their fear of the coming
States-General's attitude toward slavery and the color
line.

The first note against slavery had been sounded a full
half-century before by Montesquieu in his "Esprit des
Lois," but ever since then the chorus had been swelling
in volume. All the leaders of later French thought had

written against this institution,[19] and in the preceding year the movement (become international in scope) had assumed a practical form truly alarming to the colonies. In 1787, the English reformer Clarkson had founded in London a society advocating the abolition of slavery. It had spread like wildfire, and a propaganda had begun which within a year reached Parliament and alarmed the British colonies.[20]

And almost immediately the movement jumped the Channel, for in February, 1788, the brilliant young pamphleteer Brissot founded the famous society of the "Amis des Noirs."[21] If the English propaganda had spread fast, the French one spread infinitely faster. The mother society in Paris quickly counted among its members many of the great names of the Revolution: men already famous like Lafayette, Mirabeau, and Condorcet; coming figures like Robespierre. Furthermore, it quickly became much more radical than the English society. It affiliated with the network of secret revolutionary organizations then springing up over France, embraced abstract principles, and already formulated the "Rights of Man." It appealed to the people and soon gained many thousand adherents. By its organized network of daughter societies, it anticipated the system of the Jacobins.[22]

If even the English propaganda had disquieted San Domingo,[23] it is easy to imagine the alarm caused by the progress of the French society and by the accompanying flood of antislavery literature. "I well remember," says Moreau de Saint-Méry, "the tremendous sensation at Le Cap, when, in April and May, 1788, numbers of the

'Mercure de France' arrived giving details and comment on this question."[24]

Now all this had given the colonists food for much reflection. Judging by the paralysis of the French Government, radical thought was very likely to dominate the coming States-General. And it was equally clear that this radical thought was pronouncing against colonial ideals in no uncertain fashion. Was it, then, wise to affiliate with this assembly or raise colonial questions for its consideration? To many men the correct line of conduct had already been marked out by the recent action of their English colonial neighbors. The island of Jamaica had been as much wrought up over the efforts of Clarkson and his friends as San Domingo by the doings of the "Amis des Noirs"; — indeed, even in San Domingan opinion, the English island was at that moment considered the more menaced of the two.[25] Yet the Jamaicans expressed no desire to send a handful of representatives to be lost in the mass of the British Parliament; instead, they had been more than contented to send agents for the protection of their interests.[26] This struck the mass of the San Domingo planters as the proper solution of their own difficulty. To keep colonial questions as much as possible out of the French public eye, and to obtain reforms directly from the Crown through the quiet efforts of their agents, appeared to these men the only safe course to pursue.[27]

This opposition to colonial representation was not long in assuming concrete form. Not only was there widespread refusal to sign the petition circulated in May, 1788,[28] but a public protest was got up and presented to

THE EVE OF THE REVOLUTION

Barbé-Marbois.[29] In his correspondence with the Minister of Marine, the Intendant explains the feelings of this opposition. "Admission to the States-General," he writes, "would, in itself, be dear to all the colonists. . . . But they feel how little likeness there is between colonial conditions and those to be treated by the States-General, and they think that the voices of a few colonial deputies would be lost in those of six or seven hundred persons few of whom could have any knowledge of colonial conditions or interests." [30]

Such was the conviction of both Government and majority; yet, as has often happened, they were unable to defeat the plans of an aggressive minority which knew what it wanted and strove to a definite end. By the close of the year 1788 this minority had acquired a well-knit organization, with provincial and even parochial committees working under the guidance of the Chamber at Le Cap.[31] Accordingly, after various aggressive moves,[32] the Chamber in late December boldly defied the Government, and convoked throughout the colony electoral assemblies for the choice of deputies to the States-General.[33] The conservative majority protested,[34] but did nothing, and its natural leader, the Intendant, dared not move for lack of orders. These elections appear to have been highly irregular, packed, and sometimes secret. The planter opposition refused to vote, and of the poor whites only party henchmen were admitted. The result was the "election" of a solid delegation of thirty-seven deputies, several of whom were residents of France.[35] At the same time *cahiers* of grievances were drawn up stating the electors' wishes. These show clearly the party's aims, which were nothing less than the erection of the planter caste into a privileged aristocracy which should monopolize the public offices and rule San Domingo.[36]

As the result of these elections the Government was quite discredited,[37] and it soon fell into absolute impotence through a quarrel of Governor and Intendant. The important results of the hard winter of 1788-89 upon the course of the French Revolution have been often noted, and it is interesting to discover a direct effect upon the history of San Domingo as well. The failure of the French crops had caused a prohibition against the export of grain from France, and this threatened San Domingo with famine. To avert this famine, Governor Du Chilleau in March, 1789, threw open the ports to foreign foodstuffs. The terms of his proclamation, however, exceeded the law, and Barbé-Marbois protested. For some time the relations between the two had been growing less cordial, and this action of the Intendant completed the rupture. Du Chilleau, a weak man with a hot temper, now fell under the influence of the radical planters, who, in May, 1789, induced him to issue an entirely illegal ordinance giving the island virtual freedom of trade. The Intendant at once reported to the Home Government this nullification of the "Pacte Coloniale," and the Minister of Marine promptly annulled Du Chilleau's acts and recalled him in disgrace. But the political consequences of the quarrel were none the less serious. The ministerial orders did not arrive until autumn, and before that time the news of the first great triumphs of the French Revolution had reached San Domingo — to find the island virtually without a government.[38]

The year 1789 discovered France in the tumult of the approaching elections to the States-General, and therein the voice of the Colonial Committee was heard loudly raised among the rest. That it aroused a certain amount of interest is proved by the election of several of its supporters and by some favorable *cahiers*.[39] Yet its rather noisy propaganda also had a reflex effect which went far to justify the fears of its colonial opponents. The "Amis des Noirs" took up its efforts as a challenge, seeing in the champions of the Colonial Committee the most bitter opponents of those changes so deeply laid to heart. They therefore declaimed loudly against the oppression of the slaves and the iniquities of slavery, and they succeeded in getting a better hearing than the Colonial Committee itself.[40] The great mass of public opinion, however, refused to declare for either party.[41]

The efforts of the Colonial Committee had evoked yet another current of opposition. Among the colonists living in France there existed the same differences of opinion as among the residents of San Domingo. From the first there had been much lively dissent at the doings of the Colonial Committee, and these dissenters were rapidly drawing together into that definite organization later known as the "Club Massiac." Several of their sympathizers were elected to the States-General where they were certain to oppose colonial representation,[42] and in this attitude they were sure to be supported by the deputies of the commercial towns, already alarmed as these were at the Colonial Committee's strictures on the "Pacte Coloniale." [43]

Faced by such powerful opponents it is not surprising

that the first efforts of the Committee to seat its deputies were failures. The States-General opened on the 5th of May, and in mid-June the cause of the San Domingo deputies looked more than doubtful. In this *impasse* they were fortuitously saved by the Day of the Tennis Court:[44] in that crisis Gouy d'Arcy saw his opportunity and led his fellows to the aid of the imperilled Third Estate. The spectacle of this group of noblemen appearing in the hour of peril to share their fortunes roused a wave of grateful enthusiasm among the Commons, who admitted the principle of colonial representation on the spot.[45]

The Colonial Committee had thus won in principle, but the extent of its victory still remained to be determined. In the first debates on the size of the San Domingo delegation, it seemed as though its demand for twenty seats would go through. But the pressure of other business caused frequent adjournments, and this delay was skilfully used by its opponents. Pamphlets from influential members of the "Amis des Noirs" like Brissot and Condorcet appeared to chill opinion; a protest from the "Club Massiac" stabbed the Committee from behind; worst of all, the able pen of Mirabeau fought savagely against the San Domingans, and in the debates his great voice thundered forth words which must have caused a shudder among the colonial deputies.[46] "Have not the best minds denied the very utility of colonies?" he cried. "And, even admitting their utility, is that any reason for a right to representation? These people wish a representation in proportion to the number of inhabitants. But have the negroes or the free people of color taken part in the elections? The free colored are landowners and taxpayers;— nevertheless, they have had no vote. And as to the slaves—either they are, or they are not, men. If they be men, let the colonists free them, make them voters and eligible as deputies; if they be not men,— have we counted into the population of France the number of our horses and mules?" [47]

On July 7, it is true, the Assembly voted the admission of six deputies from San Domingo. But the gulf had already opened beneath the colonists' feet. Before those ominous words of Mirabeau, even the sanguine Gouy d'Arcy must have remembered the despised warnings of the "Club Massiac." In the words of Déschamps, "This logic was far from pleasing to the colonists. It chilled the enthusiasm of the 20th of June, and made them already regret their action in having placed themselves under the protection of the Assembly. The political rights of the mulattoes and the abolition of slavery were, in this very first hour, already looming over the horizon, evoked by the mighty orator who had thus far guided the Revolution. It was nothing less than a declaration of war, and one all the more serious in that the very utility of colonies had been questioned. From that moment the colonial deputies felt that they must separate their cause from the mother country's, must extricate their interests from its principles, and must give blow for blow to those 'Amis des Noirs' of whom Mirabeau was but the spokesman." [48]

In other words, the Colonial Committee was about to try, too late, what wiser heads had attempted from the first — to keep San Domingo out of the Revolution. At one time, this had not been an impossibility. If the great planter aristocracy had held together and consistently backed the Government, it could certainly have kept the island peaceful. And with no news from San Domingo to rouse public interest or excite discussion, it is more than likely that in the coming tumult of great events, colonial questions would have been either overlooked or hushed up by a little clever manipulation.[49] As a matter of fact, a policy very like this was actually carried out by the colonists of Île-de-France and Bourbon,[50] with the result that these islands escaped the woes of the French West Indian colonies. Even persons close to the event realized the Colonial Committee's fatal error. "To-day," writes the essayist Beaulieu in 1802, "this thoughtless step of the inhabitants of San Domingo is generally held to have been the source of those ills which wrought their ruin. If the inhabitants of San Domingo had never sent deputies to the States-General, there would have been no point of contact between them and that National Assembly which was the heart of the Revolution, or, at most, communication would have been both slow and difficult." [51]

But it was not to be. For more than a year the partisans of colonial representation had trumpeted their cause all over France, stirred San Domingo to discord and confusion, and engaged in a furious duel with French radical thought which had filled the land with a flood of oratory and pamphlets. The French public was now deeply interested both in San Domingo and in colonial questions, and the presence of her deputies in the

National Assembly had "bound the fate of the colony to that of the mother country, which was soon to impose upon that colony laws against which she would strive in vain." [52]

VII

FIRST STAGE OF THE COLONIAL STRUGGLE IN FRANCE

IN France, the Revolution moved forward with stunning rapidity. The storming of the Bastille on the 14th of July felled the Government of the King, the night of the 4th of August destroyed the power of the French nobility, and on August 20, the "Declaration of the Rights of Man" committed the National Assembly to principles which condemned the very bases of colonial society.

The colonists in France were wild with terror. "The colony," write the San Domingo deputies to their constituents on August 12, "is in most imminent peril. People here are trying to raise a revolt among our negroes, and the danger is such as to cause us the most horrible alarm. We see the danger, — and yet are forced to keep silence. Gentlemen, these people are drunk with liberty. A society of enthusiasts who style themselves the 'Friends of the Blacks' is writing openly against us; it is watching eagerly for the favorable moment to explode the mine against slavery; and should we have the tactlessness to but utter that word, its members might make it the occasion to demand the enfranchisement of our negroes." [1]

Under the pressure of this growing peril, both Colonial Committee and Club Massiac drew together. What was done, was done, and no time must be wasted in useless recrimination: positive action was necessary. It was evident that the old Government was in its death-agony and that the National Assembly would soon be supreme. Before this should happen, the best plan seemed to be to establish in San Domingo some new power which might offer resistance to anti-colonial legislation, and, by means of the still-existing royal prerogative, to "remove colonial affairs from the control of the National Assembly to that of some local body in which the slave interests would be safe." [2]

Accordingly, the two factions approached the Minister of Marine with a request for royal authorization to convoke a Colonial Assembly. This request La Luzerne was only too happy to grant, and on September 27, he despatched to San Domingo orders quite to the liking of his petitioners. These orders provided for an Assembly having competence over internal affairs and elected through a franchise so limited by property qualifications as assured planter control.[3] Best of all, from the colonists' standpoint, there was no recognition whatever of the National Assembly: the future colonial body was to be accountable only to the King.[4]

The course of events quickly showed the colonists that they had acted none too soon. It also convinced them that fresh efforts on their part were necessary. For, on October 5, the Paris mob marched on Versailles and brought both King and National Assembly back with them next day. From that moment it was plain that neither King nor Assembly was a free agent, and that the radical minority might at any time enforce its will through pressure from the Paris mob.

Indeed, this fresh victory of the Revolution soon produced important developments in the colonial question. In Paris there had long existed a community of wealthy mulattoes, come thither to obtain a European education or to escape the rigors of the color line. These men had naturally excited the sympathetic interest of French radical thought, and from the first, the "Amis des Noirs" had eagerly planned how the mulattoes might best derive advantage from the course of the Revolution.[5] Under the leadership of one of these white friends (an advocate named De Joly), the Paris mulattoes had recently organized themselves into the society of "Colons Américains." The progress of the Revolution greatly encouraged their prospects, and on October 22, the influence of the "Amis des Noirs" succeeded in getting the mulattoes a hearing before the National Assembly. On that day a delegation of the "Colons Américains" appeared at the Assembly's bar, and there demanded that the mulattoes be allowed to enjoy all the privileges of citizenship, not as a favor but as a natural right, and that the Assembly admit into its body certain delegates representing the interests of the mulatto caste. The President replied amicably that "no part of the nation should ask its rights from the Assembly in vain," and took the "Colons Américains'" petition into consideration.[6]

The next few weeks saw a vigorous controversy, both within and without the Assembly. The "Amis des Noirs" did their best to insure their protégés' admission, and the influential pen of the Abbé Grégoire did yeoman service. But their opponents were also active, and all the powerful influence of the commercial towns backed the colonists in

FIRST STAGE OF COLONIAL STRUGGLE 85

their efforts to shelve a proposal so certain to destroy the peace of the colonies. On December 3, the question came before the House, and a great debate ended in the defeat of the "Amis des Noirs." [7]

The danger was over for the moment, but the colonists saw what must speedily be done. No more such oratorical battles must be fought in the hall of the National Assembly, for in these contests, the "Amis des Noirs," with their ringing appeals to Revolutionary principles and their backing of sympathetic galleries, were certain sooner or later to sweep the Assembly off its feet and to gain some decisive victory. If such questions must come up at all, the colonists felt it absolutely necessary to get them off the floor of the House into the quiet of the committee room.[8] Accordingly, a colonial deputy [9] promptly proposed the formation of a Committee on Colonies, to be composed of colonial and commercial deputies in equal proportions.[10] The "Amis des Noirs," however, were fully alive to the importance of this move. It was quite clear that, once a body so constituted was established, every proposal affecting the colonies would be either killed in committee or reported to the House in biased form. They accordingly fought the proposal, and showed their strength by compassing its defeat.[11]

Then, for three months, colonial questions slumbered as interest centred in constitution-making and the foreign crisis over Nootka Sound. However, toward the end of February, 1790, the Assembly was brought to reconsideration by the increasingly serious news from the colonies. Violent scenes were taking place in San Domingo,[12] and still more serious tidings came from Guadeloupe and

Martinique, where the negroes were already stirring at the call of the Revolution.[13]

It was clear that the House needed full information on this complicated question, and to sift the accumulating mass of evidence, the Assembly on March 2, 1790, appointed a Committee on Colonies. On this committee only two colonial deputies found seats, but as the "Amis des Noirs" were excluded while the other members were moderate in tone, the colonists might feel that they would be given a friendly hearing.[14]

This committee reported on the 8th of March, when its chairman, Barnave, laid before the House a draft decree for the settlement of the troubles over-seas. His recommendations were very pleasing to the colonists. In his report, Barnave maintained that the late troubles were caused by the arbitrary nature of the Royal Government, the extreme rigor of the "Pacte Coloniale," and the machinations of "those enemies of the happiness of France" who had made the colonists believe that the carrying out of the national decrees involved the ruin of their fortunes and the peril of their lives. This last was, of course, a direct thrust at the "Amis des Noirs." To remedy these evils, Barnave advised that the colonies should be left to work out their own internal constitutions, that the "Pacte" should be toned down, and that the National Assembly should quiet the colonies' fears regarding the safety of their social organization.[15]

In the draft decree these ideas were embodied in no uncertain fashion. Its preamble stated that "While the National Assembly considers the colonies as part of the French Empire, and while it desires to see them enjoy the

FIRST STAGE OF COLONIAL STRUGGLE 87

fruits of the happy regeneration which has just taken place, it has, notwithstanding, never intended to include them as subject to the constitution decreed for the kingdom or laws incompatible with their local circumstances." [16] The body of the decree authorized the various colonies to make known their wishes through local assemblies, and declared "criminal against the nation whosoever should seek to foment risings against them." [17]

This was a sweeping colonial victory, but the Assembly had become so thoroughly alarmed at the condition of the colonies that it received Barnave's proposals with acclamation. Even Mirabeau's great voice was drowned by the cries of "Aux voix! Aux voix!" and the decree was voted almost unanimously.[18]

The Decree of March 8, 1790, was a crushing blow for the "Amis des Noirs." Nevertheless, they did not despair, for they saw a chance of undoing the colonists' victory. The decree was general in form and needed a set of instructions to explain its execution. These instructions did not come before the House until the 23d of March, and this gave time for the exertion of adverse pressure and for the framing of "jokers" to nullify its purpose. The effect of this two weeks' effort was very apparent when the instructions came before the Assembly, which now showed clearly that strain of moral cowardice and vacillation which was to be so largely responsible for the ruin of San Domingo.

The great struggle came over Article 4, which concerned voting qualifications. After much preliminary bickering, the article as proposed stated that "all persons" twenty-five years of age, owners of real estate or taxpayers, should be held qualified voters. Now this phrasing contained an ambiguity which might well be interpreted into a complete nullification of the decree it was supposed to explain. For, taken literally, Article 4 admitted to the franchise a very large number of mulattoes; — something which was clearly just such a revolutionary change in colonial conditions as had been expressly disclaimed by the decree.

And, in the debate which followed, this ambiguity was brought sharply to the notice of the Assembly. The Abbé Grégoire loudly hailed Article 4 as consecrating the political equality of the mulattoes, and this assertion was at once hotly denied by a colonial deputy. Now, if the decree of March 8 meant anything at all, it meant the retention of the existing colonial *status quo*: yet the Assembly simply could not bring itself to a specific contradiction of its vaunted principles, and finally shirked the point by simply voting Article 4 as it stood — ambiguity and all.[19] "Thus," says Mills, "the Assembly refused to consider the question above all others needing settlement. The decree literally interpreted would admit the free people of color to the exercise of the suffrage; but the traditions and customary law of the island were against any such concession. It is evident that the colonial deputies did not intend that the colored people should be admitted to full citizenship. The explanation of this evasive action of the Assembly is probably to be found in its unwillingness to do anything which might seem to be inconsistent with its Declaration of Rights and other enunciations of fundamental principles, while at the same time it was felt that no hasty action should be taken in the settle-

FIRST STAGE OF COLONIAL STRUGGLE 89

ment of a question affecting the commercial interests of France." [20]

Fraught with its ominous equivocation, this truly Delphic utterance of the National Assembly went forth to San Domingo.

VIII

THE FIRST TROUBLES IN SAN DOMINGO

THE close of the year 1789 found San Domingo already the theatre of growing tumult and confusion. The prestige of the Royal Government had suffered a heavy blow from the January elections, and the breach between Governor and Intendant had destroyed its power of action.[1] Still, the public peace was not really disturbed before the autumn. Impotent as was the Royal Government for repression, its hold on the machinery of government was still unbroken, and the opposition dared attempt no open attack until the result of the struggle in France should be known in the island. The Party of Representation, therefore, contented itself with perpetuating its political organization by the establishment of Provincial Committees, against which the Government took no action.[2]

Early in September, however, this truce was broken by the tidings of the 14th of July. At San Domingo, as in France, the fall of the Bastille was the signal for an explosion: in the towns, at least, the tricolor cockade was worn by all, and several persons who ventured to express their disapproval were lynched by excited crowds.[3]

But the popular nature of these disorders showed that the movement was assuming a new phase. Hitherto, the struggle had been confined to the upper classes of society, and the January elections had shown how completely the

FIRST TROUBLES IN SAN DOMINGO

lower orders of the white population had been disregarded.[4] But the ensuing months had given ample time for the Revolutionary leaven to work among the needy proletariat of the towns,[5] whose latent jealousy of the wealthy whites had been rapidly transformed into an active desire to share in the Revolution.[6] That the poor whites would have to be reckoned with in future politics was soon conclusively shown. The *cahier* of grievances drawn up in the January elections was published at this moment, and its demands for the erection of the planter caste into a ruling aristocracy aroused such a storm of popular indignation at Le Cap that the Provincial Committee hastened to convoke all classes of the white population to the election of a Provincial Assembly.[7]

The committee was emboldened to this step by the victory which it had just won over the Government. The news of the 14th of July had been hailed by the opposition as the signal for its attack upon the royal authority. Wherever its power extended it had disbanded the royalist-officered militia and enrolled its supporters into companies of National Guards,[8] and as soon as it had thus acquired a military backing it had dealt a decisive blow. Everybody agreed that the pillar of royal authority in San Domingo was the Intendant, Barbé-Marbois, — and him the opposition promptly decided to eliminate. Accordingly, a corps of Le Cap volunteers marched overland on Port-au-Prince to arrest the Intendant. Barbé-Marbois, knowing his probable fate if captured and despairing of any effective resistance to this sudden *coup*, took ship and left the island, accompanied by those other officials known for the most zealous upholders of the royal prerogative.[9] At San Domingo, as in France, the "emigration" had begun.

This flight of the Intendant had the desired effect. It left unsupported the new Governor, Count de Peynier, who had arrived less than a month before. Although personally a brave soldier, Peynier was advanced in years, somewhat lacking in resolution, and too unacquainted with local affairs to venture a determined resistance to the attacks of the opposition.[10] Accordingly, on November 1, the new Provincial Assembly of the North met at Le Cap without interference from the royal authorities. It was, of course, dominated by the opposition, which had by this time adopted the party nickname of "Patriots." The "Patriots" had now developed a directing group of reckless spirits, foremost among them being a showy nobleman named Bacon de la Chevalerie, and one Larchevesque Thibaud, an oratorical lawyer of the Le Cap Bar.[11] These two men were to be the leading spirits of the "Patriot" party down to its destruction in 1793.

The new Assembly at once declared that the powers of government for the Province of the North vested entirely in the body of its deputies, and assumed control over every branch of local administration in complete disregard of the Governor's authority.[12]

With such a party stronghold as the North Province, the progress of the "Patriots" in the rest of the colony was rapid. Early in January, 1790, an Assembly of the West Province met at Port-au-Prince, under the very eyes of Governor Peynier, and in mid-February an Assembly of the South met at Les Cayes. However, the

FIRST TROUBLES IN SAN DOMINGO   93

Governor's presence and the growing conservatism of the West and South forced these two bodies to adopt a much more modest attitude than had been the case with the Assembly of the remote and self-sufficient North.[13]

Some time in January, 1790, arrived that plan for a Colonial Assembly which had been drawn up by the Home Government at the request of the colonists in France. Its details were not wholly pleasing to the "Patriots" and were promptly modified, but its substance was quite in accord with their wishes. Therefore, in the latter part of February, the three provincial bodies convoked a Colonial Assembly, to meet at the town of Saint-Marc in the West Province on the 25th of March.[14] The tardy arrival of its members delayed the opening of this Colonial Assembly:[15] before that date, the colony had been thrown into great alarm by a rising among the mulattoes.

The ferment of the Revolution had not failed to stir the mulattoes of San Domingo. As early as January, 1789, some mulattoes of the West Province had asserted their claims to political rights in a memorial to the royal authorities, and although at that moment they did not dare publicly to avow their hopes, they were steadily encouraged by the reports received from the mulatto community in Paris.[16] However, as tidings concerning the anti-colonial tendencies displayed by the Revolutionary party in France continued to reach the island, the hopes of the mulattoes became tinged with fears for their personal safety. The alarm of the white population over the "Amis des Noirs" in 1788 has been already noted.[17] Later, this feeling had been submerged by the political crisis, although we have seen how profoundly fear for the existing social order had influenced conservative colonial opinion.[18] But when the "Declaration of the Rights of Man" arrived in late September, a fresh quiver of alarm ran through San Domingo. "To promulgate such lessons in the colonies as the declared sense of the Supreme Government," observes Edwards, "was to subvert the whole system of their establishments. Accordingly, a general ferment prevailed among the French inhabitants of San Domingo, from one end to the other." [19]

And the fears of the colonists were not confined to possible action of the mulattoes: already alarm was felt at the attitude of the slaves. "In this country," writes a colonist at this moment, "we are in the greatest fear concerning the negroes." [20] That this attitude was justified is shown by the report of a royal officer in the district of Fort Dauphin, dated so early as the 14th of October, 1789, and considered by the Governor to be of sufficient importance for transmission to the Minister of Marine. "Sir," it reads, "this word 'Liberty,' which is echoing so loudly all the way from distant Europe to these parts, and which is being everywhere repeated with such enthusiasm, is sowing a fatal seed, whose sprouting will be terrible. In France, where its application endangers despotism alone, we may hope for the best results. But here, where everything opposes the entire liberty of all classes, we should see only blood, carnage, and the certain destruction of one or other of those incompatible races of men which inhabit this colony. So long as there exists the opposition of white and black, so long it will be impossible to establish, upon a basis of liberty, any

FIRST TROUBLES IN SAN DOMINGO 95

mutual support of existing society." [21] He reports much unrest among the negroes of his district, and urges greater activity of the *maréchaussée* in searching negro "quarters" for concealed weapons and in breaking up nocturnal gatherings among the slaves. That the servile mass was thus early responsive to the Revolution was also shown by the negro risings in Guadeloupe and Martinique during these same autumn months of 1789.[22]

The news of the mulatto propaganda in France and the great debate of December 3 awakened fresh alarm. "The speech of M. de Joly and its favorable reception by the National Assembly," writes Governor Peynier, "have aroused an agitation and terror of acute intensity." [23] But if the news from France alarmed the whites, it so encouraged the mulattoes that they began to desert their passive attitude, and in November, 1789, a number of public addresses demanding political rights were drawn up by them in various parts of the colony. At this bold step, however, the growing alarm of the whites changed to a wave of fury. The framers of the addresses were lynched, and a widespread persecution of the mulattoes followed these first excesses.[24]

Yet there was more than fear behind the numerous outrages to which the mulattoes were now subjected: it was also the explosion of long-suppressed class hatred which here stood revealed. If the poor whites envied the richer members of their own color, they both envied and hated the wealthy mulattoes. Even in the past, they had never neglected an opportunity to vent their feelings, although hitherto the royal authority had protected the mulattoes against the more serious forms of outrage.[25]

But now the Royal Government was shorn of its power, and those upper-class colonial whites who controlled the "Patriot" party, alarmed as they were at the Revolutionary peril and anxious for poor white support, were not likely to embroil themselves to protect their race opponents. By this time the local offices were becoming filled with poor whites, and to the will and pleasure of these new functionaries, the mulattoes were now delivered almost without reserve.[26]

The result of all this was very serious. The mulattoes, excited as they were at the news from France and intoxicated by the principles of the Revolution, were thus at the same time subjected to an oppression not only far more severe than they had ever known, but also peculiarly intolerable to their sense of justice. To the legal discriminations of the color line, backed by a unanimous official and public conviction, they had hitherto bent as to the inevitable. But this arbitrary tyranny of ignorant and despised adventurers was insupportable.[27] The wild rage which rankled in mulatto hearts was soon to wreak its vengeance upon the entire white population.

However, the first results, though significant enough in character, were quite inconsiderable in fact. During the month of March a rising took place in the West Province among the mulattoes of the Artibonite, an inland tract of fertile plain where the numbers of the caste were very considerable. But the insurgents displayed no activity, aroused no support save a few mutterings in the South, and were promptly dispersed by the vigorous action of the local militia and *maréchaussée*.[28]

Insignificant as had been the rising, however, the les-

FIRST TROUBLES IN SAN DOMINGO   97

son was for the moment taken to heart. This is proved by the great lenience shown the insurgents. Some of the disturbances had taken place in territory controlled by the "Patriots," others in the sphere still dominated by the Government, but in both cases the rebels were granted a general pardon.[29] This was the result of new political developments of great potential importance.

Under the Old Régime, we have already seen that the royal Government had been the chief protection of the mulatto caste.[30] That the mulattoes fully realized this had been shown by their recent conduct. From the first, they had maintained a respectful attitude toward the royal authorities and had refrained from any anti-Government demonstration. Naturally, this was highly pleasing to the harassed King's officers, who soon came to regard the mulattoes as potential allies in the struggle against the Revolutionary party.[31]

Still more significant was the waning hostility to the Government now shown by the better element of the "Patriot" party. These wealthy planters and merchants were becoming more and more alarmed at the attitude of the white lower classes. For the pretensions of the poor whites were daily becoming more extreme. Composed mostly of ignorant men of narrow intelligence, this class was either too short-sighted to realize the results of white disunion or too reckless to care about consequences. Therefore the poor whites were now openly striving for political supremacy, and furthermore they were making no secret of their hostility to wealth and privilege.[32] In the recent elections to the new Colonial Assembly they had in many cases taken possession of the polls and excluded upper-class voters by violence and intimidation.[33] All the events of the last few months were thus steadily leading conservative "Patriots" to forget their feud with the Government. Alarmed at the ambitions of the poor whites, warned by their own representatives in France to heal dissension before the Revolutionary peril, and taught by the mulatto rising that a continuance of persecution would drive that class to utter desperation, these men began to approach the Government and to reënforce that strong body of Royalist opinion which was already preparing for armed defence.

Out of all this there might have sprung a triple alliance between the Government, the united planters, and the mulattoes which would very possibly have saved San Domingo. Even the "Patriot" Assembly of the North was at this moment showing a spirit of conciliation to the mulattoes, and it is probable that the majority of this caste would have been too much alive to the poor white menace and the Revolutionary ferment among the negroes not to have accepted concessions short of the abolition of the color line, and to have joined its fellow property-holders and slaveowners in the maintenance of existing society. This was what actually took place in Îsle-de-France and Bourbon, with the result that these islands were spared the horrors of race war and social dissolution.[34]

Unfortunately, this alliance never took place. The new Colonial Assembly at once assumed a constitutional position which re-formed party lines among the whites; while the ambiguous March decrees of the National Assembly

FIRST TROUBLES IN SAN DOMINGO 99

and the incitements of their French friends so roused the mulattoes that they resolved to strike for the full attainment of their hopes.[35] The gods had indeed decreed the destruction of San Domingo.

IX

THE ASSEMBLY OF SAINT-MARC

ON April 15, 1790, the new Colonial Assembly met at Saint-Marc, a port town of the West Province, some fifty miles north of Port-au-Prince. As might have been expected from the unscrupulous activity displayed in the elections, the "Patriots" were in a great majority; indeed, all the more violent leaders of this party were to be found on the roll of assemblymen. The first act of the new Assembly was to elect as its President Bacon de la Chevalerie, the arch-radical of Le Cap, and its next steps were equally significant. Rejecting the term "Colonial" as beneath its dignity, the new body assumed the title of "General Assembly," and inscribed upon its walls the motto, "Saint-Domingue, la Loi et le Roi." [1]

From the first, it was clear that the General Assembly considered itself the supreme authority in the island: as Déschamps well puts the matter, "It sincerely believed itself a miniature Constituent Assembly." [2] And unfortunately it at once imitated one of the most serious errors of its French model. The National Decree of March 8, 1790, had authorized each colony to formulate its wishes regarding its future internal status. Accordingly, the General Assembly, instead of busying itself with practical measures of conciliation and reform, plunged at once into the attractive but perilous task of framing a constitution. History shows that there is nothing which so destroys in a parliamentary body its sense of what is real and practicable as its prolonged absorption in the formulation of abstract constitutional principles. This was especially true in the case of the General Assembly, for it rapidly evolved a theory of government which rendered a struggle with the royal authority inevitable and which sharpened political divisions among the colonial whites past all likelihood of reconciliation.

The fruit of these labors was a decree, passed on the 28th of May, entitled "Constitutional Bases of the General Assembly." By this self-made charter, the Assembly arrogated to itself supreme authority in the island and transformed the royal officers into its servants: all effective control by the National Assembly was excluded, and the connection of San Domingo to the mother country was entirely through the Crown.[3]

In France, this colonial constitution was almost universally condemned as an attempt at independence, and even in San Domingo itself many persons were convinced of its secessionist character.[4] Nevertheless, these judgments seem to have been unfounded. When we consider the island's past history [5] and the nature of its government,[6] there is certainly nothing novel in the insistence upon the royal connection. The great charge aimed against the Assembly of Saint-Marc is its refusal to recognize the paramount authority of the National Assembly. But this is just where its case is strongest. The power of the French people, as distinct from that of the French Crown, was something quite as revolutionary as any of the clauses of the colonial constitution: indeed, it was to guard against just such assumptions of popular control over the colonies that the King's Ministers, in the preceding September, had drawn up that plan of convocation which was the legal basis of the General Assembly's existence.[7] We must here be more than usually on our guard not to read the future into our judgments. At that very moment, thousands of persons [8] were leaving France because they refused to recognize that supreme power lay with a popular assembly and not with the King, while still larger numbers of Frenchmen were soon to dispute the doctrine of popular sovereignty by passive resistance or armed rebellion.[9] To stigmatize as treason the colonists' refusal to accept this debated theory may have been good Revolutionary politics, but is an historical absurdity.

Garran-Coulon, the compiler of the great official report so often quoted in these pages, well expresses the conviction of the men of the Revolution. According to him, there were but two courses open to the General Assembly: either entire acquiescence in the decrees of the National Assembly with the admission that San Domingo was a subject colony, or complete independence.[10] But this argument is fallacious. As Mills well observes, "Between these two extremes was another course. The planters recognized the sovereignty of the French King, but not the supremacy of the French people. They claimed that as a matter of expediency this view was the one best suited to the interest of France and of San Domingo, and that as a matter of history this had been the real relation of the two." [11] Unfortunately, Revolutionary France was already displaying that uncompromising refusal to tolerate the slightest objection to its imperious will which was to cause the Vendée at home, and the ruin of San Domingo over-seas.

The real innovation made by the May Constitution lay in its subjection of the local royal authorities. To proclaim submission to the King, and then in the same breath turn the King's officers into the Assembly's servants was a political hocus-pocus as contradictory in theory as it was dangerous in practice. For thus, at the very moment of its defiance to Revolutionary France, the General Assembly declared war upon its one natural ally, and embarked on a desperate strife of faction when the greater struggle was already looming over the horizon.

The tension between Government and Assembly now rapidly grew more acute. Up to this time Governor Peynier, an irresolute man averse to conflict, had done his best to keep on good terms with the Assembly, and had overlooked many of its early provocations.[12] But now the issue of resistance or submission was fairly joined, and the Governor was the more encouraged to oppose the Assembly's pretensions in that he felt himself supported by a growing body of public opinion. Even before the Assembly had met, we have seen that the conservative wing of the "Patriots" had begun to break up,[13] and since then the party's conduct had caused many fresh desertions. This was especially the case in the former "Patriot" stronghold of the North. The mere departure of the "Patriot" leaders for the General Assembly had weakened that party's hold upon the provincial body,[14] while the hostility shown by the General Assembly to the existing commercial system had soon alarmed the great merchant body of Le Cap.[15] The May Constitution now capped the climax, for, by its provisions, the Provincial Assemblies were as much threatened as the Royal Government. This roused all the strong local feeling of the North, which hereupon recalled its deputies from the General Assembly and issued a manifesto which was a virtual declaration of war.[16] Furthermore, the pressure of common interests soon resulted in an understanding with the Governor, and a species of alliance was formed between the two against the General Assembly.[17]

Nevertheless, Peynier, averse as ever to violent measures, attempted to turn the difficulty. The National Decree of March 8 provided that in cases of Colonial Assemblies chosen before its passage, elections might be held to determine whether these assemblies should continue or be replaced by new bodies. In mid-June, therefore, Peynier took advantage of this to order a referendum on the question,[18] although his official correspondence shows him to have been doubtful of the result. "The colony," he writes to La Luzerne, "is at this moment in the greatest agitation. Two parties divide it. The one, entirely devoted to the General Assembly, demands its continuation: the other seeks its dissolution. This latter party is the more numerous, and contains the most intelligent and responsible citizens; nevertheless, I very much doubt whether it will be successful. For the other party is made up of the discontented, the declaimers against pretended despotism, and the mass of workingmen and artisans, who are persuaded that their opponents are composed solely of those persons wishing to maintain abuses." [19] Peynier's fears were justified by the event. In the elections the North came out strongly against

THE ASSEMBLY OF SAINT-MARC 105

renewal, but elsewhere, save in a few Government strongholds, the poor whites voted solidly for the General Assembly. The "Patriots" won a clear victory, and on July 13, Peynier reluctantly proclaimed the Assembly renewed.[20]

Flushed by this triumph, the General Assembly now forgot all moderation and determined to coerce the Governor by force. Accordingly, it at once seized the royal arsenals within its jurisdiction, and on July 27, it decreed the disbanding of the regular troops, who were invited to re-form as "paid National Guards of San Domingo."[21] This was, of course, an open declaration of war.

But the struggle had no sooner begun than it became apparent that vigor and determination had passed from the "Patriots" to the Government. This state of things was largely due to the fact that the Government party once more possessed a head. Since the flight of Barbé-Marbois, almost a year before,[22] the conservative forces, though growing in strength, had been quite destitute of leadership. But early in June the Chevalier Mauduit had arrived to take up his duties as colonel of the Royal Infantry Regiment "Port-au-Prince," and in the short space of two months he had become the acknowledged leader of the conservatives. Mauduit had none of the bureaucratic caution of the late Intendant. A man of great courage, his love of action was spurred by his hatred of the Revolution; for the Chevalier Mauduit was an ardent Royalist. Only a short time before this he had written, "I love my country passionately; — and I love the blood of my kings as men knew how to love two hundred years ago."[23] Just previous to his departure for San Domingo he had gone to Turin for a conference with the Comte d'Artois, the leader of the *émigrés*.[24] Such was the Chevalier Mauduit, to whom the irresolute Peynier surrendered himself, now that decisive action had become a necessity.[25]

That Mauduit had already gained the affection of his soldiers was proved by the failure of the General Assembly to sap their loyalty. But the regiment "Port-au-Prince" did not number over twelve hundred men,[26] — scarcely a sufficient force to meet the large bodies of National Guards at the General Assembly's disposal. Fortunately, however, Mauduit had found another instrument ready to his hand. Ever since the proscription of Barbé-Marbois, the more determined Royalists of the West Province had enrolled themselves into volunteer companies known as the "Pompons Blancs," from a white decoration worn in their *chapeaux*.[27] These organizations Mauduit now heavily recruited, and the Government soon possessed a considerable force of thoroughly reliable troops.[28]

Events soon showed that Mauduit had acted none too soon. In the campaign which he had planned against Saint-Marc, he had intended to use the naval forces then in San Domingan waters to blockade the town by sea. But it now appeared that the sailors had been tampered with, for the crew of the flagship Léopard mutinied and sailed to Saint-Marc, where the vessel was greeted with hysterical delight and rechristened Sauveur des Français.[29]

The Government leaders now realized that the under-

THE ASSEMBLY OF SAINT-MARC

taking was even more serious than they had imagined, and that before striking at the Assembly they must make sure of their own ground. For a dangerous centre of disaffection existed in Port-au-Prince itself. The Committee of the West Province had always remained in "Patriot" hands, and the mutiny of the Léopard had so encouraged this body that it had now begun to assemble its partisans for a rising in the very capital of the colony. But Colonel Mauduit was just the man for the situation. At two o'clock on the morning of July 30, he led a strong force of regulars and Royalist volunteers [30] against the headquarters of the Western Committee, stormed it after a bloody skirmish, and stamped out all signs of disaffection within the limits of the town.[31]

The road was now clear for a direct stroke at Saint-Marc, albeit the Government leaders realized that the bloodshed already attendant upon the *coup d'état* was likely to produce a dangerous effect upon French public opinion, becoming daily more hostile to the suppression of disorder. In his report to La Luzerne, Peynier foresees that people in France will be demanding his head "for having shed the blood of citizens." "Yet, sir," he continues, "I should have held myself a traitor had I not put down those in rebellion. . . . You, sir, know by your own experience how dangerous are such movements in a country like this. . . . Had I not acted thus, the mutual hostility was such that I feel sure one part of the town would soon have been massacred by the other." [32]

But this danger from France made it the more necessary to finish the business quickly. Fortunately, the Government was assured of active aid from the north.

In the person of the Baron de Cambefort, colonel of the Royal Regiment "Le Cap," Mauduit had found a colleague after his own heart, and this man's able efforts had resulted in the formation of a compact little army which, under the command of a zealous young officer named Vincent, had already left Le Cap by sea to coöperate with the main body of the Government troops.[33]

The campaign was short, bloodless, and decisive. Mauduit moved rapidly on Saint-Marc from Port-au-Prince while Vincent's army landed north of the town, thus taking it between two fires. The General Assembly had issued a proclamation calling on the citizens to rise in its defence, and this appeal roused widespread response, especially in the South. But the South was far away, Saint-Marc itself was full of disaffection, and the Assembly soon recognized that resistance was impossible.[34]

In its perplexity the General Assembly took a daring resolution. Thanks to the Léopard the sea remained open, and the Assembly now resolved to go to France, there to seek aid and protection from its quondam rival the National Assembly. Accordingly, on the afternoon of the 8th of August, the General Assembly — now thinned by desertions to a mere rump of eighty-five members — met in its old hall for the last time, and thence, amid long lines of troops, marched to the shore and embarked on the Léopard. Next day the "Eighty-five," accompanied by their most zealous followers, sailed for France.[35]

The General Assembly was gone, but its partisans remained. At the very moment of its embarkation, an army some two thousand strong was advancing from the

THE ASSEMBLY OF SAINT-MARC 109

South to its aid, gathering numerous recruits on its march through the inland parishes of the West. But the departure of the General Assembly for France had obviously carried the matter before a higher tribunal, and until the decision of the national body should be known, neither party desired to prejudice its case by further acts of aggression. Accordingly, negotiations were begun, which on August 23 ended in the so-called "Treaty of Léogane"; really a truce in which both parties promised to abstain from hostilities until the arrival of the National Assembly's decision.[36]

It was obvious that the "Treaty of Léogane" settled nothing: indeed, the course of the next few months merely deepened the gulf between the parties. San Domingo was now divided between three factions, the bounds of whose authority coincided roughly with the provincial frontiers. The West was pretty generally subject to Government control, and Mauduit's vigorous measures, backed by his regulars and Royalist "Pompons Blancs," effected a species of counter-revolution. The old King's officers were restored and all disaffection sternly repressed. But there was nothing healing or constructive in these measures, and this blind reaction merely compressed the latent discontent till some future moment of explosion.[37]

In the South, the "Patriots" were absolute masters. The General Assembly's appeal for aid had here been the signal for a general rising, and the last royal officers had been deposed or murdered. Now that the "Treaty of Léogane" had given them undisturbed authority, the "Patriot" leaders proceeded to organize the Southern parishes into a regular confederation, with an executive council, a treasury, and an army.[38] This was of great significance for the future. We have already noted the peculiar nature of the South; its isolation, its backward economic and social conditions, and the strong influence exerted by the neighboring English island of Jamaica.[39] This traditional separatism was greatly enhanced by the practical independence now enjoyed, which did much to bring about the Confederation of the Grande Anse and the appeal to the English, in 1793.

The North, we have seen, had zealously aided Governor Peynier against the Assembly of Saint-Marc, but it was perfectly obvious that this action had been dictated by hatred of the common enemy and in no sense by submission to the royal authority. Therefore, as soon as the reason for joint action had vanished, its alliance gave place to watchful neutrality. Peynier, however, was too cautious to make any attempt against the North, and the relations of the two remained outwardly correct. The Northern Assembly assumed full control over its province, although here as elsewhere the other factions were represented by minorities ready to make trouble at the first opportunity.[40]

One thing was clear — the white colonists were entirely forgetting the necessity of union in face of the French Revolution. Indeed, the recent action of the defeated "Patriots" in appealing to the judgment of the National Assembly had shown a complete disregard of all the warnings from cooler heads on both sides of the Atlantic. At the time of Mauduit's *coup* against the Western Committee, De Wimpffen had ably voiced this body of opinion. "I see," he writes, "but one way of saving

THE ASSEMBLY OF SAINT-MARC 111

the colony: it is to bring about the Revolution by the hands of those who are ineffectually employed to retard its progress. They can no longer check; they may still direct it. The bulk of the colonists, the merchants, the different departments of the administration, have all an equal interest to maintain order: let them speedily join themselves to the Government, to baffle and counteract the dark intrigues carried on by the disaffected to excite an insurrection of the people of color and the negroes."[41]

The truth of these words was soon made evident. Failure to obtain political rights had infuriated the Paris mulattoes; the excited declamations of their numerous sympathizers convinced them that they were victims of an intolerable injustice; and the very air of Revolutionary Paris taught them the gospel of violent measures. Under these circumstances it is not strange that one of their number, a young man of ardent temperament named Ogé, presently became convinced that he was destined to lead a successful rising of his caste. Accordingly he left for England, whence, with the aid of Clarkson, he succeeded in reaching San Domingo in the early part of October. His presence in the island was kept a profound secret until, on October 28, he raised the standard of revolt in the mountainous district of the North Province near the Spanish border. With a force of about three hundred men he kept the field for several days, but was finally beaten after a sharp engagement by the strong column of regulars and militia sent against him from Le Cap. Ogé and his principal followers fled into Spanish territory, but were soon surrendered to the French authorities under the terms of the extradition treaty then in force. Nearly all the insurgents were apprehended and punished in proportion to their share in the movement. Ogé and his lieutenant Chavannes suffered the usual penalty inflicted upon insurgent leaders, — that of being broken on the wheel; a score of others were hanged, and a large number were sentenced to various terms of imprisonment.[42]

This second rising of the mulattoes was a very much more serious affair than the abortive attempt of the preceding March.[43] Not only had the insurgents stood their ground; their call to arms had awakened widespread response throughout the colony. In the West large numbers of mulattoes had taken arms, and only the vigorous action of Mauduit and the prompt collapse of the Northern rising had avoided serious consequences.[44] Still more ominous was the fact that this rising had been the direct result of incitement from France.

Its results were more serious still. The numerous executions which followed the suppression of the revolt roused a furious desire for vengeance among the mulattoes, and made any common action of the two castes against future Revolutionary slave legislation impossible.[45] Lastly, the news of Ogé's tragic death excited in France such a wave of sympathy for the mulattoes and hostility to the colonists as greatly furthered the passage of the momentous National Decree of May 15, 1791.[46]

But all this was lost upon the minds of excited partisans. The one fact which appeared on the surface was that this second mulatto effort had been repressed almost as quickly and easily as the first, and a feeling of confidence ensued which blinded the colonists to future dangers and persuaded them that they might safely continue their

THE ASSEMBLY OF SAINT-MARC   113

internal quarrels. In November, 1790, the decision of the National Assembly on the troubles of Saint-Marc had reached the island. The specious pleading of the fugitive colonial legislature had been unable to gloze over the manifest tendencies of its actions, and on October 12 the National Assembly had issued a decree which completely vindicated the Government, nullified all the acts of the colonial legislature, and declared its dissolution.[47] But the "Patriots" refused to submit to this decision, and the island remained in its condition of unstable equilibrium [48] until a sudden shock from without destroyed the existing balance of parties in the spring of 1791.

The disturbed conditions revealed by the reports on the troubles of Saint-Marc had convinced the National Assembly that an increase of the military forces in San Domingo had become a necessity, and in consequence of this decision, on the 2d of March, 1791, a squadron appeared in the harbor of Port-au-Prince with two regiments of the line on board. But by this time the Revolutionary spirit had thoroughly infected the French army. Even on the voyage the troops had got quite out of hand, and the appeals at once made to them by the oppressed "Patriots" of the town roused the soldiers to furious mutiny. In the preceding winter the breakdown of Governor Peynier's health had caused his replacement by the Vicomte de Blanchelande, but the new Governor was no stronger than his predecessor and displayed in this crisis a total lack of resolution. The result was inevitable. Left without orders, the soldiers of the regiment "Port-au-Prince" succumbed to their comrades' appeals to join in overthrowing this counter-revolution, and on March 4,

Blanchelande fled, while Mauduit, who refused to desert his post, was murdered by the mutineers.[49] A "Patriot" revolution followed throughout the province. The Government officials were everywhere deposed, the "Pompons Blancs" disarmed, and the Royalist régime completely overthrown throughout the West.[50]

The "Patriots" were now supreme in both West and South; but this naturally revived the alliance of their opponents. Blanchelande and the leading members of the Government party fled to Le Cap, where they were received in most friendly fashion, and as the "Patriots" did not feel strong enough to attempt the reduction of the North, this new balance of parties continued[51] until, early in July, all quarrels were forgotten in presence of the National Decree of May 15, 1791.

X

THE DECREE OF MAY 15, 1791

THE National Decrees of March, 1790, had really begged the question of the colonies.[1] But the attitude of the Assembly of Saint-Marc, the alarm caused by Article 4, and the pressure of conservative opinion in France, all showed the National Assembly that any blow aimed at the existing social order in the colonies would entail the most serious consequences. Until the spring of 1791 the National Assembly consistently refused to touch either slavery or the color line.

The attitude of conservative Frenchmen on the colonial question is well expressed by De Wimpffen in a letter written at the very beginning of the Revolution. "My sentiments, sir, with regard to the slavery of the blacks are no secret to you," he writes a French correspondent in March, 1789. "You are apprised, then, that I have always agreed, and still agree with those writers who reprobate so strongly the infamous traffic we maintain on the coasts of Africa. But, while I do justice to the purity of their motives, . . . our age is unfortunately too full of political reformers; who are in a violent haste to pull down an irregular edifice, without having either the talents or the materials necessary to construct it again upon a better plan. One simple argument shall suffice for all. Your colonies, such as they are, cannot exist without slavery. This is a frightful truth, I confess; — but the not recognizing it is more frightful still, and may produce the most terrible consequences. You must, then, sanction slavery or renounce your colonies: and as 30,000 whites can control 460,000 negroes only by the force of opinion (the sole guaranty of their existence), everything which tends to weaken or destroy that opinion is a crime against society." [2]

And the attitude of the colonists themselves was now explained to the National Legislature by no less a body than the Provincial Assembly of the North. This body had accepted the supremacy of the National Assembly and had declared war upon the autonomists of Saint-Marc: and yet, at the height of the crisis, in the very moment when it was equipping Vincent's army for an invasion of the West, it had drawn up an address to the French Assembly which frankly stated how easily its action might have been reversed. This address, dated July 13, 1790, begins by a vigorous condemnation of the Assembly of Saint-Marc. "But," it adds, "what has led the General Assembly into such a rash and disloyal course? Let us, who have proved our loyalty, tell you with the frankness permitted a friend speaking truth. Gentlemen, the reason is an unfortunate suspicion of the National Assembly itself: you have the proof of this assertion in the Decree of the 28th of May,[3] . . . and in the precautions taken against the National Assembly." This suspicion, declares the address, has been caused by the agitation of the "Amis des Noirs" within and without the National Assembly, by the favorable reception granted by that body to the mulattoes,[4] by Article 4, and by the strong negrophil sentiment displayed by so large a section of French public opinion.

"Pardon our frankness, gentlemen," continues the address. "Never was frankness more necessary. The misfortune of the General Assembly is that it does not believe that your Decree of March 28 safeguards the colony, and that it distrusts your attitude. We think the contrary, and we believe that you could never lay a snare for your brothers. But, had we believed as the General Assembly, our conduct might well have been different.

"This is no time for mincing matters. Gentlemen, San Domingo will never sacrifice her indispensable prejudice regarding the mulattoes. She will protect them; she will ameliorate their lot: of this intention she is daily giving proof, and time will doubtless afford more extensive opportunities. But of both time and means, she must be the absolute mistress, the only judge. . . . As to the negroes, our self-interest is allied to their well-being; but the colony will never suffer this sort of property, which it holds by the law and which guarantees all other species, to be called in question, now or at any future time.

"The greater part of the colonists have misinterpreted your intentions. It is therefore of supreme importance that you remove these doubts, because long delay in so doing might engender the idea of secession from France. Forestall, then, these dangers, by a new act of wisdom, confidence, and justice. Gentlemen, we have every confidence in you; — but who is to assure us of the future? Place subsequent legislatures in the happy impossibility of listening to the enemies of our well-being; grant the colony, in advance, an unchangeable article of the French

Constitution, to the effect that no law concerning its internal condition (notably as regards the status of the different classes which compose it) can be decreed except on the specific demand of the colony itself. Then the colony is quiet forever. Then the doubters can no longer doubt. Then the ill-intentioned will have no more excuse. Then, but then only, our ties will be unbreakable."[5]

All this greatly influenced the National Assembly, and its Decree of October 12, 1790, although concerned primarily with the troubles of Saint-Marc,[6] also contained a very important declaration of its general intentions toward the colonies. "No laws upon the status of persons shall be decreed for the colonies," reads a clause of this act, "except upon the specific, formal demand of their Assemblies."[7] Thus, at least in general terms, the National Legislature promised to respect the social system of the colonies.

But with the opening months of 1791 there came a turn of the tide. The wave of Revolution was rising fast and the King was now but waiting the moment for flight: that the radical flood should once more threaten the conservative edifice of colonial society was inevitable. The "Amis des Noirs" had never relaxed their efforts. Besides their general appeals for loyalty to the fundamental principles of the Revolution, they maintained that, by passing Article 4 of the March Instructions, the Assembly had actually decreed the political equality of the mulattoes, and they insistently demanded that the Assembly, by some unequivocal act, should confound those persons now barring the mulattoes from political rights in defiance of the national will. To all this the colonists made reply, and a great controversy raged during the opening months of 1791. In March, the learned Moreau de Saint-Méry published his "Considérations"; the ablest exposition of the colonial thesis in all the voluminous literature of the time. He is especially emphatic in combatting the assertions of the "Amis des Noirs" to the effect that the National Assembly must legislate on the status of the mulattoes, and he predicts that if the Assembly should reverse its decision as expressed in the Decrees of March 8 and October 12, negro emancipation and the destruction of the colonies must soon follow of themselves. "If the National Assembly," he writes, "has the misfortune to legislate on the mulatto status, all is over. The colonists will believe themselves betrayed; the mulattoes, instigated by their friends, will go to the last extremity. And then the slaves, who possess the same friends and the same means of action, will seek to attain the same results. The colonies will soon be only a vast shambles: and France —? Yes! The mulattoes themselves are but pawns in a larger game. For, if our slaves once suspect that there is a power other than their masters which holds the final disposition of their fate; if they once see that the mulattoes have successfully invoked this power and by its aid have become our equals; — then France must renounce all hope of preserving her colonies." [8]

However, as time passed, public opinion declared itself more and more in favor of the "Amis des Noirs," and early in April the news of Ogé's execution caused a veritable storm of anti-colonial feeling. The terrible death of the young enthusiast was just the sort of thing to rouse popular passion in that feverish time. Paris hailed Ogé as a martyr to liberty, enacted his death upon the stage, and grew so hostile to the colonial whites that a planter scarcely ventured to appear upon the streets.[9]

All this quickly reacted upon the National Assembly, and presently a Grand Committee was appointed, consisting of the five Committees on the Constitution, Marine, Colonies, Commerce, and Agriculture, for a thorough consideration of the social system in the colonies. On the 7th of May this Grand Committee reported to the Assembly,[10] — but its recommendations were favorable to colonial desires. It urged the Assembly, as an act of both justice and necessity, "to fulfil toward the colonies an engagement which you have already solemnly taken; an engagement from which your loyalty forbids you to escape; — that is to say, to decree and transform into a constitutional provision your promise of last October.[11] One thing cannot be gainsaid: the convulsions which now rend the colonies have been caused first and foremost by the fears there roused at the moment of the Revolution as to your political intentions; fears which have been ever since inflamed by the most culpable methods." The report then went on to explain why these fears had not been allayed by the Assembly's pronouncements in the Decree of March 8, 1790: because, aside from Article 4 of the instructions, its enemies had at once asserted that it was only temporary in its nature and that it might be revoked any day at the Assembly's pleasure. Then came the Decree of October 12, stating explicitly "the Assembly's firm resolution to establish as an article of the French Constitution the principle that no laws concerning the status of persons should be decreed for the colonies except upon the precise and formal demand of their Assemblies."

And that promise, asserted the report, it was high time to fulfil. "Gentlemen, it is in vain that you are told that what you have already decreed is sufficient. Without doubt it ought to suffice, but as a matter of fact it does not suffice at all." For, the report continued, the opponents of the present colonial system were now asserting that the promise of October 12, like the pronouncement of March 8, was merely provisional and liable to instant revocation. The colonists, therefore, should have their fears finally allayed by a positive constitutional decree which would settle the matter beyond possibility of doubt. "If this be not done," the report ended, "you will put all in jeopardy; — rich possessions, a fleet, an army, and the good order and prosperity of islands which, by a word, you can return to peace and happiness. Lastly, you will drive the colonial deputies to despair of the safety of their country. . . . We repeat, gentlemen: the circumstances are grave; they are imperious. The measure which we propose has become a necessity; — and above all, a prompt necessity. Gentlemen, discuss if you will, but do not adjourn: the fate of your colonies, of your commerce, consequently of your political future, are bound up with your decision."

Nevertheless, the Assembly did adjourn after a lively preliminary skirmish; but on May 11 the decisive battle began. Never before had such a battle been fought on the colonies. Day after day its greatest orators strove upon the floor of the House, and yet neither side could carry the victory. But at last, suddenly and unexpectedly, the end came.

It was the evening of the 15th of May. For five days the National Assembly had winced beneath the threats and warnings of the commercial and colonial deputies; for five days it had writhed under the appeals of the "Amis des Noirs" and the taunts of the roaring galleries. Of a sudden, in a momentary lull, the radical deputy Rewbell sprang to his feet and offered the following "amendment": "The National Assembly decrees that it will never deliberate upon the political status of the people of color *who are not born of free father and mother* without the previous free and spontaneous desire of the colonies; that the Colonial Assemblies actually existing shall continue; but that the people of color born of free father and mother shall be admitted to all the future parish and Colonial Assemblies, if in other respects possessed of the required qualifications."

The Rewbell "amendment" was really a substitute for the Grand Committee's bill; but its clever phrasing and the small number of persons covered by its provisions made it just the sort of compromise which appealed to a body smarting in its conscience and worn down by exhaustion into a sullen agony to have done. Therefore, in spite of the desperate efforts of Barnave, Malouet, and the colonial deputies, the Rewbell amendment, amid a thunder of applause, passed the House and became the famous National Decree of May 15, 1791.[12]

The rout of the colonists was complete. The number of mulattoes thus decreed political equality was, it is true, very small: not over four hundred voters, according

THE DECREE OF MAY 15, 1791   123

to Governor Blanchelande.[13] And yet, given a conflict of irreconcilable principles in a time of revolution, this decree was just that symbolic act which, if accepted by the beaten side, ensured the other's complete victory. But it was soon clear that no thought of submission lay in colonial hearts. On the very next day [14] the colonial deputies solemnly withdrew from the House,[15] and presently the tidings from over-sea told the National Assembly that it was face to face with rebellion.

It was on the 30th of June that the news of this decree arrived at Le Cap, together with reports of the official explanation drawn up by the victorious party in the National Assembly.[16] This latter document was an uncompromising statement of Revolutionary principles which but added fuel to the flames. Almost at the start its language excited misgivings as to the permanence of even the decree's concessions on slavery; for, while it pointed out the Assembly's decision not to legislate on the status of the "non-free," it condemned slavery in principle, and stated that the Assembly condoned the undoubted evils of this institution only in consideration of the fact that the persons involved were ignorant aliens whose immediate emancipation would provoke great evils, and whom the Assembly would therefore leave to the ameliorating effect of time. How much any promise of the National Assembly was worth in a matter which violated its principles the colonists might decide from the appended explanation of its recent action regarding the mulattoes. For this document not only assumed that by Article 4 of the March instructions the Assembly had decreed the political equality of free-born persons; it also went on to say that the Assembly would have been powerless to deprive any such persons of political equality: for, "the rights of citizens are anterior to society, of which they form the necessary base. The Assembly has, therefore, been able merely to discover and define them; it finds itself in happy impotence to infringe them." After a severe condemnation of the colonial deputies for their bolting of the Assembly, the document closed as follows: "The National Assembly has granted all to the colonies: all, except the sacrifice of the imprescriptible rights of a class of citizens which nature and law render an integral part of political society; all, except the reversal of the life-giving principles of the French Constitution."

At the news of this revolutionary decree, the excitable population of San Domingo rose in a delirium of furious resistance. Governor Blanchelande seems to have been almost as much shocked as the rest, for his letter of July 3 to the Minister of Marine not only unsparingly condemns the decree, but asserts his absolute refusal to enforce it.

"I would, sir," he writes, "that I were not obliged to report to you the sensation made by this news and the rapidity with which it is flying to all parts of the colony. ... Three powerful motives combine to excite the present feeling: offended pride, fear for the colony's safety, and indignation at a broken promise. Sir, do not force me to repeat the threats which are upon every tongue; threats each more violent than the one before. The most loyal hearts are estranged, and a frightful civil war or the loss of the colony to France may well result from the present state of opinion. . . .

"The first part of the decree, concerning the slaves and

freedmen, does not reassure people even as to their property; for it is regarded as a mere temporary disposition which a subsequent decree will abrogate, just as this one has annulled the promise of the 12th October. Wherefore, there has occurred that greatest of all misfortunes: the colonists' trust in the National Assembly is absolutely destroyed.

"The same letters also announce that England is despatching to West Indian waters a fleet of forty-five sail; and my pen refuses to report the speeches, perhaps the prayers, to which this circumstance gives birth. To-morrow the Provincial Assembly meets. I have had proof of its patriotism; — but the National Assembly has already seen its principles regarding the mulattoes from its address of last July; [17] and these principles have not changed. On the other hand, the mulattoes may take action, and if they move, all is lost. Judge, then, sir, of my position. It is not my province to criticize decrees; my duty is to enforce them. And yet, sir, I am resolved to spill my own blood rather than that of my fellow citizens and brothers. I pray to Heaven that the retirement of the colonial deputies from the National Assembly and the remonstrances of commerce may bring about the withdrawal of this fatal decree. . . . But, sir, if it be not at least materially modified, I have every reason to fear that it will prove the death-warrant of many thousands of men, including those very persons who are the objects of its solicitude." [18]

These were Blanchelande's reflections after observing public opinion at Le Cap; as news arrived from other parts of the colony, his reports bespoke still deeper alarm.

"This decree is regarded as murderous to the colony," he writes the Minister of Marine on the 31st of July; "and men's minds are growing more inflamed instead of calming down. Popular resentment shows itself in the most violent speeches, the most extraordinary proposals, and people here speak only of resistance to the injustice and ingratitude of the representatives of the nation. Men ceaselessly invoke those promises contained in the Decrees of March 8 and October 12 never to legislate on the status of persons; promises, be it said, not yet explicitly revoked, and here regarded as sacred. But these promises being broken by the utterance of the 15th of May, men say they are thereby quite absolved from their allegiance. In fine, sir, despair is growing from day to day, and counsels only armed resistance to the execution of this law, however large the forces which may be sent hither." [19]

That the Governor had not exaggerated is abundantly proved both by other official writings [20] and by the large number of private letters still preserved in the Archives Nationales. One of these letters, dated Le Cap, July 5, notes such intense indignation that the writer fears a universal explosion. "The colony is resolved on secession if the mother country attempts to enforce this decree." [21] Still more alarming is a letter from Port-au-Prince. This also predicts a war between the castes, for the whites will never yield. "Do you think," exclaims the writer, "that we will take the law from the grandson of one of our slaves? 'No! Rather die than assent to this infamy!' — that is the cry of all. If France sends troops for the execution of this decree, it is likely that we will decide to abandon France." [22] "Desolation is stamped upon every

THE DECREE OF MAY 15, 1791

face," reads a letter from Léogane. "All business has ceased, and people busy themselves only with this affair."[23] Correspondence from the South Province is but the echo of that from the North and West. "This decree has electrified the whole colony," reads a letter from Les Cayes, which closes with the gloomy prophecy that "the colony is doomed."[24]

The best rallying-point for future resistance was obviously a Colonial Assembly. Accordingly, the Provincial Assembly of the North promptly issued election writs throughout the colony, and on August 9 the new body met at Léogane, a town of the West. Its members displayed great unanimity, but soon adjourned after a few proceedings of a formal nature, fixing the regular session for the 25th of August at Le Cap. It was felt that the crisis demanded the presence of the Colonial Legislature in the chief centre of population, especially since Blanchelande's friendly attitude left nothing to be feared from the royal authority.[25]

But before the appointed day the mulattoes of the West were in general revolt, while the negroes of the North had lighted a conflagration never to be put out.

XI

THE NEGRO INSURRECTION IN THE NORTH

It was just before dawn on the 23d of August, 1791, that a stream of dishevelled fugitives waked Le Cap to terror and affright, while over the great North Plain a lurid glow bore ominous witness to their tidings. These refugees reported that the negroes were burning the cane-fields and plantations, and that they themselves were but the survivors of a frightful massacre.[1]

So absorbed had the colonists been of late in their preparations for resistance to the May Decree that this rising seems to have taken them quite unawares. And yet for full two years the colony had been vouchsafed a whole series of premonitory symptoms which a more observant people would have seriously laid to heart.

We have already had a glimpse of the alarm caused by the conduct of the negroes as far back as the autumn of 1789,[2] and what was there quoted is by no means all the evidence which even now remains. "The troubles in France have reached here," writes Julien Raymond from the South Province to his brother, the mulatto leader in Paris; "the whites have taken the tricolor cockade. As you may well imagine, this has not occurred without considerable disturbance and bloodshed. The most terrible thing about this business, however, is the attitude of the negroes, who, hearing that the cockade means liberty and equality, have wanted to rise themselves. In several districts a considerable number of them have been executed."[3] Several other letters from this period speak of similar disturbances, and throughout the year 1790 sporadic mutinies occurred on plantations in various parts of the colony.[4]

But early in July, 1791, that sullen wave of unrest passed over the negro population which heralded the great rising: it is plain that at this moment the negroes throughout the colony knew that something was in the wind. The disaffection seems to have been spread by the great Vaudoux cult,[5] which accounts for the secrecy and obscurity of the whole affair, whose details will probably never be known. In the West the disturbances were widespread and called for vigorous measures. "The negroes are stirring in astonishing fashion," writes a colonist from Port-au-Prince to the Club Massiac on the 18th of July. "Regular armed rebellions have occurred at several points hereabouts, . . . and at one place some twenty miles from here they had to call out the whole neighborhood and summon the *maréchaussée*. At this place they had to fire a volley and charge the rebels, who stood their ground and did not surrender until their leaders had fallen. A dozen of them have since been hanged."[6]

Still more alarming signs appeared in the North. On the 11th of August a rising occurred at Limbé, a parish of the Plain. The local *maréchaussée* stamped out the trouble, but the testimony gathered from prisoners taken during the next few days was of a very disquieting nature. It appeared that three days after the Limbé rising a meeting had taken place, at which negroes from most of the parishes in the Plain had assembled, "to fix the day for the outbreak of the insurrection decided upon long before."[7]

But all these warnings were disregarded. The risings were repressed with great severity, it is true, but these very successes appear to have inspired a feeling of overconfidence.[8] And yet this is not so singular as it appears to us, who judge in the light of future events: sporadic plantation mutinies could not have been supremely alarming to men accustomed to maroon incursions[9] and absorbed in the alarming prospect of rebellion against France. Furthermore, any alliance between negroes and mulattoes was thought unlikely in the extreme, for it was held impossible that the slaves could so far forget the hatred which they bore toward their hardest taskmasters.[10] In the words of Mirabeau, the colonists "slept on the edge of Vesuvius."[11]

Whatever may have been its antecedents, the rising which took place over the North Plain on the night of the 22d of August was well planned and systematically executed. The insurgent leader in the vicinity of Le Cap was one Boukman, said to have been high in the Vaudoux cult; and reports, apparently legendary, tell of preliminary ceremonies of a savage and bloody nature.[12] The scattered white population of the plantations could offer no resistance. The men were at once killed, often with every species of atrocity, while the unfortunate white women were violated — frequently upon the very bodies of their husbands, fathers, and brothers.[13] The full horror of the situation was soon brought home to the people of Le Cap itself. A reconnoitring party of National Guards which ventured a little way out into the

NEGRO INSURRECTION IN THE NORTH

Plain was suddenly overwhelmed in the half-light of dawn by a horde of negroes whose ghastly standard was the impaled body of a white child: only two or three of the soldiers escaped to carry the dreadful tidings.[14] Within a few days the whole of the great North Plain was to be only a waste of blood and ashes.[15]

On that very morning of the 23d a strong column of regulars and militia entered the Plain, but it was soon compelled to retreat before the swarming negro masses, and thereafter for some time the whites of Le Cap attempted no aggressive measures. This lack of initiative was due to several causes. In the first place, the colonists seem to have been literally paralyzed by the magnitude of the catastrophe and by the peculiar horror of the attendant circumstances. Carteau, an eye-witness of these events, has left us a vivid description. "Picture to yourself," he writes, "the whole horizon a wall of fire, from which continually rose thick vortices of smoke, whose huge black volumes could be likened only to those frightful storm-clouds which roll onwards charged with thunder and with lightnings. The rifts in these clouds disclosed flames as great in volume which rose darting and flashing to the very sky. Such was their voracity that for nearly three weeks we could barely distinguish between day and night, for so long as the rebels found anything to feed the flames, they never ceased to burn, resolved as they were to leave not a cane nor house behind. The most striking feature of this terrible spectacle was a rain of fire composed of burning cane-straw which whirled thickly before the blast like flakes of snow, and which the wind carried, now toward the harbor and shipping, now over the houses of the city, plunging us in the greatest fear of its effects and wringing our hearts with an agony of grief as it disclosed the full extent of our misfortunes." [16]

Edwards, who arrived at Le Cap about a month after the outbreak of the insurrection, corroborates Carteau's testimony. "We arrived in the harbor of Le Cap," he writes, "at evening of September 26, and the first sight which arrested our attention as we approached was a dreadful scene of devastation by fire. The noble plain adjoining Le Cap was covered with ashes, and the surrounding hills, as far as the eye could reach, everywhere presented to us ruins still smoking, and houses and plantations at that moment in flames. It was a sight more terrible than the mind of any man unaccustomed to such a scene can easily conceive." [17] Any one who has seen a burned district in the tropics can appreciate the force of this description.[18]

But there were also very practical reasons for renouncing all immediate thought of reducing the rebels of the Plain. The resident white population of Le Cap was not over four thousand, the regular troops did not exceed twelve hundred, and of the three thousand sailors in the port nearly a third were foreigners.[19] Even counting the refugees, the total number of whites in Le Cap during the first days of the insurrection could not have been over ten thousand, and their confidence was not increased by the fact that the city also contained not less than fourteen hundred mulattoes and from ten to twelve thousand negro slaves.[20] The loyalty of the mulattoes was doubtful, while the negro population was certainly ripe for revolt and massacre.

NEGRO INSURRECTION IN THE NORTH 133

It would seem that for some days previous to the fateful 23d of August, the Government had scented trouble. On the very evening before the rising, several suspected persons had been arrested and brought before the Governor. "From their admissions," writes Blanchelande to the Minister of Marine, "I became convinced that some conspiracy was on foot against the town." [21] As the result of his fears he quietly took strong precautions, which probably averted a terrible disaster.

But the most alarming fact remains to be told. Among the prisoners there had been several whites, and Blanchelande says that at the moment he "could not quite make out whether the suspected plot was among the whites, mulattoes, free negroes, or slaves." One thing, however, seems clear: a certain section of that low rabble of criminals and aliens which had always given so much trouble [22] was of so desperate and depraved a character that it was willing to see Le Cap go down in blood and fire, provided it had a share in the plunder. Indeed, by the following morning, Blanchelande considered the situation so critical that he placed an embargo on all vessels, "to serve as a refuge in case of disaster," and ordered sorties into the Plain to cease. "If the means at my disposal had allowed," he continues, "I should not have contented myself with this mere defensive attitude; I should have immediately marched against the negroes and reduced them. But Le Cap contained within itself a number of dangerous elements, of all colors. I discovered then — I am still daily discovering — numerous plots which prove that the town negroes are in league with those in arms on the Plain: hence, we must be continually on our guard lest some spark within the town itself flame rapidly into a general conflagration."

However, imminent danger to the city itself lessened with every day. Le Cap, of course, had been an open town with no fortifications on its landward side, but the heights which lay between it and the Plain offered natural advantages for defence quickly strengthened into regular fortified lines.[23] On September 13, Blanchelande was able to write that he considered the city fairly safe from attack, "although the whites almost without exception are the prey of a discouragement whose intensity you can hardly conceive; in addition to which it is undeniable that this town contains a very large number of poor and disaffected whites, who would welcome disorder in the hope of bettering their lot by plunder. This class has clearly shown its evil intentions by its formal refusal to fight the rebels." [24]

Very different was the spirit displayed by the whites of the country. In the Plain, it is true, the sudden rising of its dense negro population had swept the unsuspecting colonists off their feet; but elsewhere the whites flew to arms with astonishing rapidity, and succeeded in stemming the black torrent for the time. Before long every exit from the Plain was barred by military posts, while along the mountain-crests the labor of numerous slave *corvées* rapidly erected lines of strong forts and block-houses, called "cordons," which were successfully to bar all insurgent intercourse with the West down to the collapse of white authority in 1793. The white women and children were rapidly gathered into fortified "camps," where they might be safe from chance raiding parties[25].

NEGRO INSURRECTION IN THE NORTH 135

Then began a struggle obscure in detail but horrible in character. "To detail," writes Edwards, "the various conflicts, skirmishes, massacres, and other scenes of slaughter which this exterminating war produced, were to offer a disgusting and frightful picture; a combination of horrors wherein we should behold cruelties unexampled in the annals of mankind; human blood poured forth in torrents, the earth blackened with ashes, the air tainted with pestilence. It is computed that, within two months after the revolt first began, upwards of two thousand whites had been massacred; that one hundred and eighty sugar-plantations and about nine hundred coffee, cotton, and indigo settlements had been destroyed (the buildings thereon being consumed by fire); and twelve hundred families reduced from opulence to abject destitution. Of the insurgents, it was reckoned that upwards of ten thousand had perished by the sword or famine, and some hundreds by the hand of the executioner — many of these on the wheel."[26] And he thereupon gives a vivid picture of such an execution held beneath the very windows of his lodging.[27]

A British army officer who visited Le Cap in the early autumn of 1791 has left a striking account of its condition. "The city," he writes, "presents a terrible spectacle; surrounded by ditches and palisades, the streets blocked by barricades, and the squares occupied by scaffolds on which captured negroes are tortured, — the whole forming a depressing picture of devastation and carnage."[28]

The aspect of the country was more dreadful still. The Great Plain was a silent waste of blackened ruin infested by bands of prowling savages,[29] while farther inland the debatable hill country was studded with white and negro "camps," both of which must have been veritable dens of horror. The negro stockades were garnished, in the African fashion, with the skulls of prisoners killed after unspeakable tortures, while the tree-lined roads leading to the white "camps" were festooned with the bodies of hanged rebels.[30]

However, as the months passed it became evident that the insurgents were slowly gaining ground. By the month of October, it is true, expeditions issued from Le Cap; but in these sallies the rabble took no part, and the *bourgeois* National Guards, though brave and willing, died like flies before the climate and could not long keep the field. The brunt of the fighting fell upon the regulars, whose numbers were, however, soon terribly reduced.[31] Even the country whites suffered greatly from tropical campaigning, and this continual drain upon their small number was of course irreparable. How the country whites wasted away is well shown by a letter from the inland parish of Le Borgne. The district was quiet for the moment, as the negroes had drawn off to resist a sortie from Le Cap; "but sickness continues its war, and our privations make of us an easy prey. Of the ten members of our local committee, only three are able to be about, and this is but typical of the rest. One of our most vital posts kills every week some five or six of our men." [32]

The way in which the hill country was gradually lost is well described by the official diary of the Parish of Le Trou. It begins with that general arming of the whites and establishment of camps to guard exposed points which occurred during the last days of August. Till mid-

NEGRO INSURRECTION IN THE NORTH 137

September the parish was outwardly peaceful, though a lengthening list of negro emissaries caught and shot among the slave *ateliers* is daily recorded. On September 16, however, a stream of fugitives announced the capture of the neighboring parish of Saint-Suzanne by the terrible mulatto leader Candy. Now that Le Trou had become a frontier parish things rapidly grew worse, and a week later the mulatto companies of militia murdered their white officers and went over to Candy. Then follows a gallant two months' struggle against the inevitable. Every night plantations are sacked and the slaves carried over to the enemy: sometimes a whole canton is thus devastated. Finally, on November 16, the whites evacuate their posts and retire towards the sea. Only the priest remains behind, and Candy promptly occupies the country.[33]

The first leaders of the negro rising were Boukman [34] and one Jeannot. But Boukman was killed by the whites at the very start, and Jeannot was not only a monster of cruelty, but such an insufferable tyrant that he was soon done away with by his own followers. These first leaders were replaced by two others named Jean-François and Biassou, of whom the former was ultimately to become the acknowledged insurgent head. Of course the rebel organization was at this time very crude, and these men were only the two most prominent members of a whole group of guerilla chiefs.[35] Rather alongside this negro organization were the mulatto bands of Candy; for, throughout the Plain, the mulattoes had risen at the same moment as the slaves.

The negroes naturally adopted guerilla tactics, and

never faced the whites in the open except when possessed of overwhelming numbers. Such a negro attack is described by the anonymous but well-informed author of the "Désastres de Saint-Domingue." "Their enterprises," he writes, "have about them something truly terrifying by the very manner of execution. The negroes never mass in the open: a thousand blacks will never await in line of battle the charge of a hundred whites. They first advance with a frightful clamor, preceded by a great number of women and children singing and yelling in chorus. When they have arrived just out of gunshot from the whites, the most profound silence suddenly falls, and the negroes now dispose themselves in such a manner that they appear six times as numerous as they are in reality. The man of faint heart, already daunted by the apparent multitude of his enemies, is still further shaken by their noiseless posturings and grimaces. All this time the ominous silence continues; the only sounds coming from the magicians, who now begin to dance and sing with the contortions of demoniacs. These men are working their incantations ['Wanga'] to assure the success of the coming attack, and they often advance within musket-shot, confident that the bullets cannot touch them and desirous of proving to the other negroes the power of their magic charms. The attack now takes place with cries and howlings which, notwithstanding, should not shake the courageous man." [36]

Both existing evidence and the trend of events combine to show that the great negro uprising of August, 1791, was but the natural action of the Revolution upon highly inflammable material.[37] This is the opinion of

NEGRO INSURRECTION IN THE NORTH 139

Garran-Coulon [38] and of the Colonial Committee in the National Assembly; [39] both of them contemporary verdicts rendered after the careful examination of an enormous mass of evidence. Yet naturally there were a number of contributing factors to the great disaster which the prevalent suspicion of the Revolutionary period raised to the rank of primary causes.

Many conservative writers charged the outbreak to the deliberate plottings of the "Amis des Noirs." [40] Now there seems to be no doubt that the writings and speeches of the French radicals did have a considerable effect upon the negroes. In spite of all the colonists' efforts, a good deal of incendiary literature found its way into the island: a very violent open letter of the Abbé Grégoire to the negroes was certainly known to them, and Carteau states that on several occasions he saw Revolutionary pamphlets in the hands of slaves.[41] The conduct of persons newly arrived from France must also have had a very exciting effect. Blanchelande writes that when the mutinous soldiers landed at Port-au-Prince in March, 1791,[42] "they gave the fraternal embrace to all the negroes and mulattoes whom they met, telling them that the National Assembly had declared them free and the equals of the whites"; [43] while a colonist writes that some of the Western disturbances of July, 1791, were due "to the civism of the sailors who were constantly about." [44] Nevertheless, it is quite certain that no accredited emissary of the French radicals was ever captured among the rebels, and the Colonial Committee states that its investigation had discovered no incriminating evidence of actual complicity on the part of the French society.[45]

Perhaps the most telling indirect evidence in the radical's favor, however, is the fact that the insurgents rose to the cry of "God and the King," assumed Royalist insignia, spared the clergy, and were shown benevolent neutrality by the Spaniards. The later events of the Vendée formed too striking a superficial analogy not to be seized upon by many Revolutionary writers, who make the charge that the Royalists incited the negroes to revolt in the hope of frightening the colonists back to the Old Régime.[46] But as bitter a hater of Royalism as Garran-Coulon absolves them of the charge and holds that the negroes' adoption of the outward signs of the Old Régime was merely the imitation of the only insignia of authority then known to them.[47] The clergy, whom the negroes regarded with superstitious reverence, did generally remain unmolested among the rebels, and it is certain that some of them actively aided the negroes;[48] but these were probably zealots whom the religious schism then existing in France had roused to extreme fanaticism. As to the Spaniards, it is certain that they refused to give the aid called for by treaty obligations, and that the frontier officials winked at an extensive contraband traffic with the negro rebels.[49] But the Spanish attitude is sufficiently explained by horror at the French Revolution, rage at the French attitude over Nootka Sound, and the corrupt character of Spanish officialdom.

The colonists themselves were indirectly much to blame. It was their factional quarrels which did so much to make the negroes' opportunity, while the flood of rash political discussion carried on among the whites in season and out of season must have given their slaves much food for reflection. As far back as July, 1790, De Wimpffen is greatly alarmed at the imprudence of the colonists. "I see with pain, sir," he writes, "that the Revolutionary vertigo has already made such progress amongst the inhabitants that even at table, surrounded by mulattoes and negroes, they indulge themselves in the most imprudent discussions on liberty, etc. Very soon the slaves of the neighboring plantations, connected with those of the town, will carry home the discourses they have heard, and comment upon them in their own way. 'If these whites are free only to-day,' they will say, 'What were they then yesterday? — Slaves like ourselves'; and God preserve me from being a witness of the consequences of this mode of reasoning! To discuss the 'Rights of Man' before such people; — what is it but to teach them that power dwells with strength, and strength with numbers!" [50]

To resume the thread of events: the North Plain was the prey of a slave revolt which was blockading Le Cap and eating into the mountain parishes; the West and South were aflame with a mulatto insurrection which had just laid Port-au-Prince in ashes; [51] when, on the 26th of November, three Civil Commissioners landed at Le Cap, charged by the National Assembly to quiet the troubles of San Domingo.

XII

THE MULATTO INSURRECTION IN THE WEST

If the news of the May Decree had roused the whites of San Domingo to furious resistance, it had as inevitably inspired the mulattoes to revolt. Although technically the Decree of May 15 had granted equality to only a small number of the caste, the mulattoes realized as well as did the whites that once this decree went into effect their cause was morally won. As soon, therefore, as the whites proclaimed their determination to resist the decree, the mulattoes resolved to strike, assured as they were of French approval at this blow against professed rebels. By early August they had begun to assemble in various parts of the West, especially in their stronghold of the Artibonite, though so quietly that the preoccupied whites seem to have given the matter little attention.[1]

Both the state of mind and future plans of the mulattoes are well shown by a letter from Léogane, dated the 27th of August, addressed to the mulatto leader Raymond at Paris. It is especially significant because the writer is evidently still ignorant of the negro insurrection which had broken out four days previously in the North. "On all sides," writes this mulatto, "the whites are saying that the Decree of May 15 will never be executed, and that they would sooner lose the island than see it go into effect. Nevertheless, they are so weakened by their own dissensions that I for my part am convinced that our class, which is almost as numerous as the whites, could if properly led execute all the National Decrees on our own account. So many of our young men are coming forward ... that I am quite sure we can put three thousand men in line; and I flatter myself that these three thousand, led by a man like the late Monsieur Mauduit, would prove a torrent that Lucifer himself could not resist." [2]

The closing lines of this letter foreshadowed the next step of the mulattoes. Ever since the overthrow of the Government at Port - au - Prince in March, 1791,[3] the Western Royalists had been a minority suffering from increasing oppression. The mutinous soldiery which had expelled Blanchelande and murdered Mauduit had remained in the capital, had fraternized with the mob, and had set up a turbulent democracy whose leading spirit was one Praloto, a Maltese by birth and a thorough scoundrel by character.[4] The town merchants dared make no resistance to this government, but the country gentlemen had soon banded together and had established a centre of opposition at the neighboring town of La-Croix-des-Bouquets, the chief inland centre of the Plain of Cul-de-Sac.[5]

These men the mulattoes now approached with offers of an alliance against their common enemies. And to these Royalist gentlemen the offer must have greatly appealed. Many of them had commanded the mulattoes for years in the militia or the *maréchaussée*, understood the mulatto character, and felt that they would be able to guide a movement which would undoubtedly be full of peril to themselves if left to ignorant colored leaders.

It was, of course, evident that the mulattoes would insist upon the May Decree, but the doings of the National Assembly did not greatly trouble men who regarded it as a nest of traitors soon to be snuffed out by the Counter-Revolution. "Before three months," a member of the Club Massiac had written to his fellows in San Domingo, — "before three months, I say, your slaves will rise, your plantations will be sacked, and your houses will be burned. There is but one way of safety. Pin on the white cockade, and rest assured that France will soon come to your aid; for by that time fifty thousand Germans will have thrown out of the windows this legislative *canaille*." [6]

The leader of the Western Royalists was one Hanus de Jumecourt, a wealthy planter and a man of great energy. His efforts soon brought his associates to accept the offer of the mulattoes of the Artibonite, and in the last days of August the two parties signed a formal alliance known as the "Confederation of La-Croix-des-Bouquets." This compact was eagerly signed by the mulattoes throughout the province, while the signatures of the country whites of all classes were obtained either willingly or by violence. The news of the negro insurrection in the North seems to have been very efficacious to this end.[7]

The news of this confederation greatly alarmed the democrats of Port-au-Prince, who determined that sharp action must at once be taken. Accordingly, on September 2, a disorderly column of regulars, National Guards, and ruffians, loosely organized under the name of "Flibustiers," marched on La-Croix-des-Bouquets.

MULATTO INSURRECTION IN THE WEST 145

The expedition, however, quickly ended in disaster. The Confederates laid an ambush into which the column unsuspectingly marched, the rabble fled at the first volley, and the regulars, after a good fight, were cut to pieces.[8] The temporary disorganization which ensued among the democrats of Port-au-Prince was cleverly taken advantage of by the merchant classes, who were so exasperated at their own position and so terrified for the future by the news from the North that they were willing to make almost any agreement with a party headed by such reliable persons as De Jumecourt and his associates. Accordingly a conservative deputation was sent to negotiate with the Confederates, and on the 11th of the month the conference resulted in the so-called "Concordat of September." By this document the whites of Port-au-Prince agreed not to oppose the National Decree of the 15th May, and promised to admit mulattoes to the franchise under the terms of the famous Article 4.[9]

The Concordat of September was couched in fair words, but it seems unlikely that either party took it very seriously. De Jumecourt and his aristocratic associates appear to have been really willing to see its execution, for they realized that with the restoration of absolute government all the clauses anent mulatto political equality would become so much waste paper, since there could be neither franchise nor assemblies under the Old Régime. Their hopes and plans are revealed in a letter written by the Royalist commandant at Saint-Marc on the 21st of September: "You have three classes of brigands to fight. First, the white brigands, who are the most to be feared. Leave them to be destroyed by the mulattoes, if you do not care to destroy them yourself. Next, with the aid of the mulattoes, you will reduce the rebel negroes. After that, you will gradually restore the old laws, and by that time you will be able to suppress the refractory element among the mulattoes themselves." [10] The other white signatories of the Concordat, whose adhesion had been obtained "under persuasion of torch and poniard," as the Colonial Assembly put it,[11] were well aware that this same Assembly would never assent to the Concordat's provisions.

Neither did the more intelligent mulattoes believe that the gulf of race hatred could be bridged by a sheet of parchment. Upon the arrival of that decisive National Decree of April 4, 1792, which was finally to ordain full mulatto equality, a leader of the caste wrote to Raymond: "You cannot imagine the sensation which this beneficent decree has made among the whites; for, although those of them allied with us had carried out the Concordat, it is certain that they had never taken it seriously. They rightly counted upon the fact that the General Assembly would never pronounce in our favor." [12] In spite of all this, however, the mulattoes had good practical reasons for desiring an outward reconciliation. Besides the fact that the Concordat was a moral victory, there were so many wealthy slaveowners among the Western mulattoes that the negro uprising in the North and the agitation then going on among the negroes of the West had excited almost as much alarm among them as among the whites themselves. These mulattoes were only too anxious to preserve order in the West until the arrival of the forces then expected to be sent from France to overawe colonial defiance of the mother country.

The West, however, was not to be long preserved from new disorders. The Concordat and the Royalist reaction effected by the Confederates in the country parishes of the West [13] had alarmed both racial and political feeling at Le Cap. The Colonial Assembly denounced the Concordat and its authors in no uncertain terms; and Blanchelande, who had drawn away from the extreme Royalists during his residence in the North, wrote a severe letter to the Confederates, pointing out the impossibility of his executing the May Decree until after its official arrival in the colony,[14] and ordering them forthwith to disperse.[15]

The above action of Governor and Assembly was probably only what the Confederates had expected; but what now occurred at Port-au-Prince was quite a different matter. By the mass of the town population the Concordat had been received with fury, while among the democratic leaders the news of the Counter-Revolution effected throughout the West had aroused lively fears for their personal safety. "The popular leaders here," reads a letter of mid-October, "have so much to fear from a return of the Old Régime that they prefer to expose the colony to possible ruin rather than yield." [16] Accordingly the democratic leaders denounced the merchant negotiators of the Concordat as traitors, regained their old ascendancy, and broke off relations with the Confederates. De Jumecourt, however, acted with great energy. He at once blockaded Port-au-Prince with an army of several thousand mulattoes, and as the town was not provisioned for a siege it was soon forced to submit and sign the "Concordat of October" on the 23d of that month. In this second treaty not only were all the provisions of the September Concordat reaffirmed; the city also agreed to admit fifteen hundred mulatto troops as part of its garrison.[17]

Such was the condition of the West when, only a few days later, the news of the National Decree of September 24 upset the calculations of both parties, and rendered a new crisis inevitable.

We have already seen under what peculiar conditions the Rewbell amendment had passed the National Assembly and become the Decree of May 15, 1791.[18] But, as usual, no sooner had a definite stand been taken on the thorny question of the colonies than an increasingly large number of moderate deputies began to repent of their action. The defiant secession of the colonial deputies was a very ominous portent, while the Assembly was immediately deluged with addresses and appeals which soon produced a marked effect. Also, the colonists and their commercial allies still had one chance of repairing their defeat. Until the decree had been officially sent to Blanchelande for execution the matter was not irreparable; and this delay the changed temper of the House enabled them to accomplish.[19]

The feelings of the wavering majority may be imagined when in mid-August there arrived the news that San Domingo and its Governor were in open rebellion. The worst predictions of the colonial deputies were thus fulfilled, and an intense revulsion of sentiment took place which emboldened the colonists to strike for the reversal of the hated decree. To detail the parliamentary struggle

MULATTO INSURRECTION IN THE WEST 149

which followed would be but the tedious repetition of what had gone before: suffice it to say that after a final grand debate the National Assembly, then on the very verge of dissolution, passed the Decree of September 24, 1791, which granted all the demands of the colonists. By its terms the status of both the mulattoes and the slaves was left to the discretion of the colonial assemblies whose decisions were to be ratified solely by the King, the National Assembly having no voice in the matter. Lastly, in order to take this question out of politics, the decree was declared an unalterable article of the French Constitution.[20]

It was in the first days of November that the news of this final *volte-face* of the Constituent Assembly reached San Domingo. The effect was tremendous. The confidence of the mulattoes in the French nation was as much shattered by the Decree of the 24th September as the faith of the whites had been by that of the 15th May. The mulattoes now felt that their only chance lay in violent measures, especially as the whites had been so encouraged that they were now breathing vengeance rather than conciliation. With the full tide of race hatred thus unloosed on both sides, a general explosion in the West was inevitable.[21]

The natural theatre for the new crisis was Port-au-Prince. As soon as the news of the September Decree had arrived, the mulattoes demanded that the inhabitants should signify their continued adhesion to the Concordat — which had of course been nullified by this reversal of the Decree of the 15th May. In the city itself feeling was at the boiling point, for the mass of the inhabitants (who of course loathed the Concordat) had been greatly excited by the new decree, and had been roused to fury by the insolent conduct of the mulatto soldiery quartered in the town. It is not strange, therefore, that, when on November 21 the question of reaffirmation was put to the vote, the polling ended in a riot followed by a pitched battle. After several hours' fierce fighting the mulatto troops were driven from the town: before sunrise the greater part of Port-au-Prince lay in ashes. The cause of the terrible conflagration has always remained obscure. From several conflicting versions, it would seem that the retreating Confederates set fire to the outskirts of the town while at about the same moment the white rabble, bent on plunder and vengeance, fired the business quarter. At any rate, the shops and houses of the merchant classes were thoroughly sacked by the mob, several wealthy whites were murdered, and a large number of unarmed mulattoes were massacred.[22]

The consequences of all this were terrible. Hitherto, as we have seen, the policy of De Jumecourt had kept the Western troubles within the bounds of politics. But the struggle which now began was predominantly one of race. It is true that De Jumecourt and his aristocratic associates nominally continued to head the Confederates, but they could do little to restrain the passions of their mulatto allies. The country whites were everywhere subjected to plunder and outrage, and the slightest resistance was followed by torture and massacre. The spirit of the mulattoes is well shown by the following frantic letter of Augustin Rigaud, brother of the mulatto leader soon to become so prominent: "The Parish of

MULATTO INSURRECTION IN THE WEST 151

Acquin has just accepted our terms, but no reliance can be placed upon such perverse men. Watch them! Leave town! Take to the bush! At the least sign, kill, sack, burn! No terms except the Articles of La-Croix-des-Bouquets. I ride to vengeance. If I do not die on this expedition, I shall soon return. Rise, I say; and we will conquer these brigands who wish to massacre and enslave our party. Vengeance! Vengeance! I embrace you all. My last word is to wreak vengeance on these barbarians. Fly to the succor of our murdered brothers. Vive la liberté! Vive l'égalité! Vive l'amour!" [23]

The horror of the race war in the West now almost surpassed that of the North. The mulatto Confederates, in hideous token of their Royalist sentiments, fashioned white cockades from the ears of their dead enemies.[24] The atrocities perpetrated upon the white women and children are past belief. "The mulattoes," writes the Colonial Assembly to its Paris commissioners, "rip open pregnant women, and then before death force the husbands to eat of this horrible fruit. Other infants are thrown to the hogs." [25]

The condition of Port-au-Prince was also terrible. The demagogue Praloto and a bodyguard of desperadoes, mostly foreigners like himself, had established a veritable reign of terror. A merchant captain who sailed for France on the 29th of December pictures vividly the state of the town; strictly blockaded by the Confederates, "the inhabitants living on salt meat and putrid water, yet resolved to be buried beneath the ashes of their town rather than yield to the mulattoes." The mob was daily forcing the jails and lynching mulatto prisoners there confined.[26] Edwards records a horrible atrocity committed upon a mulatto leader captured in a skirmish. He was paraded through the town nailed to a cart, then broken on the wheel, and cast still living into the fire.[27]

And by this time the South was also aflame. This remote province seems to have been little affected until the great explosion in the West at the end of November; but from then on its troubles rapidly grew acute. The mulattoes rose *en masse* and drove the bulk of the white population into Les Cayes; but at the mountainous extremity of the peninsula, the region known as the "Grande Anse," the whites killed or expelled the mulattoes. The negroes of this remote quarter seem to have been entirely unaffected by the Revolutionary ideas, and to have entertained only their natural hatred toward the mulattoes. Taking advantage of this, the whites armed their slaves, and at the head of their *ateliers* began the reconquest of the South.[28]

Such was the state of San Domingo at the beginning of the year 1792.

XIII

THE FIRST CIVIL COMMISSIONERS

As early as November, 1790, the National Assembly had entertained the thought of sending a commission to San Domingo to investigate and to appease the troubles which there prevailed. But no such commission was actually formed until the summer of 1791, and even then its departure for the island was delayed till October by the struggle for the repeal of the Decree of the 15th May.[1] This delay, however, had an important bearing upon the commission's subsequent action. Chosen at the time of the May Decree, its members were what might be termed moderate radicals; that is to say, they were opposed to the immediate destruction of slavery, but favored mulatto equality. Now had come the Decree of the 24th September. It should have been plain that a change in personnel had thereby become a necessity: as a matter of fact, nothing of the sort took place, and there followed the anomalous spectacle of a commission sent to support principles which it had been created to overthrow. Thus handicapped from the start, its success might be deemed most problematical.[2]

And neither its instructions nor its membership brightened its prospects. The directions of the National Assembly were vague; the powers conferred so general that conflict with the existing island authorities was almost a certainty.[3] As to the three "Civil Commissioners,"

Mirbeck, Roume, and Saint-Leger, they were all devoid of past distinction or future capacity. Mirbeck was a person of rather unedifying habits who proved a nonentity; Saint-Leger soon gained a venal reputation; Roume alone showed forth an honest and upright nature, albeit one marred by dogmatism and weakness.

On the 29th of November, 1791, the Commissioners landed at Le Cap, stunned with horror at the awful conditions which there prevailed, no tidings of the negro insurrection having reached France at the moment of their departure for San Domingo.[4] They were well received by both Governor and Assembly,[5] made a fairly good impression,[6] and wrote home their thorough approval of the various measures taken for the stemming of the insurrection.[7]

But this era of good feeling was not of long duration. The Commissioners were so depressed by the condition of the colony that they yearned for an occasion to exercise their rôle of peacemakers, — and it was not long before an apparently golden opportunity presented itself. Immediately upon their arrival the Commissioners had issued a proclamation announcing the speedy arrival of large military forces for the restoration of order.[8] This, together with the imposing ceremonies of their installation, had been duly reported to the rebel negroes, and produced a considerable effect. In their devastated territories the insurgents were by this time suffering great privations, and many of them despaired of the future. In consequence of all this, on the 10th of December a rebel flag of truce appeared before Le Cap, bearing from the negro chiefs Jean-François and Biassou a

THE FIRST CIVIL COMMISSIONERS 155

letter to the new Commissioners expressing a desire for peace.⁹

A gracious answer from the Commissioners brought forth a most astonishing reply: in return for liberty granted to themselves and their principal followers, the insurgent leaders promised nothing less than to force the main body of the negroes back into obedience. "By simply commanding each one of us to return to his own place, as stated in your proclamation," reads this letter, "you are ordering that which is impossible and perilous at the same time. One hundred thousand men are in arms. We are dependent upon the general will; — and what a general will! That of a multitude of negroes from the coast,¹⁰ who for the most part do not know two words of French yet who have been warriors in their own country." If peace is to be restored, the letter goes on, the Commissioners must grant liberty to the several hundred chiefs whom the writer shall name. Thereupon, with all the natural leaders of the negroes working to this end, the thing can probably be done; although the writers do not deny that it will be dangerous. "For false principles will make the slaves very obstinate; they will say that they have been betrayed, and the result may be fatal, no matter what precautions are taken." Still, concludes the letter, if the King's troops will occupy the open country, the writers think they can hunt down those obstinate negroes "who, refusing obedience, will infect the woods." ¹¹

The Commissioners were naturally overjoyed at this offer, and on December 21 they had a personal interview with Jean-François a short distance out in the Plain.

Herein the negro leader expressed the greatest desire for peace and agreed to send envoys to negotiate the terms of a general pacification.[12]

But at this point the Commissioners were surprised to encounter the vigorous disapprobation of the colonists. This attitude is well set forth in a letter written by a prominent planter to Moreau de Saint-Méry: "Did you ever hear anything more audacious than Jean-François' demands? These wretches not only ask to escape the punishment they so richly deserve; they want to be rewarded as well. But, would not the granting of such terms be a premium put upon the subsequent rebellion of those excluded from the first, yet desirous of obtaining the reward of murder and brigandage? Then, again, how can we allow at large persons known to have incited their fellows to insurrection; men ever destined to be a terror from their present authority strengthened by future impunity? How can we thus suffer among us those who have murdered and ruined their masters? Can such crimes be pardoned?" [13]

This feeling was plainly shared by the Colonial Assembly, for when the insurgent envoys appeared at its bar, they were received with haughty severity and were offered little beyond vague promises. Furthermore, the Assembly took pains to emphasize the fact that by the National Decree of the 24th September the status of persons had been left entirely in its hands, and spoke of the Civil Commissioners as mere "intercessors." The result of this was soon apparent. The Civil Commissioners' prestige with the negroes was destroyed, and the rebels broke off negotiations.[14]

THE FIRST CIVIL COMMISSIONERS 157

Whether the offers of the negro leaders were either sincere or even practicable, it is impossible to say. Blanchelande seems to have been somewhat sceptical,[15] and it must not be forgotten that Jean-François and Biassou were at this time merely the leaders of the two largest bands of the Plain. Nevertheless, the colonists' attitude certainly appears unwise: Jean-François' letter of March 12 has the ring of sincerity, and a few hundred liberties would seem a small price to pay for even a slight chance of quelling the insurrection, whatever the ultimate risks of such a course. The *intransigeance* of the colonists undoubtedly arose from the long months during which they had seen their homes destroyed and their families devoted to every species of outrage and torture. Their wild thirst for vengeance may be imagined when, as late as February, 1792, the very Civil Commissioners wrote the following lines to the Minister of Marine after detailing some peculiarly horrible atrocities of the negro and mulatto insurgents: "Their crimes are so atrocious that it is impossible to pardon them; and even if we did so they would not believe it. . . . It will be necessary to exterminate very many of these wretches, both free and slave, before San Domingo can be pacified." [16] As the Colonial Assembly itself expressed it, "We could not bring ourselves to treat with men armed against every law; with incendiaries still covered with the blood of our constituents." [17]

However, the consequences of this rupture were serious. The rebels answered by a fresh burst of activity, not only before Le Cap, but against the military lines along the inland mountains as well. The Eastern Cordon was broken through and the Plain of Fort Dauphin sacked and fired: in the peninsula of the Môle occurred a revolt of both negroes and mulattoes, which took in rear the vital Cordon de l'Ouest and culminated in the storming of a large "camp" and the massacre of its hundreds of helpless refugees. On the 25th of January, Blanchelande wrote in the most pessimistic vein: "The state of the colony grows worse every day. If powerful succors do not speedily arrive, I shall regard it as absolutely doomed." [18]

The failure of these negotiations also marked the beginning of the breach between the Civil Commissioners and the Colonial Assembly. The Commissioners, at least, had been certain of success; [19] and they were furious at the Assembly both for causing their failure and for minimizing their powers.[20] They immediately informed the Colonial Legislature that their authority was practically unlimited, and began a quarrel which by late February culminated in a virtual ultimatum. After stigmatizing as "lèse nation" the appointment of a committee to investigate their powers, the Commissioners went on as follows: "Understand, then, and never forget, that the nation and the King have commissioned us to bring peace and order to San Domingo; and that to this end our powers have no limits except the terrible responsibility which they entail. Our authority is a veritable dictatorship." [21]

This quarrel with the Colonial Assembly had the further effect of altering the Commissioners' attitude toward the mulatto insurgents of the West. We have already seen the dreadful condition to which that province had been reduced by the opening days of 1792; — the capital terrorized by an irresponsible mob and closely invested by several thousand equally irresponsible insurgents.[22] The spirit which animated these besiegers is well shown by the appeal from the mulatto leaders before Port-au-Prince to their brethren of the Artibonite. "Hasten, dear friends," reads this letter, "to the siege of Port-au-Prince; and there plunge your bloody arms, avengers of treason and perfidy, in the breasts of these European monsters. Too long have we been the sport of their wiles and passions; too long have we groaned beneath their yoke of iron. Come, then, and destroy our tyrants; bury them beneath our former shame; and pluck up by the roots this upas tree of Prejudice." [23]

Shortly after their arrival at Le Cap the Commissioners had received deputations from both parties to this desperate struggle, though at the moment they were so absorbed in their negotiations with the negro rebels that they had done little beyond sending stern addresses to both sides.[24] But the horrible reports which continued to arrive from both West and South so worked on the Commissioners that, despite their quarrel with the Assembly, they determined that one of their number must go to Port-au-Prince to see what could be done. Accordingly, on the 29th of January, 1792, Saint-Leger landed at the besieged capital.

Saint-Leger's first impressions were apparently horror at conditions in the town and terror at the state of the province. For in addition to the awful struggle going on between the whites and the mulattoes, symptoms were now appearing among the negro population which betokened downright social dissolution. In the high mountains south of Port-au-Prince a Spanish half-breed had founded a genuine religious sect. Calling himself, with extraordinary inconsistency, "Romaine *the Prophetess*," inspired by the Virgin, his fanatic bands were spreading terror and desolation throughout the hill country.[25]

All this convinced Saint-Leger that the warring factions must compose their differences at any price; but his tactless efforts to accomplish this reconciliation merely drew upon him the suspicions of the white population. These suspicions the violent demagogues of Port-au-Prince took no pains to conceal: on the other hand, the Confederate emissaries cleverly profited from these misunderstandings by showing him the greatest deference. The upshot of the matter was that the vain and irascible Saint-Leger left Port-au-Prince in a rage, and established himself among the mulattoes at La-Croix-des-Bouquets. His favor was further assured the Confederates by the alacrity with which they obeyed his orders to disperse the bands of "Romaine the Prophetess." The breach between Saint-Leger and the whites of Port-au-Prince was soon complete.[26]

Saint-Leger still hoped to accomplish great things, but he was soon reduced to utter despair by the general explosion which now took place in the Artibonite. The incendiary appeals from La-Croix-des-Bouquets [27] had done their work only too well, for in mid-February the mulattoes of the Artibonite suddenly rose and massacred many of the white inhabitants. The refugees, however, soon found an able leader in an adventurer named Borel, and a war of extermination then began which virtually

THE FIRST CIVIL COMMISSIONERS 161

dissolved the Confederation of La-Croix-des-Bouquets; the mass of the country whites preferring the most desperate struggle in the open field to further association with the treacherous mulattoes. Lastly, this break-up of the Confederation encouraged the whites of Port-au-Prince to a bold stroke. A strong column swept triumphantly out over the Cul-de-Sac and occupied La-Croix-des-Bouquets itself. But at this the mulattoes summoned the slave population to revolt, attacked the whites, and on March 31, after a terrible battle in which two thousand of the half-armed negroes are said to have fallen, forced their enemies to retire once more to Port-au-Prince. However, this general rising of the negroes had completed the disorganization of the province, which sank for the moment into utter anarchy. Overwhelmed with terror and despair, Saint-Leger took refuge on a warship off the coast and sailed on the 9th of April for France.[28]

When the despairing Saint-Leger dropped the Western mountains below the horizon he did not know that his colleague Mirbeck was already far on the homeward voyage in an almost similar frame of mind. The Commissioners' claim to a dictatorship [29] had infuriated the Colonial Assembly to such a degree that its radical wing had determined to rid the island of their presence. But forcible deportation of the nation's representatives was no easy task: the Governor and his troops would certainly protect the Commissioners from any such attempt. It was therefore necessary to find allies outside the Assembly. Allies, however, were to be had — for a price. Up to this moment Blanchelande's orders and Cambefort's regulars had kept fair order at Le Cap. But this had been increasingly annoying to the mob of the town. The sack of Port-au-Prince and the plundering democracy there established had whetted the appetites of the proletarians of Le Cap, who hated the Governor as much as the Assembly did the Commissioners. It is therefore not strange to find that an alliance between mob and radical Assemblymen was soon established.

How great was the alarm among conservative citizens is shown by a letter of this period. "Our ills," it reads, "grow steadily worse, with no signs of betterment for the future. All those whose means permit are leaving this unhappy colony, — with the result that the *canaille* continues to gain in power. Honest men will soon no longer dare show themselves. Things have come to such a pass that at any moment we fear they will cut our throats." [30]

The conspirators were, however, greatly aided by the growing unpopularity of the Commissioners with all classes of the white population. Saint-Leger's favor to the mulattoes of the West was rousing race-feeling to a high pitch, while the attempts of Mirbeck and Roume to induce the Assembly to grant political rights to the mulattoes completed the general exasperation. "Behold us," writes an Assemblyman to a friend in the West, "irrevocably embroiled with the Civil Commissioners. Their negrophil principles, their partiality for the mulattoes, their pretensions to be the sovereign repositories of all authority, are absolutely unmasked. Their influence can be but fatal to this unhappy country." [31]

The crisis came on the 26th of March. All night long

THE FIRST CIVIL COMMISSIONERS 163

the conspirators had plied the rabble with drink in the low taverns of the water-front, and about sunrise a cursing, shrieking mob poured toward the Governor's mansion, yelling "To arms, citizens! Rid yourselves of your enemies! Were this Port-au-Prince it would already have been done!" [32]

Faced by this sudden peril Blanchelande showed the same weakness as in the Western crisis of the year before,[33] and was made prisoner after a half-hearted resistance. Carrying the unhappy Governor in its midst, the mob next invaded the Colonial Assembly and for many hours held the trembling legislators in its grasp. After a really brave stand, the conservative members were forced to vote Blanchelande's embarkation: as to the Civil Commissioners, voices from the galleries yelled that the easiest way would be to drown them.

All this time, however, the respectable elements had been gathering under the vigorous appeals of Cambefort, who finally ventured to call out his regulars. The mob, too, was steadily thinning, as the drunken ruffians tired of the business and went home to sleep off their debauch. Accordingly, about two o'clock on the morning of the 27th of March, Blanchelande was rescued, and the Assembly promptly reversed its embarkation decree. Within a few hours order was restored.[34]

The *coup* had failed, it is true, but there was every prospect that another might be tried in the near future. The Civil Commissioners had come very near assassination and felt their position to be a hopeless one. Accordingly, on **March 30**, Mirbeck embarked for France, Roume agreeing to follow three days later.[35]

As a matter of fact, Roume did not sail, but remained for many months in San Domingo. The very day after his colleague's departure he had a conference with some conservative members of the Assembly, from which he came away convinced that Le Cap was menaced by a Royalist counter-revolution. And from the evidence which remains it would seem that he was right. There had always been a Royalist minority among the population of the North, while Colonel Cambefort and his officers had shown themselves partisans of the Old Régime on many occasions — notably by their zealous coöperation with Mauduit in the Western troubles of the year before.[36] These Northern Royalists had been encouraged by the triumphant reaction at Martinique and were infuriated by the violence of the new National Assembly which had met at Paris in the preceding October.[37] Furthermore, they had succeeded in converting to their views an ever larger portion of conservative opinion. All moderate men were disgusted at the excesses of the town mobs, and in addition were so alarmed at the hostility of the new National Assembly that they were becoming more and more willing to forget their liberal ideas in a longing for the strong arm of military authority. At this moment, then, it seems clear that all classes except the rabble were ready to join the Royalists in their plans for an alliance with the Western Confederates and the reëstablishment of the Old Régime throughout San Domingo.

This, however, Roume resolved at all costs to prevent, and he felt that his presence might keep the wavering Blanchelande from going over to the movement. In this,

THE FIRST CIVIL COMMISSIONERS 165

by rather clever temporizing, he actually succeeded; and Le Cap remained in uneasy disquietude until in mid-May it was stricken by the tidings of the National Law of April 4, 1792.[38]

XIV

THE LAW OF APRIL 4, 1792

ON the very day after the passage of the Decree of September 24, 1791, occurred an event which boded ill for its future: Barnave and others prominent in its passage were formally expelled from the Jacobin Club. "The Society," it was said, "could preserve upon its membership-roll only true friends of the Constitution and of Humanity." This action was invested with still greater future significance from the fact that the expulsions had been moved by Polverel, one of the men who within a year were to be sent as dictators to San Domingo. Furthermore, this was but the last of a series of steps already taken by the Club in avowed hostility to the colonial system. On June 10, Danton had obtained the expulsion of Gouy d'Arcy for "forfaiture nationale," and the Club had striven as desperately as the "Amis des Noirs" to compass the September Decree's defeat.[1]

And yet it was this Society which had already set out to capture the coming Legislative Assembly, and which within the year was to be the real Sovereign of France. That its unscrupulous election methods had been a success was shown when the new "Législatif" met on October 1, 1791. Instead of the Jacobin handful in the late Constituent Assembly, 136 "Législatif" deputies were on the books of the Club, while the whole Assembly was distinctly more radical in tone. The pronounced conservatives had taken little part in the recent elections. Many had by this time emigrated; still larger numbers had been kept from voting by conscientious scruples or Jacobin violence. Lastly, the Constituante's self-denying ordinance made the Législatif a body of entirely new men, and the inexperienced mass of moderate deputies had small chance of acquiring the capacity for organized resistance to the disciplined driving-power of the great Club backed by the Paris mob.

The Législatif had not been long in session when tidings of the great negro rising in San Domingo began to arrive in France; tidings coupled with frantic appeals for aid which grew in intensity and volume. Blanchelande's initial report on the situation estimated six thousand regular troops, fifteen thousand stand of arms, and an immense *matériel* of war as the absolute minimum required to save San Domingo from destruction.[2] And these colonial appeals were vigorously endorsed by the Civil Commissioners recently sent from France. Their very first letter emphasized the need of large and speedy succors,[3] and their recommendations grew more insistent with every despatch sent home. When on February 20, 1792, the Colonial Assembly drew up an appeal for twenty thousand troops,[4] the Commissioners appended their earnest endorsement. "Twenty thousand men," it reads, — "this figure, we certify, is but the absolute necessity." [5]

But against these appeals the Jacobins and the "Amis des Noirs" [6] set themselves like flint, and in fact succeeded in preventing the despatch of any real aid to San Domingo. They first denied the existence of the insurrection, declaring it a ruse to assure a Royalist asylum over-seas; then, when forced to admit the fact, they branded it as the work of *émigrés*. "The massacres," cried Brissot triumphantly, "began on the 21st of August; — just at the moment when the news had arrived of the King's flight to Varennes. Evidently they were organized by the Counter-Revolutionists."[7] Month after month frantic letters and petitions poured by hundreds into the Hall of Assembly, and these not only from over-seas, but also from thousands of Frenchmen reduced to ruin and trembling for the lives of kindred in San Domingo.[8] These appeals, coupled with the horrors contained in every report from the island, might well have moved hearts of stone; — but not the hearts of the Jacobin opposition. Time after time a grim tragi-comedy was enacted on the floor of the Assembly. Some fresh batch of reports and petitions on San Domingo would move moderate members to propose the sending of aid. Instantly the Jacobins would be upon their feet with a wealth of fine phrases, patriotic suspicions, and a whole armory of nullifying amendments and motions to adjourn; — the whole backed by gallery threats to the moderate proponents. And in the end, nothing would be done.[9]

The effect of all this upon the wretched inhabitants of San Domingo may be conceived. On the 25th of January, Blanchelande writes that the news of this continual obstruction in the National Assembly "is reducing the people to absolute despair."[10] The Minister of Marine, Bertrand de Molleville, did what he could, but this was little enough. So late as the 20th of February, the Civil

THE LAW OF APRIL 4, 1792

Commissioners wrote that up to that moment only eleven hundred soldiers had arrived; while Commissioners, Governor, and Colonial Assembly all joined in asserting that such poor driblets were useless, since the men had to be at once scattered among the most exposed points where, unacclimated and crushed by excessive service, they quickly melted away.[11]

Of this opposition to the relief of San Domingo it is difficult to speak with moderation. For not even on grounds of fanaticism can the Jacobin policy be palliated; their attitude was largely due to a mere factious desire to discredit the existing Government. The Jacobins had vowed the destruction of the moderate "Feuillant" Ministry of the day, and they realized the excellent political capital to be made out of the troubles in San Domingo. Besides their ability to "point with alarm" to the Feuillants' inability to restore order, the Jacobins had been quick to realize the fact that these colonial disasters were producing much discontent at home. The price of sugar and coffee was going up every day, and complaints were rising from every French breakfast table. The one thing that can be said for the Jacobin opposition is that it possessed the virtue of consistency: it fought the rescue of suffering Avignon as stoutly as the salvation of martyred San Domingo, and richly earned the bitter gibe of Pitt that these Frenchmen preferred their coffee "au caramel."

But the programme of the Club was by no means a wholly negative one: the hateful September Decree was also the logical object of consistent Jacobin attack. The story of the long six months' struggle which preceded complete Jacobin success is vividly narrated in the correspondence of those commissioners sent to France by the Colonial Assembly in the early autumn of 1791.[12]

The Jacobin attack was both direct and indirect in character. We have seen that the September Decree had been made an article of the French Constitution of 1791, and that it had been declared irrepealable except upon the express desire of the colonies themselves. But history teaches nothing more certain than the impossibility of forbidding any action of the sovereign power for all future time. This anomaly was promptly insisted on by the Jacobin orators, and besides declaring the September Decree illegal, as contravening fundamental principles and the imprescriptible rights of citizens, they urged the Législatif to vindicate its honor by repudiating this attempt to trammel its sovereignty.

The news of the Concordat made in September between the whites and mulattoes of the West Province gave the Jacobins an opportunity for indirect attack. Ignoring the fact that the September Decree had specified only requests from Colonial Legislatures, the Jacobins now asserted that by making the Concordat the colony had expressed its desire for a change, and they urged the National Assembly to ratify this instrument and make it the law for all San Domingo.[13] Of course it was quite evident that any such action would completely nullify the September Decree.

The upshot of all this was that the whole question was referred to the Committee on Colonies. This body was by no means as friendly to the colonial whites as its predecessor of the Constituante;[14] nevertheless, on January

THE LAW OF APRIL 4, 1792

11, 1792, it rendered a report which affirmed the constitutionality of the September Decree and advised against either ratifying the Concordat or extending its provisions to the whole of San Domingo.[15]

This blow checked the Jacobins — but only for a time. For as the winter waned so did the Feuillant Ministry, and every day revealed more clearly the coming Jacobin ascendancy over France. By mid-February the grand assault on the colonial system began. The letters of the San Domingo commissioners tell of desperate efforts to stem the tide, but their tone is one of ever deepening despair. "There is no use denying the fact," they write on the 14th of February, "the Législatif will never grant us aid until it has annulled the constitutional law of the 24th September. . . . The most influential members of this Assembly are indeed of the opinion that the law is not even constitutional, and any day may see our safeguard destroyed." [16]

In their final campaign the Jacobins were greatly aided by the growing irritation among even conservative French circles at the steady refusal of the colonial whites to accept the mulattoes as their political equals. The very commercial classes were now estranged from their former allies, since the French merchants had no desire to be ruined for the upholding of the color line. What appeared to colonists a vital principle seemed to Frenchmen a foolish prejudice, and the whites of San Domingo were more and more regarded as a stiff-necked generation in great part responsible for the woes which overwhelmed them. It was perfectly clear that the mulattoes were as much opposed as the whites themselves to negro emancipation; consequently, if the whites would frankly and fully accept the mulattoes as their equals, it was certain that the freedmen would join whole-heartedly in the suppression of the rebel slaves.

Another idea widely held among Frenchmen at this moment contributed to favor the Jacobin campaign. The opponents of the colonial system had long asserted that when the Constituante passed the September Decree it was with the tacit understanding that the Colonial Assembly would itself grant the mulattoes political rights. This claim appears to have been entirely without foundation; nevertheless, the feeling grew in France that the Colonial Assembly was bound to adopt some such line of action, at least on grounds of policy and humanity. The Civil Commissioners had made no secret of such convictions, and their efforts to this effect had done much to rouse the island whites against them. In their "ultimatum" of February 19,[17] they had said, "Representatives of the colony of San Domingo and its unfortunate inhabitants, remember that the mother country is watching you, and that she will demand a reckoning for the precious time which you are losing in vain debates. Hasten, then, to repair your errors by busying yourselves with that internal status which cries so loudly for a remedy." [18]

The colonists were well aware of the increasing peril; nevertheless, they grimly refused to abandon their position. Their attitude is well set forth in a memorial written at this moment by the Assemblyman De Pons.[19] He contends that the mulattoes' claim for political rights is only the first step in their deeper determination to obtain social equality and the mixing of the bloods by intermarriage. And, asserts De Pons, once grant political equality and all the rest will follow in time: the mulattoes will soon outvote the whites, establish mulatto political supremacy, and then by coercive legislation force the whites either to admit social equality or leave the island.[20]

De Pons's claim that the mulattoes were certain to obtain political supremacy if given the vote is strikingly echoed by the mulatto leader Raymond. Writing to his brethren at San Domingo, in censure of their support of the Old Régime and dislike of popular assemblies, he urges that such bodies are the surest instruments of victory, since the mulattoes would soon outvote the whites and thereafter dominate the island.[21]

Given such irreconcilable ambitions inflamed by so much bloodshed and race hatred, it is not strange that the colonial whites grimly resolved to keep San Domingo a "white man's country" or to be buried in its ruins.

However, deserted as the colonists now were by even conservative French opinion, the Jacobin triumph was only a question of time: when the Feuillant Ministry went down on March 10, 1792, the prompt overthrow of the colonial system became a certainty. In fact, on the 24th of March, the House passed that drastic project of the Jacobin Gensonné which the terrorized King's signature transformed into the National Law of April 4, 1792.[22]

This law absolutely nullified the Constitutional Decree of September, 1791, and pressed the Act of May 15 to its logical conclusion.[23]

"The National Assembly," reads its preamble, "acknowledges and declares that the people of color and free negroes in the colonies ought to enjoy equality of political rights with the whites; in .consequence whereof it decrees as follows: —

"1. Immediately after the publication of the present decree, the inhabitants of each of the French colonies of the Windward and Leeward Islands shall proceed to the reëlection of Colonial and Parochial Assemblies, after the mode prescribed by the Decree of March 8, 1790, and the Instructions of March 28.

"2. The people of color and free negroes shall be admitted to vote in all the primary and electoral assemblies, and shall be eligible to the legislature and to all places of trust, provided they possess the qualifications prescribed in Article 4 of the aforesaid instructions.

"3. Three Civil Commissioners shall be named for the colony of San Domingo . . . to see this decree enforced."

That the Jacobins were determined to have no half-measures was plain from the articles which followed: the Commissioners thus decreed for the new law's enforcement were given the powers of dictators and the backing of an army to compel entire obedience to the Législatif's will.[24] The white colonists were given the curt warning to bend or be broken.

By the whites of San Domingo, indeed, the Law of April 4, 1792, was regarded as a virtual sentence of death. "With the most profound sadness," write its commissioners to the Colonial Assembly, "we must inform you that on the 24th of this month M. Gensonné's draft decree was adopted almost unanimously. Both deputies and public galleries were at such a pitch of frenzy that it would have been highly dangerous for any one to have

THE LAW OF APRIL 4, 1792

manifested a contrary opinion, so that the minority offered no opposition. The Minister of Marine is deeply afflicted by this decision, and sees therein the certain ruin not only of San Domingo, but of the Windward Islands [25] as well." [26] However, Bertrand de Molleville's opinion was a matter of small importance, for within a few days he was replaced by the Jacobin Lacoste.

"You may announce unreservedly that it is all over with San Domingo," writes a returned colonist from Bordeaux. "One of three things will follow: the whites will exterminate the whole mulatto caste; the mulattoes will destroy the whites; or the negroes will profit by these dissensions to annihilate both the whites and the mulattoes. But in any case, San Domingo should be erased from the maps of France." [27]

When the tidings reached the island, the white population of San Domingo was crushed as by a thunderbolt. "On May 11," writes the Colonial Assembly to its commissioners, "the news arrived, — the news of the final ruin of this unhappy country. Desolation is upon every face; rage and despair may occasion something terrible." [28] Its letter upon the law's official arrival is a veritable cry of agonized despair. "What!" it reads, "after having been slaughtered, burned, ruined by these monsters, we must now take them to our hearts like beloved brothers? We are, then, to be forced by bayonets to sign our death-warrant? This is the climax of horror, tyranny, and despair!" [29]

Very significant was the attitude of Governor Blanchelande. He flatly refused to give the new Minister of Marine his opinion on the Law of the 4th of April, saying

176 FRENCH REVOLUTION IN SAN DOMINGO

that he knew himself suspect to many members of the National Assembly and that, in consequence, unpalatable remarks might be used against him.[30] Henceforth his letters are quite unreliable on the race question. They are obviously written for effect.

The joy of the mulattoes was, of course, as great as the colonists' despair. Raymond's letter to his friends in San Domingo is a pæan of victory,[31] and their letters to him are equally jubilant. "Behold, then," writes his brother François, "the decree which finally settles our political status, so long disputed by abominable prejudice. Good God! how this country is convulsed. Just imagine: there are still some parts where people hope to see this decree treated like that of the 15th May! But this time they will have to obey the law." [32]

The Civil Commissioner Roume was as delighted as the mulattoes themselves and took no pains to conceal the dislike he had always felt for the Decree of the 24th September. "I cannot bring myself to speak of petty details," he writes the new Minister of Marine, "when discussing an event which restores to its pristine dignity one of the three great families of the human race and enriches France with an intermediate species in which are crossed and blended two of these ancient families. Oh, that the September Decree had never been!" [33]

It is plain that the Law of the 4th of April was as abhorrent to the white colonists as the Decree of the 15th May, yet its arrival was followed by nothing except low cries of despair. For there was a world of difference between their situation in the two periods. A year before the whites had been masters of the whole island; now they were crowded into a few port towns or prostrate beneath the knives of the mulattoes of the West. Lastly, they could hope for no foreign aid, since at the moment there was no sign of an English war. To offer armed resistance to the coming army of Jacobin France was clearly to court immediate destruction. Therefore the white leaders resolved to bow for the moment in the faint hope of a better time to come, and the Colonial Assembly formally counselled submission to the national will.[34] "We are so dispersed," writes this body to its commissioners, "that there is nothing left but submission." [35] Hopeless as was the situation, however, it seems that this surrender of the Assembly alone prevented a supreme outburst of despair, for Roume writes that the absence of resistance was wholly due to the conduct of the Assembly. "It is certain," he adds, "that if the Colonial Assembly had shown the least insubordination to this law, we should have seen flowing torrents of blood." [36]

By mid-June, Commissioner Roume was assured that the whites of Le Cap were too crushed in spirit to make any immediate trouble. He therefore felt free to turn his undivided attention to the West. That province had not long remained in the anarchy consequent upon the mulatto appeal to the slave population and the battle of La-Croix-des-Bouquets.[37] For to all parties it had been perfectly clear that the explosion of the West had left the vital military cordon along the Western mountains quite in the air; and it was absolutely certain that once the black tide of the Northern rebellion burst through that mountain wall and flowed over the seething negro population of the West, all was over.[38] And no one was more conscious of this fact than the commandant of the Western Cordon, De Fontanges. This officer, by his high character and unimpeachable Royalism, succeeded in bringing together the white and mulatto planters of the Artibonite, and on April 19 he mediated the so-called "Treaty of Saint-Marc," [39] — really a revival of the Confederation of La-Croix-des-Bouquets. This was quickly joined by the other country parishes of the West, and early in May an executive body called the "Council of Peace and Union" met at Saint-Marc for the settlement of the province. Its efforts were successful. The Cordon de l'Ouest was once more made secure, and the slave disturbances suppressed.[40]

Nevertheless, these events had been viewed by Roume with very mixed emotions. For the "Council of Peace and Union" was as Royalist a body as the old Confederation had been, and the Bourbon Lilies were flying over many a camp of the West.[41] Roume, therefore, set himself to win the mulattoes for the Revolution. To this end he now came out squarely in favor of political equality.[42] On May 9 he wrote warmly to the new League, praising their "holy union," which if generally adopted would "save San Domingo." He offered the League his "most fraternal greetings," and assured its members that France would soon grant their wishes, "reducing to nothing the work of the Colonial Assembly." [43]

The Law of the 4th of April made Roume certain of success. He now determined to go in person to the West to break the alliance between the mulattoes and the Old Régime; and on this journey he was accompanied by Blanchelande, who desired to profit by mulatto satis-

THE LAW OF APRIL 4, 1792 179

faction to raise troops among them for use against the negro rebels of the North. Accordingly the two landed at Saint-Marc on the 20th of June, where Roume was greatly edified at observing whites and mulattoes "sitting together like good brothers." [44] It is true that the Confederates soon gave them to understand that no aid would be granted against the Northern rebels until they had helped capture Port-au-Prince; but as neither Roume nor Blanchelande had any love for that turbulent democracy, they immediately accepted the terms of the League. Roume, therefore, journeyed overland to the besieging mulatto army, while Blanchelande with the warships which had brought them from Le Cap sailed to blockade Port-au-Prince by sea. The position of the town was now hopeless, and on July 10, Port-au-Prince sullenly surrendered. It was sharply dealt with. The mutinous soldiery which for more than a year had terrorized the town was embarked for France, the most prominent mob leaders were expelled the country, and the arch-demagogue Praloto was murdered. Held down by a strong mulatto garrison, Port-au-Prince seemed unlikely to give further trouble.[45]

However, notwithstanding this triumph, the Western mulattoes still seemed quite indisposed to follow Blanchelande against the negroes of the North. They now demanded that before receiving the promised aid the Governor should help their brethren in the South. The mulattoes of that province were, indeed, in need of assistance, for the hard-fighting planters of the Southern mountains and their black followers had by this time pretty well mastered the whole country. These Southern whites had already formed that "Confederation of the Grande Anse" soon to play such an important rôle, and had absolutely refused to obey the Law of the 4th of April.

Blanchelande visited the South, it is true, but in a vacillating mood that foreboded failure. He had no heart to enforce the new law; he probably realized that he had been duped by the League; and yet his platonic counsels of submission and his release of mulatto prisoners infuriated the Southern whites against him. Resolved to do something to justify his presence, he attempted to clear the high mountains of their bands of half-maroon negroes, but the local whites gave little aid and the expedition ended in a bad disaster. Discouraged and discredited he sailed back to Le Cap, not only without mulatto recruits, but deprived of the few soldiers who had followed him to the West.[46] Roume, meanwhile, remained at Port-au-Prince trying to convert the mulattoes from Royalism to the Revolution, although subsequent events proved that his efforts were crowned with very mediocre success.

Such was the state of San Domingo when, on September 18, the Jacobin Commissioners and six thousand troops sailed into the harbor of Le Cap, to enforce throughout the island compliance with the Law of April 4, 1792.

XV

THE SECOND CIVIL COMMISSIONERS

THAT the new Jacobin rulers of France were determined that their enactments should be no idle statements of principle is shown by a glance at the Law of April 4, 1792; if the preamble and first two articles laid down the doctrine of mulatto equality, the next eight were concerned with measures for its strict enforcement. The closing paragraph alone contained concessions to the colonists, for by this final clause slavery was still maintained and slave legislation left to the Colonial Assemblies.[1]

The cardinal idea in these coercive measures was the sending of new Civil Commissioners to direct the law's enforcement, and the powers granted these Commissioners, especially as amplified by the supplementary decree passed on the 15th of June,[2] created nothing short of a dictatorship. With such plenary powers, the new Commission's future action depended entirely upon the character of its members. And nothing shows more clearly Jacobin *intransigeance* toward the feelings of the colonists than the selection of persons which now took place. Indeed, the first idea of the Jacobin party was actually to appoint, as one of the trio, Raymond, the leader of the Paris mulattoes; and although moderate opposition finally defeated this project, the terrified letters of the colonial delegates [3] and the regretful comments of Garran-Coulon [4] show how near it came to success. The defeat of this proposal undoubtedly spared much bloodshed in San Domingo, for the state of mind there prevailing was such [5] that if the whites had learned that the chief mulatto leader was to have been one of their future dictators, it is almost certain that they would have risen in some supreme convulsion of despair.

But even though no mulatto was appointed, the choice of persons finally selected did little to quiet the alarm of white San Domingo.[6] Polverel, Sonthonax, and Ailhaud, the new Civil Commissioners, were all Jacobins, and the first two had already shown their sentiments toward the colonists in no uncertain fashion. It was Polverel who in the Jacobin Club had moved the expulsion of Barnave and the other supporters of the distasteful decree of September 24, 1791. Yet Polverel was by far the best of the three. His Jacobinism, though fanatical, was sincere, his personal honesty was never questioned, and ripening years had brought some insight and reflection in their train. To Polverel is due the fact that the succeeding pages of San Domingan history were not even more lurid than the terrible reality. Ailhaud was a mere cipher who played no part in coming events.

In the sinister figure of Sonthonax, however, all the worst traits of the Jacobin type stood revealed. An obscure country lawyer from the Savoyard border,[7] the Revolution had been his opportunity, and from the first he had identified himself with that extreme wing of the Jacobin party then known as the "Enragés," and later still more famous as the nucleus of the "Mountain." A mere mouther of phrases, corrupt in both public and private life, his one real talent lay in a certain sly ability

THE SECOND CIVIL COMMISSIONERS 183

to trim with the times which was to bring him safe through the storms of the Revolution. In that dreadful company of Jacobin Proconsuls, history should rank Sonthonax beside Carrier of Nantes and Joseph Lebon of Arras.

If such a man can be said to have real convictions, his ideas on colonial questions may be gathered from a signed article published in one of the ultra-radical sheets about a year before. "The ownership of land both at San Domingo and the other colonies," reads this article, "belongs in reality to the negroes. It is they who have earned it with the sweat of their brows, and only by usurpation do others now enjoy the fruits." [8] The new Minister of Marine, member of the Jacobin Ministry though he was, remonstrated strongly against Sonthonax's appointment as Commissioner to San Domingo; but his objections were overruled.[9]

The personnel of the new Commission was naturally very pleasing to the mulatto colony at Paris. In his jubilant letter of the 18th of June to his friends in San Domingo, Raymond remarks, "As to the new Commissioners, you may rely on the purity of their principles and on their resolution to enforce the law." [10]

The feelings of the white colonists in France are shown by the following remarkable letter to the Colonial Assembly from one of its commissioners.

"I send you, gentlemen," he writes, "a decree of the National Assembly which will give you the key to the operations by which its Commissioners are to bring about the general enfranchisement of the negroes. Do not doubt these words, gentlemen; I know whereof I speak; and I swear upon my honor that my words are true. The plot is already hatched within the National Assembly, and will be carried out the moment the Commissioners have attained complete authority. The plan is to enfranchise all the negroes in all the French colonies; then, with these first freedmen, to bring about enfranchisement in all the foreign colonies; and thus to carry revolt and independence throughout the New World, — a thing which, according to its authors, will give them supremacy over all the Powers of Europe. And this atrocious plan producing such torrents of blood will certainly be executed if you do not join haste to resolution, concord to preparation, and to your resistance the courage of despair. Gentlemen, beat off these tigers athirst for blood; crush in these wretches' hearts their barbarous projects; and thereby earn the love of your countrymen and the blessings of an entire world saved by your courage from the atrocious convulsions which these madmen have in store.

"If you are sufficiently united to follow my counsel, I guarantee the salvation of San Domingo. But, in any case, let no one cherish the hope of mercy from these men, let no one be deluded by their sly tricks of policy; the negroes alone find room in their affections, and all the whites without distinction, all the mulattoes as well, are doomed; all alike are dangerous to their projects, all alike will be sacrificed as soon as these men shall have disposed of the officers, gotten rid of the troops of the line, and become at last the undisputed masters." [11]

The closing lines of this letter are a remarkable prophecy, for they accurately foreshadow those progressive steps which culminated in Sonthonax's emancipation

THE SECOND CIVIL COMMISSIONERS 185

proclamation of August, 1793. It is, indeed, far from impossible that some such scheme was actually entertained by the extreme Jacobin leaders, for it is quite in line with their avowed programme for the universal triumph of the French Revolution and the regeneration of the world. And, if such a plan did in fact exist, Sonthonax must have been privy to it, since he was the friend and candidate of the "Enragés." Such schemes were certainly widely believed in at the time, and this letter is only one of a number of similar predictions uttered during the summer and autumn of 1792.[12] But of such a plan no actual trace apparently remains, and Polverel at least must certainly be exonerated from any intention of so far exceeding his instructions.

These instructions were the logical sequence of the law of April 4 and the Decree of the 15th June. After sketching the terrible condition of San Domingo, the instructions point out the difference between the situation of the first and second Civil Commissioners. The first Commissioners, read the instructions, had to execute the Law of the 24th September, "which placed the fate of the colored citizens at the will of the Colonial Assembly"; the second Commissioners are "being sent to execute the Law of the 4th of April which pronounces equality of political rights." The first Commissioners "had to conciliate the rigor of the Law with the counsels and pleadings of Equity"; the second Commissioners are "going forth strong in a new Law which permits neither the one party to demand nor the other to temporize or refuse." The first Commissioners were without soldiers; the second Commissioners will come to San Domingo with six thousand troops, which should suffice "to stifle the very murmurs of dissent." The new Commissioners are to use every persuasion, yet armed resistance is more than likely. In that case they are to use most vigorous measures, and "disobedience shall be regarded as high treason." In the elections which will follow the dissolution of the existing Assemblies, the Commissioners are to take the greatest care that the Law is strictly enforced, and shall see to it that mulattoes and free negroes are everywhere not only voters but candidates as well. Lastly, the Commissioners are directed to prosecute a most rigorous investigation to discover the authors of the late troubles, who are to be sent prisoners to France.[13]

Armed with these instructions the second Civil Commissioners sailed in late July for San Domingo accompanied by six thousand men; two thousand of them troops of the line to give consistency and discipline, the other four thousand National Guards carefully chosen for the soundness of their principles. The temper of these new Commissioners was well shown even on the voyage. Their first report is characterized by the Revolutionary attitude of suspicion, — suspicion that officials in the French ports have given them slow ships to delay their arrival at San Domingo; suspicion that many officers are seeking to debauch the soldiers' principles; lastly, grave suspicion of General Desparbés, the commander of the troops.[14] Desparbés's instructions had enjoined subordination to the Commissioners in matters of policy, but had specifically given him full control over the technical handling of the troops. But the Commissioners promptly began to trespass upon this province, and the very day of their arrival at Le Cap saw an open breach. The Commissioners sent Desparbés directions on how to land his troops, at which Desparbés, with the proverbial short temper of an old soldier, swore roundly, sent the Commission word to mind their business, and expressed his opinion of meddlesome civilians before his assembled staff. The Commissioners' report to the Minister of Marine expresses grave doubts as to the "civism" of the general.[15]

Uncertainty as to their reception had led the Commissioners to send on a fast ship which brought back letters from the various high officials at Le Cap while the fleet was still at sea. And the contents of these despatches should have given the Commissioners much food for reflection. There was first of all a report from Blanchelande giving a detailed statement of conditions in the island. He reported less than fifteen hundred regular troops fit for duty, and placed the numbers of the Northern rebels at sixty thousand, albeit scattered in many bands. The Ordonnateur,[16] in his report, urged that, as there was no formal opposition to the new law, the Commissioners should postpone their reconstructive measures until the suppression of the negro revolt; adding that he thought it might really be put down if the colonists were not further alienated and if the new troops were used at once before the climate had enfeebled their strength. Both the Governor and the commander of the naval station wrote special memoirs on the dangers of the political situation, stating that the soldiers and sailors shared the colonists' repugnance to the Law of the 4th of April, and that unless the Commissioners acted tactfully and avoided allying themselves to any of the existing parties, a terrible explosion was almost inevitable.[17] How the Commissioners acted upon these advices was soon to be seen.

It was on the 18th of September, 1792, that the fleet dropped anchor in the harbor of Le Cap. The Commissioners were impressively received by both Governor and Assembly, though the speech of President Daugy showed the deep alarm felt as to their intentions. "Gentlemen," he cried, "we are in your hands as a jar of clay, which you may break at will. This is, then, perhaps the last moment vouchsafed us to warn you of a vital truth ill understood by your predecessors. This truth, already recognized by the Constituent Assembly in its closing moments, is that there can be no agriculture at San Domingo without slavery; that five hundred thousand savages cannot be brought as slaves from the coast of Africa to enter this country as French citizens; lastly, that their existence here as free citizens would be physically incompatible with the coexistence of our European brethren." [18]

To this address both Polverel and Sonthonax replied in terms designed to quiet all fears regarding the abolition of slavery. Polverel's speech was undoubtedly sincere,[19] but the words of Sonthonax, when contrasted with the arguments so soon to be addressed to the National Convention, are a revelation of his consummate hypocrisy. "We declare," he cried dramatically, "in the presence of the Supreme Being, in the name of the mother country, before the people and amid its present representatives, that from this time forth we recognize but two classes of men at San Domingo — the free, without

THE SECOND CIVIL COMMISSIONERS 189

distinction of color, and the slaves. We declare that to the Colonial Assemblies alone belong the right to pronounce upon the fate of the slaves. We declare that slavery is necessary to the cultivation and prosperity of the colonies; that it is neither in the principles nor the will of the National Assembly of France to touch these prerogatives of the colonists; and that if the Assembly should ever be so far misled as to provoke their abolition, we swear to oppose such action with all our power. Such are our principles. Such are those given us by the National Assembly and the King. We will die, if need be, that they may triumph!" [20]

That the Commissioners were generally satisfied with their reception is clear from their first despatch to the Minister of Marine. "Every one," it reads, "seems disposed to obey the Law of the 4th of April. Nevertheless, prejudice is not yet destroyed. Time will do the business, — but we will not neglect measures for its acceleration." [21]

The Commissioners' first act was highly significant. Ever since the March riots [22] the white rabble of Le Cap had been kept down by the strong hand of Colonel Cambefort, and their feelings toward the royal authorities after six months of this military rule may be imagined. To the Commissioners, however, this was highly pleasing, for they thus perceived an unlooked-for chance to divide the white inhabitants. Accordingly they at once showed marked favor to the poor whites, who were soon enrolled in a popular club [23] quite on the Jacobin model. The fraternal greetings of Polverel and the mob oratory of Sonthonax were delightful to men smarting under the aristocratic aloofness and military severity of the old Government; and as the Commissioners momentarily refrained from pressing "Citizens of the 4th of April"[24] upon its membership, the relations of club and Commissioners were of the best.[25]

Having broken the ranks of the colonial whites, the Commissioners now began aggressive measures against the existing authorities. Governor Blanchelande, whose weakness and half-measures had had the usual result of arousing the dislike of all parties, was quickly shipped off, "suspect," to France, where the unfortunate man perished on the guillotine in April, 1793.[26] Roume had hastened up from the West and had offered the new Commissioners the benefit of his experience, but they soon showed him he was not wanted, and he hastily embarked for France.[27] On October 12, the Commissioners took the still bolder step of dissolving the Colonial Assembly; but instead of ordering elections for a new body, as prescribed in their instructions, they set up a "Commission Intermédiaire," a species of advisory council composed of six whites, five mulattoes, and one free negro.

However, the effect of this act upon public opinion was obscured by the political crisis now caused by the latest news from France. For at this moment came tidings of the momentous "Tenth of August": the storming of the Tuileries, the practical deposition of the King, and the call for the Convention. The news roused the Royalists to fury and spread terror among all moderate men. For it was only too clear that the "Tenth of August" was a matter of vital concern to San Domingo,—what the Jacobins and the mob of Paris had done yesterday, that the Jacobins and the mob of Le Cap would surely do to-morrow. That the recent measures of the Commissioners had roused political passions is shown by the letter of one of their partisans from the distant Cordon de l'Ouest. "The principal inhabitants of this parish," it reads, "are extremely envious of the lot of Martinique,[28] and are doing their best to foment a civil war from which they expect the happiest results after the destruction of the brigands.[29] What I have expected is coming to pass: the more energetically your love for the common weal is manifest at Le Cap, the more your watchfulness unmasks the perfidy of bad Frenchmen, — the more these strive to form a party in the parishes. You can have no idea of the tricks they play to seduce the troops of the cordon. 'Monsieur Cambefort is a god, Monsieur Desparbés is a booby, and the Civil Commissioners are rascals'; — such are their opinions." [30]

If this was the state of a country parish, it is easy to imagine the condition of Le Cap. The Royalists, realizing that it was their last chance to imitate Martinique, began to concert measures for getting rid of the Commissioners. And for such a stroke they were assured the backing of most of the regular troops. Cambefort's ability had kept the old regiment "Le Cap" absolutely Royalist in feeling, and it was clear that the "Le Cap" veterans did not stand alone. Some time before the Commissioners' arrival there had landed two battalions of the Irish regiments "Dillon" and "Walsh"; and these, like most of the foreign troops in French service, had remained loyal to the King. Lastly, Desparbés had grown so furious at the Commissioners' conduct that he listened receptively to the proposals now made against them.

The crisis was prematurely evoked by a trivial incident. On the morning of the 17th of October, Le Cap was placarded with libels representing the officers of these Royalist regiments hanged in chains. An Irish officer of "Walsh" lost his temper at the sight, began tearing down the placards, and told an angry group of clubmen that "he thanked God he was no Frenchman." As he was about to be lynched a number of his soldiers arrived, and a free fight followed. Both sides now took action. The Royalists demanded the dissolution of the club, the club demanded the embarkation of Cambefort and the Royalist officers. Finally, before dawn of the 18th October, the mob seized the arsenal, and thereupon, by Cambefort's advice, Desparbés ordered out the troops. The regiment "Le Cap" and the Irish battalions responded with a will, but the four thousand French National Guards declared for the Commissioners. One of their officers has left us a vivid picture of how he harangued a battalion, asking the soldiers if they were going to shoot their brothers "to satisfy the barbarous humor of a handful of aristocrats who wished only the destruction of the human race." [31]

It is probable that the discipline of the regulars would have given them the victory; but Desparbés, an old man of seventy-three, could not face the terrible struggle which would certainly follow a Royalist attack. He refused to give the necessary orders, and the affair ended in a fiasco. The Commissioners hereupon took vigorous measures; Desparbés, Cambefort, and the chief Royalist officers were sent prisoners to France, while most of the junior officers of "Le Cap" and the Irish battalions threw up their commissions and left the country.[32] The Royalist party in the North had ceased to exist, and the Commissioners were freed of their most dangerous enemy.

XVI

SONTHONAX'S RULE IN THE NORTH

It was less than a week after the Royalist plot that a squadron entered the harbor of Le Cap with General Rochambeau [1] and two thousand men on board. Having been repulsed from Royalist Martinique, Rochambeau received a fine reception at Le Cap and was appointed Governor-General in place of Desparbés. The stanch Revolutionary sentiments of these new troops still further encouraged the Commissioners, who now proceeded to further measures for the strict enforcement of the Law of the 4th of April.

A month's residence in the island had already convinced the Commissioners that much must be done if this law were to become a reality. Their tactics had divided the colonists on political questions, it is true, but they had made no progress in rallying any white support for measures against the color line. "Strange, indeed," they write the Convention on October 25, "is the error prevailing in Europe that there has ever been a single colonial white who has shown himself the true friend of the colored citizens. The famous Confederation of La-Croix-des-Bouquets, the Union of Saint-Marc, the cajolery of the military officers, have all been so much Counter-Revolutionary speculation." [2]

However, the Commissioners' conduct in these last days of October bore witness to their zealous employment

SONTHONAX'S RULE IN THE NORTH 195

of those "measures for the destruction of the ruling prejudice" promised in their first letter to the Minister of Marine.³ The colored members of the "Commission Intermédiaire" were but the first of a lengthening list of official appointees from the ranks of the "Citizens of the 4th of April." And how white disrespect to these new appointees would be treated was soon made plain by the striking case of the Sieur Théron.

The Sieur Théron was captain-general of a parish in the region of Fort Dauphin, and held a brilliant record for bravery and military skill. The captain-general of the adjoining parish was none other than the mulatto leader Candy who had gained so sinister a reputation in the rising of the Plain. Candy had later quarrelled with the negro chiefs, had made his peace with the authorities, and was now high in the Commissioners' favor. It appears that Théron did not show much respect to the mulatto officers sent through his district with Candy's official reports, in consequence of which Candy made some personal remarks about the Sieur Théron. When the white leader heard of this he lost his temper and wrote Candy the following letter: "If the National Assembly has granted you the political rights you now enjoy, we on our part know how to bear it. Of this, you yourself are the best proof; our conduct in your case should convince you that we know how to sacrifice to time and circumstance. But the whole nation has not the power to tear from our hearts the feeling of superiority toward you which we have always held and ever shall hold while there remain at San Domingo those negro slaves from which you spring. This is a fact you now overlook, —

and which it is good some one should teach you. Sir, you make a great mistake if you think that any of us will ever live in friendly familiarity with you and yours. 'Good-day'; 'Good-bye'; politeness, but exceeding reserve; that, sir, is all you can ask of us, — and the law itself can force us to nothing more, because the law cannot command the feelings of the heart. If this same law subjects us to your orders, we will obey you with resignation, but also with a certain dignity which will still maintain us at a great distance from you." The letter closed by explicitly stating that as this was a private affair the writer trusted Candy would not stir public feeling by showing these words to others, but would keep the quarrel a personal one.

The infuriated Candy, however, instead of seeking satisfaction of Théron, promptly forwarded the letter to Le Cap. The Commissioners felt that Théron had expressed only too well what all the white colonists were thinking, and the captain-general's very prominence increased their resolve to make an example of him. Accordingly, the Sieur Théron was summoned to Le Cap for trial. Sonthonax opened the examination by asking Théron why he had written Candy such an insulting and provocative letter; to which the captain-general replied that he had wished to abate the pride of Candy. To this Polverel observed that the air of superiority in the letter was a manifest violation of the Law of the 4th of April, which had established equality between all citizens regardless of color. Théron replied that he had expressly wished to keep this matter between Candy and himself, and that he could not see how he had violated the law, "which commanded execution and resignation, — not the feelings of the heart"; and that therefore he had considered himself free to choose his friends. But the Commissioners observed severely that this was not a case of "feelings kept carefully within the heart, but an overt act squarely against the law"; and to Théron's further objection that this act, though overt, concerned only Candy and could never hinder the law's execution, the Commissioners answered that by showing Candy his sentiments Théron had increased race hostility and had been guilty of sedition. Thus the trial proceeds for many pages, in which it is instructive to note both the cold severity of Polverel and Sonthonax's brutal invective. The verdict was, of course, certain from the start: "Considering that it is necessary to take severe measures to repress a prejudice whose annihilation can alone save the colony," the Sieur Théron was degraded from his office and shipped a prisoner to France to answer for his "incivism" before the bar of the Convention. When we remember that this same Candy had torn out the eyes of his wretched prisoners with a corkscrew and had been guilty of unspeakable outrages upon white women, it is easy to understand the wild despair that settled down upon white San Domingo. The Sieur Théron had been in error: Jacobin law did "command the feelings of the heart."[4]

The condemnation of the Sieur Théron was almost the last joint act of the Civil Commissioners for many months to come: on October 29, Polverel and the cipher Ailhaud sailed for the West. The "Tenth of August" had so intensified the Royalism of this province that the Commissioners had decided something must speedily be done, and the quiet then prevailing at Le Cap encouraged them to think that the North would give little further trouble.[5]

This momentary lull at Le Cap encouraged the energetic Rochambeau to begin those operations against the negro rebels which until then had been entirely forgotten in face of the necessity for holding down the white population of the city; but his successes were ephemeral, for ever larger numbers of troops had to be held in Le Cap itself to face the storm raised by the character of Sonthonax's rule.[6] Relieved of his colleague's relative moderation, Sonthonax, as sole dictator of the North, now displayed to the full the reckless and arbitrary violence of his nature. Every ship for France carried numerous suspects, while a forced loan to cover his lavish expenditure struck terror to the propertied classes. Most significant of all, however, was the hostility of his former allies the poor white clubmen. Their dreams of exploiting the aristocrats and monopolizing public office had proved but fond illusion; they now saw themselves more and more discarded for "Citizens of the 4th of April." Officials, counsellors, intimates, mistresses, — all about Sonthonax was now mulatto. The white proletarians of Le Cap discovered that in the eyes of Sonthonax they too were aristocrats — "Aristocrates de la Peau." [7] As the poor whites took no pains to conceal their rage at this new state of things, a series of violent quarrels with Sonthonax ensued which ended in the closing of the club and the deportation of its prominent agitators. Sonthonax, however, seems to have realized the growing difficulties of his position, for he attempted to veil his most arbitrary measures by making the suggestions come from his crea-

SONTHONAX'S RULE IN THE NORTH 199

ture, the "Commission Intermédiaire." But this petty ruse deceived no one, and popular hatred became merely dashed with contempt.[8]

His state of mind was probably not improved by his colleague's remonstrances. These are particularly sharp in Polverel's letter of the 14th December.[9] In this Sonthonax is sharply censured both for his wholesale deportations and for his manner of bringing them about. Sonthonax's method was to have the "Commission Intermédiaire" draw up proscription lists of those who had "lost the confidence of the People"; whereupon Sonthonax would yield to the voice of the "People's representatives," declare the accused "suspect," and order them deported to France for examination by the Convention. This practice Polverel condemned as both illegal and impolitic. The West had cried that Sonthonax was trying to hide behind his tool, and the Commissioners' prestige was being ruined in consequence. Polverel also condemned Sonthonax's closure of the club. "This act is a manifest violation of the rights of man and the citizen," reads the letter, "in addition to which, you have remedied nothing; for by dissolving the club you have not annihilated its members." He also expressed indignation that Sonthonax should have taken general measures without his assent, and announced that he had forbidden in the West and South the execution of that forced loan decreed by Sonthonax for the whole of San Domingo.

Sonthonax's reply was characteristic. He complained bitterly that his colleague should have listened to the "voice of calumny," and justified his arbitrary measures on the broad ground of "necessity." As to the club, it was a "nest of aristocrats"; in addition to which he expressed astonishment that Polverel should "quote the Rights of Man in a slave country." He had consulted the "Commission Intermédiaire" "to have virtually the desire of the colony by the mouths of its provisional representatives"; and he closed by stating that "his heart was torn" by Polverel's action.[10] In other words, Sonthonax intended to persevere in the course he had laid down.

But before Polverel had even written his protest a fresh explosion had occurred at Le Cap. That Sonthonax had scented trouble is plain, for during the month of November he had recruited a large body of mulatto soldiers. It was further action in this same line which brought on the explosion of the 2d of December. It will be recalled that after the failure of the Royalist attempt in late October, most of the officers of the old regiments had thrown up their commissions and left the country. Sonthonax now announced that in conformity with the Law of the 4th of April a number of lapsed commissions in the regiment "Le Cap" would be given to mulattoes. But at this even the veterans of "Le Cap" forgot their discipline and broke into open mutiny. On December 1, Sonthonax sent the popular young general, Laveaux, to recall them to their duty, but his appeals were fruitless. A committee of the oldest soldiers met Laveaux at the barrack gate and flatly refused to receive the mulatto officers, while a great crowd encouraged their resistance with cries of "Bravo, Régiment du Cap," and a thunder of applause.

Next day the regiment was ordered to parade on the

SONTHONAX'S RULE IN THE NORTH 201

Champ de Mars. The command was obeyed, but when the regulars arrived they found themselves confronted by the new mulatto companies. Voices in the crowd cried "Massacre," for the regiment was without cartridges. At this moment a negro was seen moving toward the mulatto lines with a bag over his shoulder, and was at once seized by the crowd. General Laveaux rode up, crying that the bag contained bread, and when ripped open the bag was, indeed, found to contain bread on top, but beneath was a mass of cartridges. Then came a general explosion. The white mob and the mulattoes engaged in a general mêlée which ended by the sudden retreat of the mulattoes from the town and their seizure of the fortified lines at the entrance to the Plain. The threat was unmistakable, and beneath the awful menace of destruction by the wild rebel hordes the whites of Le Cap bowed in trembling despair. Sonthonax himself acted as the messenger of peace and returned to town at the head of the triumphant mulattoes.[11]

Le Cap now lay apparently crushed beneath the yoke of Sonthonax and his mulatto battalions. The regiment "Le Cap" and a great number of civilians were deported, and for the next few months the white population lived under a veritable reign of terror. Sonthonax presently set up a miniature Revolutionary tribunal, the prisons were jammed with suspects, and every ship carried batches of deported persons for trial in France.[12]

Sonthonax's state of mind during this period is well shown by his letter of December 8 to the Minister of Marine. After detailing his repressive measures consequent on the rioting of the 2d of December, he says, "It is hard for Frenchmen to rule by terror; but one must so rule here at San Domingo, where there are neither morals nor patriotism, neither love of France nor respect for her laws; where the ruling passions are egoism and pride; where the chain of despotism has weighed for a century on all classes of men from Governor to slave. I have arrested the evil in its course. I have chastised; I have struck down: all the factious are in fear before me. And I shall continue to punish with the same severity whosoever shall trouble the public peace, whosoever shall dare deny the national will, — especially the holy law of equality!" [13]

And the violence of Sonthonax seemed but to increase with time. Some three weeks later, in his report to the Convention, he exclaims, "Herein the Convention may see the efforts of pride to destroy the holy doctrine of equality among free men; its members may convince themselves that the French Revolution will triumph over the league of kings before it succeeds in crushing infernal prejudice at San Domingo. Oh! that I might die a martyr to that equality which it is my first duty to preach and to defend. I shall never flinch before the rage of its detractors." [14]

Crushed as the white population appeared, however, Sonthonax continually dreaded some supreme convulsion of despair. His anxiety appears in a letter of January 11, 1793, to explain the sending of an unusually large batch of suspects for trial in France. "At the time of our arrival in San Domingo," he writes, "there existed two factions — the Royalists and the Aristocrates de la Peau. The former were crushed in October, but the latter are more

SONTHONAX'S RULE IN THE NORTH 203

audacious than before. Everywhere, especially at Port-au-Prince, they prate of independence." [15] The opening weeks of the year 1793 brought ever deepening troubles in their train. The sullen fury of the whites, the stubborn Royalism of the West,[16] the melting away of the French troops under bad management and disease, and the total failure to accomplish anything against the negro rebels, — all these combined to form a picture of deepening gloom. Sonthonax's letter of February 8 confesses to utter exhaustion in both credit and supply.[17]

But most ominous of all was that storm-cloud which now peered over the horizon-line of the ocean. To say nothing of the crisis with Spain, Revolutionary France was fast drifting toward war with England; and Sonthonax knew only too well that the infuriated whites were dreaming of an English war. "The independents and the Royalists breathe only the hope of foreign fleets," he writes the Minister of Marine on February 18, 1793.[18] "However, France may count upon the Citizens of the 4th of April. She has no better friends, and they alone would suffice to repel all the valets of all the tyrants with islands in the Antilles." [19]

As recently as the December riots, Sonthonax, to quiet uneasiness at his rule, had affirmed with his usual exuberance of statement his conviction as to the necessity of slavery. "Such are my principles, such my profession of faith," he had cried, pointing to his maiden speech before the Colonial Assembly; [20] "may the day on which I change be the last of my life." [21] However, on the same day that he had written the letter last quoted to the Minister of Marine, he penned a report to the Convention the knowledge of which would have alarmed his allies, the "Citizens of the 4th of April," almost as much as the whites themselves. This letter begins with a confession of complete failure against the rebel negroes, who, "aided by the perfidious Spaniards, brave our cannon and our troops. The worst of the matter is that among these rebels are a large number of genuine irreconcilables to the Republic. These follow blindly a number of despotic chiefs who are devoted Royalists. Stupid agents of the furies of a sanguinary Court, these wretched negroes fight only for their religion and for that King whom they imagine themselves destined to restore upon his throne. The thought of Liberty never enters their heads. Only the chiefs have such ideas; and even they think less of being free men than of themselves reigning over slaves. It is, therefore, not at all the noble sentiment of Liberty which inspires them; they even speak of it as but an accessory thing." The real persons to blame, continues the letter, are "the wretches who misled the Constituent Assembly in its last moments; those who snatched from it the fatal Decree of the 24th September"; thus giving the Royalists the chance to tell the negroes that the National Assembly had abandoned them to the tender mercies of the Colonial Legislature and that their only hope lay in the King.

Sonthonax now comes to the point. Of course, he continues, he and Laveaux will fight bravely on; but he can no longer conceal "a conviction that the Convention should hasten to legislate on the lot of the slaves, without awaiting the demand of those Colonial Assemblies, which will always entertain their ridiculous pretensions to rival

SONTHONAX'S RULE IN THE NORTH 205

the Convention and which will probably never possess sufficient enlightenment and wisdom to feel the necessity for a new régime. Everything, then, demands that the Convention should break the bonds which the Constituante has laid upon the national sovereignty."

"I do not pretend," concludes Sonthonax, "to point the exact moment for effecting an entire reform in the colonial system. But if this be not promptly modified, if the lot of the slaves be not ameliorated, it is impossible to foresee the duration of the woes of San Domingo. Last of all, such a decree will be only the natural sequence of the Law of the 4th of April." [22] Thus did Sonthonax foreshadow his future action, when, six months later, without authority from home and despite Polverel's opposition, he was to proclaim the freedom of all the negroes in the North Province of San Domingo.

With Sonthonax action followed so quickly on the heels of thought that had he continued to remain at Le Cap it is more than likely his desire would not have waited six months for its translation into fact. However, the explosion which had just occurred at Port-au-Prince determined him to yield to Polverel's entreaties, and early in March he committed Le Cap to the trusty Laveaux and sailed for the West.

XVII

POLVEREL'S GOVERNMENT OF THE WEST

It was on the 2d of November, 1792, that Polverel and his shadowy colleague Ailhaud landed at the Confederate stronghold of Saint-Marc. The Commissioners had hoped that their presence "would awaken the patriotism of its inhabitants, still too warmly attached to the Old Régime and its agents"; [1] but they soon found that report had not belied the Royalism of the West. Polverel's explanation of the "Tenth of August" and the late troubles at Le Cap "did not produce the effect we had expected"; instead of applauding, the assembled crowd shouted, "Vive le Roi!" Next day things grew still more serious. An angry mob of both whites and mulattoes surrounded the Commissioners' house and so alarmed them by its threats that they hastily took refuge on shipboard. It is true that they had brought a small body of troops under the command of a reliable officer named Lasalle, but they dared not use this slender force against the angry inhabitants, and covering their humiliation by talk of "leniency to the unenlightened," they sailed for Port-au-Prince.[2]

Here their reception was very different. The favor shown by the Commissioners to the poor whites of Le Cap had aroused the greatest enthusiasm among the democrats of Port-au-Prince, and the news of the "Tenth of August" had excited as much rejoicing in the city as fury in the Royalist hinterland. Polverel and Ailhaud were therefore given the warmest of welcomes, and the tone of the reception speeches must have been delightful indeed to persons still smarting from Saint-Marc hospitality.

"This city, so grossly libelled by Monsieur Blanchelande and the former agents of despotic authority," the Commissioners inform the Convention, "appears to us full of a great number of patriots." [3] "Here is the state of things in the West," they write Sonthonax on the same day; "except Port-au-Prince, all is aristocrat. Monsieur de Jumecourt holds in his hand all the planters and *ateliers* of the Plain.[4] Up till now he has kept things intact; but the slaves are armed, and at the first sign from Monsieur de Jumecourt, or at the least move against him, all would be on fire." [5] The Confederate leader, it is true, received the Commissioners with formal respect, but Polverel was not deceived by his attitude, and, despairing for the moment of reconciling the mulattoes to the Revolution, he leaned more and more upon the whites of Port-au-Prince. This explains much of his criticism at Sonthonax's closure of the Le Cap Club and other anti-white measures.[6] In his protest already quoted, Polverel says as much. "The only dependable patriots," he assures Sonthonax, "are the whites of Port-au-Prince and Jacmel.[7] Despite their resistance to the Law of the 4th of April, all the whites here are 'patriotes enragés.'" [8]

That Polverel had not overstated the matter is shown from a letter written by a member of the Port-au-Prince Club to a brother clubman at Le Cap describing the welcome accorded Borel, the famous partisan fighter of the

Artibonite.⁹ The writer was evidently a man of little education, as the script is bad and the spelling worse. Put into grammatical language, this letter runs as follows: "The clubs, my brother, the clubs may yet save this unhappy country, covered with all possible crimes, the victim of the greatest rascals and the most infernal plots. . . . At Borel's arrival the town was all lighted up, — except a few houses of aristocrats. The sight was very pretty, but I was hoping for something prettier still; — that is to say, after the fashion of Le Cap, the entire annihilation of the aristocrats, who, to the disgrace of good citizens, dare inhabit the city of Port-au-Prince. I had thought that only patriots had the right to breathe the air of this town. Nothing of the sort: not a single deportation, not a single holy proscription; no change. The public offices are still partly held by aristocrats, by enemies of the Revolution; and Port-au-Prince, my dear brother, reeks with aristocrats; incredible to you, of course, but true." ¹⁰ It is certainly a strange irony that Sonthonax at this very moment was showing the recipient of this effusion, worthy of the Cordeliers Club, that the San Domingo clubmen were also aristocrats: "Aristocrates de la Peau."

Thus for two months Polverel remained in Port-au-Prince; closely allied to the town whites but daring no move against the solid Royalism of the inland country. In mid-January, however, tired of inaction, he resolved to visit the South, — a resolve made doubly urgent by the desertion of his colleague Ailhaud. The Commissioners had been only a few days at Port-au-Prince when Polverel had directed his colleague to take command of

POLVEREL IN THE WEST

the South. Ailhaud, however, proved but a broken reed. His weak nerves had entirely gone to pieces under the horrors of San Domingo, and he was no sooner at sea than he ordered his ship to sail forthwith to France.[11]

The South was more than ever under white control, and the policy of the Commissioners had stimulated the Royalism of the hard-fighting planters of the "Grand Anse" to a pitch which reduced Polverel to despair. In a detailed report on the South by parishes he describes one of these as "a sterile land where the seed of Revolution will not grow. It is the abode of a great number of *ci-devant* nobles who are openly addressed by their former titles, and since they and their creatures form almost the whole population, they find few persons to contradict their liking." The adjoining parish was also full of these "hommes à parchemin." In Les Cayes itself he had made some progress by founding a club "which walks in the right line of patriotism, — hatred of the Counter-Revolutionists, love for the Republic, submission to its laws and respect for its representatives. But the great planters and the inhabitants of the Plain,[12] just as in all the other parts of the colony, view with pain an order of things which places them upon a level with their fellow citizens." [13]

However, before Polverel could accomplish much, he was forced to leave Les Cayes by alarming tidings from the West. During his absence Sonthonax's mulatto rule at Le Cap had been doing Polverel's work, and the Western Royalists were at last splitting along the color line. For while there were a good many genuine Royalists among the mulattoes, the race question so overshadowed politics with the bulk of the caste that Sonthonax's ultra-radical measures were fast bringing the mulattoes to see that they had more to gain from the Commissioners than from their white Confederate allies. And, conversely, Sonthonax's treatment of the Northern whites had roused such terror throughout the colony that the whites of the West felt they must sink every political difference before a peril which menaced their very existence.

Accordingly, about the end of January, 1793, Borel, who had become the acknowledged head of the whites of Port-au-Prince, held a conference with De Jumecourt, the Confederate leader, at which they agreed to forget the past and to form a new Confederation including both parties. Polverel was greatly disturbed at the news and forbade any such action, but his unavailing protests were presently supplemented by an unlooked-for diversion in the shape of a negro rising in the West.[14]

We have already noted the existence of that powerful maroon community among the mountains of the Spanish border, whose political individuality had been recognized by the Royal Government some years before the Revolution.[15] This people had been powerfully recruited during the late troubled years, and had not remained an idle spectator of events. Its ravages had hit the mulattoes even harder than the whites, since the maroons bore a special hatred toward their old enemies of the *maréchaussée*.[16] At this moment these people had become still more formidable through the adhesion of an able negro leader named Hyacinthe, who succeeded in raising many of the slaves and who carried his ravages to the outskirts of Port-au-Prince itself. This negro rising had important political consequences. Hyacinthe had recently been in Confederate service, and the town whites, fearing some treachery on the part of De Jumecourt, drew away from the white Royalists for the time. Furthermore, the race feeling of the town mob was so aroused that they began to maltreat mulattoes, and when General Lasalle undertook to suppress these disorders the pent-up rage at Sonthonax's conduct burst into flame. Lasalle was expelled the city, and Port-au-Prince stood in open defiance of the Civil Commissioners.[17] It was the report of these troubles that induced Sonthonax to come to the West.[18]

Sonthonax landed at Saint-Marc on the 9th of March, and was received with rapture by the mulattoes who had recently made themselves absolute masters of the town. He at once saw that quick action was necessary before the Western whites should cement their alliance once more. His feelings toward them are shown by his letter to the Minister of Marine. "The crimes of Port-au-Prince begin again," he writes on March 10; "the town is forming an alliance with the heads of the Royalist party. . . . The negroes have risen, and the Plain of Cul-de-Sac lies in ashes. Such, citizen, are the fruits of the stupid and frantic pride of a handful of Europeans whom the National Assembly and its representatives have treated altogether too leniently." [19]

That Sonthonax did not intend to display much lenience in the future was plain from the manifesto drawn up with his approval by his followers at Saint-Marc and published throughout the West. "Hasten," it reads; "hasten from all parts of the colony, regenerated citizens. Surround the organs of the Law, and may our bodies fall a thousand times beneath the blows of our miserable enemies rather than allow them to abate one jot the laws of the Republic. Put forth all your strength; let our enemies tremble with fear at sight of the ardor with which we shall crush and annihilate that insolent faction which centres at Port-au-Prince. Swear never to return till the last of them are exterminated. No more peace, friends, no more pardon; crush this foul vermin which carries desolation to the most distant mountains. Remember that the foreign enemy make compromise with domestic agitation impossible, and purify with death this land still reeking with crimes." [20]

The response to this appeal was so general that when Polverel arrived from the South he found a considerable force assembled for the march on Port-au-Prince. The exclusively racial character of this new struggle is shown by the fact that "there were not thirty whites in the whole army." [21] The campaign which followed was short and decisive. The mulattoes soon surrounded Port-au-Prince from the landward side while the Commissioners and their fleet blockaded it by sea. The inhabitants knew that they could expect little mercy, but after nearly two days' terrific bombardment by the fleet their forts were silenced; to avert the general massacre which would probably have followed an assault, Port-au-Prince surrendered on April 13, 1793. Borel and several hundred of the most determined whites cut their way through the mulatto lines and escaped to the South.[22]

The conquered city was treated with extreme severity. The Commissioners' mulatto and negro troops plundered and murdered almost at will; hundreds of the inhabitants were confined in the prisons or upon hulks in the harbor, and great numbers were deported. A letter written on the 24th of April and smuggled out of the town by a friendly sailor [23] gives a vivid picture. "I have lost hope," cries the writer to his brother in France; "I am convinced that we are the destined victims of the most execrable horrors that hell itself can invent. . . . Behold our reward for all the sacrifices we have made for the Revolution. We are good citizens; we flatter ourselves that we are good Republicans: and we can speak only by signs. Should we dare make a murmur, we are thrown aboard ship like bags of dirty linen and sent to France without a word to those left behind." [24]

The West as well as the North now lay crushed beneath the heel of the Civil Commissioners and their mulatto soldiery. But the South still defied them and refused obedience to the Law of the 4th of April This last centre of resistance was now taken in hand. During the weeks which followed the surrender of Port-au-Prince a considerable army was formed for the conquest of the South and the command entrusted to André Rigaud, a Southern mulatto who had shown considerable ability in the various struggles of the South and West. But the fighters of the Grande Anse proved more formidable than before: Rigaud's army was completely cut to pieces and hundreds of mulattoes were left dead on the field. Rigaud's report to the Commissioners shows how serious had been his defeat and how momentous might well be its consequences. "If the South be not conquered," he asserts, "the whole colony will try the same course. In all the parishes our enemies openly rejoice, — and you know very well what such rejoicing means. . . . Citizens, if you want any peace you must deport half the white population of San Domingo. The mask is off at last; it plays the aristocrat to our face." [25]

But many days before Rigaud wrote these lines the Commissioners had hastened from Port-au-Prince to face a new storm-cloud in the North, and it was plain that action against the whites of the South would have to be postponed.

XVIII

THE DESTRUCTION OF LE CAP

WHEN Sonthonax sailed for the West in the opening days of March, 1793, Le Cap appeared so crushed in spirit that he anticipated little resistance to the stern rule of General Laveaux. And yet the very first report of this trusted deputy must have stirred Sonthonax to fresh disquietude. In his letter of March 7, Laveaux reported quiet, it is true, but added that this was "thanks to the watchfulness of the Commission Intermédiaire and to his own military patrols." He also reported so much veiled hostility and seditious language that a projected sally against the rebel negroes had been indefinitely postponed.[1]

And his subsequent letters were more ominous still. The very next day arrived the tidings of the execution of Louis XVI, which produced "commotion" suppressed only by redoubled patrols,[2] while ten days later the news of the English war caused him to ask Sonthonax for further orders in case of extreme necessity.[3] Before March was out the situation had grown so bad that Laveaux wrote, "You must repress the disaffected; their numbers grow with every day. Count on us, but do not lose a single instant in your return. . . . We fear a violent explosion."[4]

Such was the state of Le Cap when on the 7th of May a new Governor-General arrived from France. The outbreak of war with both England and Spain [5] placed distracted San Domingo in a highly perilous situation, and made the presence of an able military head a matter of prime necessity. Realizing this obvious fact, the Convention despatched to San Domingo one Galbaud, an officer free from political entanglements and with a professional reputation of the best. His instructions were the counterpart of those issued to Desparbés, — subordination to the Commissioners in political matters, but a free hand in the technical handling of the troops.[6]

Galbaud was a quiet, steady soldier who had always kept out of politics and who asked nothing better than absorption in his professional duties. But the excitable population of Le Cap, goaded to despair by the long months of Sonthonax's brutal rule, welcomed the new Governor-General as a deliverer: when it discovered that his wife was a San Domingo Creole it greeted Galbaud as an avenger as well. Madame Galbaud has left a vivid picture of her husband's triumphal progress through the streets of the city and of the frantic enthusiasm which met him on every side.[7]

Galbaud's soldierly instincts were greatly shocked at the terrible condition of Le Cap. He found everything in the greatest dilapidation; the magazines empty, the soldiers destitute and mutinous for want of pay, the treasury completely looted by Sonthonax and his corrupt associates. Madame Galbaud relates her horror at the Commissioners' conduct in both North and West, and the General himself seems to have shared her feelings. He at once took measures to remedy the situation, quieted the troops, and confirmed the inhabitants in their favorable opinion of his character.

THE DESTRUCTION OF LE CAP 217

At the news of Galbaud's arrival the Civil Commissioners' jealous and despotic temper at once took alarm: when they learned of the new Governor-General's measures and increasing popularity, fear gave place to fury. Galbaud's letters expressed the utmost respect, it is true, but it was clear that he intended to be master in his own department and that he was not the type of man to become their unresisting tool. The Commissioners resolved to hasten back at once to deal with this dangerous rival. Their state of mind may be gauged by a letter sent the Commission Intermédiaire announcing their coming. "Be of good heart, brave citizens," it reads, "soon the colony shall be purged of this frightful lethargy which now consumes it. Yet a few days and we shall appear once more at Le Cap; and we are there resolved to display a severity which our principles have too long restrained. The agitators of all parties will soon be annihilated, and a better order of things shall then succeed to this destructive chaos. Let not discouragement seize true Republicans. Yet a little while and they shall triumph. Let public functionaries tremble who have abused and still abuse the power of place to mislead the people! Their reign is almost over." [8]

At Le Cap itself the Commissioners' partisans breathed the same frantic menaces as their chiefs. Madame Galbaud relates how Dufay, one of Sonthonax's closest intimates, "often made remarks to me like this: 'The white population must disappear from the colony. The day of vengeance is at hand. Many of these colonist princes must be exterminated.' His tone," concludes Madame Galbaud, "was one of frenzy." [9]

It was on the 10th of June that the Civil Commissioners and their long column of mulatto soldiery entered Le Cap amid the frantic applause of their partisans and the sullen silence of the whites. Even before their arrival they seem to have made up their minds that Galbaud must at all costs be disposed of, for their attitude toward him was hostile in the extreme. Their plan of action was soon revealed. After a short examination of his credentials they pronounced these invalid, and after an angry altercation they declared him deposed and ordered him to embark for France. To all this, despite the prayers of the white population, Galbaud submitted. He realized that with men like these the only alternative to obedience was armed rebellion, and he was too much the disciplined soldier to seek a struggle with the civil authorities.

Unfortunately the Civil Commissioners began their work of vengeance before Galbaud had put to sea. Never before had Le Cap witnessed such deportations *en masse*, and within a few days every ship of the departing squadron was crowded with the condemned. Nevertheless, the impending catastrophe might still have been averted had it not been for the conduct of the Commissioners' mulatto soldiery. These men proceeded to treat the whites of Le Cap as they had those of conquered Port-au-Prince, and they made no distinction between the civilian population and the sailors of the fleet. Seamen on shore leave were insulted, and resistance was answered by murder. This was too much. In the harbor of Le Cap were nearly three thousand sailors, and the whole body now rose in a furious cry for vengeance. The movement spread like wildfire, the naval officers were swept off their feet, and

THE DESTRUCTION OF LE CAP 219

Galbaud himself yielded to the universal cry. On the evening of the 19th of June, Galbaud was borne in triumph through the fleet amid thunderous cheers of "Vive la République! Vive Galbaud!" and summoned the sailors to land for the overthrow of the tyrants.

About dawn on the 20th of June, Galbaud landed with over two thousand sailors of the fleet. The regulars who garrisoned the harbor forts went over without firing a shot, but the French National Guards held firm for the Commissioners. Then a terrible struggle began. Every street, every house, was furiously defended by the Commissioners' white and mulatto troops. Furthermore, these regular combatants were soon reënforced by the whole civilian population: the whites rising for Galbaud, the mulattoes and town negroes for the Commissioners. At the end of the day, however, it was plain that the discipline of the regulars and the wild courage of the sailors were gaining the victory, and at dawn next day Galbaud's columns pierced the main line of defence while the Commissioners fled to the fortified lines at the entrance to the Plain.

But the shouts of victory soon died in the terrible cry of "The Brigands are in the town!" The dreadful news was only too true. During the night the Commissioners, knowing that they would be beaten on the morrow, had offered plunder and liberty to the eager rebels of the Plain, and dense masses of howling savages were now pouring into the town. Against the pressure of these black hordes Galbaud and his followers could do nothing, and by nightfall they held only the harbor forts and the water-front. But the fall of night made little difference in the scene, for harbor and shipping lay bright as day in the awful glare of the burning city: Le Cap was in flames, and those of the white population not huddled along the quays were dying amid their burning homes or under the torments of the savages. Next day fully fifteen thousand more of the rebels poured into the city, and Galbaud, recognizing that the case was hopeless, set sail for the United States. Every ship that could keep the sea followed his flag, and soon the great fleet with its ten thousand despairing refugees on board had dropped the empty harbor and blazing city below the horizon. Fortunately the voyage was fair, and when this tragic armada cast anchor in Chesapeake Bay the sufferings of the wretched fugitives were over. Public and private benevolence vied in the work of mercy, and even distant Massachusetts supplemented the federal grant by special legislative provision.[10]

During all those scenes of horror which marked the fall of Le Cap the Commissioners remained immovable, and true to their promise allowed the rebel negroes the absolute sacking of the town. They would neither stir themselves nor allow any one else to do so. On the evening of the 22d, General Lasalle had arrived from the West with two hundred mulatto dragoons, and he had implored the Commissioners to let him take command of the French National Guards and the mulatto battalion to fight the fire and stop the massacre. This request, however, the Commissioners absolutely refused, and only on the evening of the 24th was Lasalle allowed to enter the city with a single squad of his dragoons; "with whom," he writes, "I marched amid flames and corpses." [11] The

THE DESTRUCTION OF LE CAP 221

Commissioners' responsibility for this awful disaster seems to be complete.

The best picture of the catastrophe is that left us by Carteau, at that moment on duty at a military post upon the heights overlooking the Plain. "For four days and nights," he writes, "we watched the fire consume this rich and famous city, the glory of the French colonies. ... We were stupefied at sight of the immense clouds of black smoke which rose by day; at night we were awed by the flames which, striking the bold promontory that overhangs the town, lit up with reflected light the whole vast immensity of the Plain. During the first two days we did not know the meaning of this terrible spectacle. Deep in our own thoughts, therefore, we whites, mulattoes, and free negroes who made up the post instinctively ranged ourselves by colors, — each against the others, each prepared to sell life dearly. In this uncertainty we awaited impatiently the outcome of this tragic event; although we whites, so long the butt of the Commissioners' injustice and cruelty, had the keenest dread of that which lay in store." [12]

XIX

EMANCIPATION

THE destruction of Le Cap was interpreted by white San Domingo as a virtual sentence of death: save within the parishes controlled by the white Confederates of the Grande Anse, all sought to quit the land accursed. Every merchant ship from the ports of North and West bore its sad freight of refugees; every Spanish outpost received a stream of despairing fugitives. But there was something still more serious. The Commissioners' deliberate summons to the savage hordes of the Plain had horrified the regular troops almost as much as the civilian population, and wherever their position allowed, these also resolved to forswear allegiance to such authorities. The results of all this were at once decisively apparent upon the Spanish border. The Spaniards had begun hostilities as far back as early May, but the small number of their troops and the scanty population of Spanish Santo Domingo [1] had confined their efforts to a few border skirmishes. Now, however, things became very different. The whole Cordon de l'Est went over in a body, while the Spaniards bestirred themselves to take the Royalist negro chiefs into their pay and laid plans for the complete conquest of the "Partie française de Saint-Domingue."

The desperate state of the French colony is disclosed by Sonthonax himself in his letters during the month of

July, 1793. A long report to the Convention, written July 10, describes the general exodus of the white population, the departure of the whole naval station, and the desertion of a thousand regulars and French National Guards to the Spaniards. "Such, citizens," he concludes, "is the disastrous condition to which Galbaud has reduced us in the Province of the North. Without ships, without money, with only a month's supply, — still we do not yet despair of the safety of the *patrie*. We ask no troops, no ships, no sailors; it is with the real inhabitants of this country, the Africans, that we will yet save to France the possession of San Domingo." [2]

However, despite this characteristic flourish, Sonthonax's reports grow more and more hopeless as he describes the triumphant progress of the Spaniards and their allies, black and white. "The slaves remaining in the party of kings," he writes on July 30, "march in company with a great number of white *émigrés*. After every action we find these people among the dead. The corsairs which infest our coast are armed and manned by Frenchmen. Well may we say that morally, as well as physically, all that is European becomes tainted and rotten in this unhappy country." [3]

When Sonthonax penned these lines he was once more in sole command of the North, Polverel having hastened back to the West. Accompanied by his mulatto troops and the few hundred French National Guards who still remained faithful to the Republic, Sonthonax lay on the heights overlooking the ruined city, surrounded by swarming thousands of negro savages. The terrible condition of Le Cap is described in a letter from an officer of the French National Guards. Although the Americans were bringing in enough supplies to keep them from actual starvation, "all the whites are leaving for New England [4] who can possibly get away. This country will in future be little suited to Europeans, and will have no lasting tranquillity. Battalions of negro slaves have been formed and have been given their liberty. They will be the future armed force of this country. Also, a general emancipation and division of the land will soon take place." [5] So appalled was the writer at the future and so worn down by privation that he closes his letter with the statement that he was about to throw up his lieutenant-colonel's commission and sail for the United States with the rest.

This French officer was a true prophet, for Sonthonax had already taken the first steps of that momentous action secretly advocated since February, 1793. "The flames which devoured Le Cap," says Carteau, "marked the triumph of the yellow caste; they were also the harbingers of black supremacy." [6] The same author tells of a number of white refugees who, despairing of mercy from the Commissioners, sought and found refuge with the terrible mulatto Candy: "for," he adds, "this gentleman, grown suspicious of the Commissioners' real aim, had begun to look upon them with an evil eye." [7]

Candy had, indeed, good cause for his disquietude. On that very 21st of June, when the rebel negroes of the Plain swarmed into Le Cap at the Commissioners' summons, there had appeared the following astounding proclamation: "The will of the French Republic and its representatives being to give liberty to all negro warriors

EMANCIPATION

who shall fight for the Republic under the Civil Commissioners' orders, . . . all slaves declared free by the Republic's delegates shall be the equals of all men, white or any other color. They shall enjoy all the rights of French citizens. Such is the mission which the National Convention and the Executive Council of the Republic have given the Civil Commissioners." [8] Furthermore, on the following day, another proclamation promised liberty to individuals who, "wishing to become free, should enroll themselves in the forces of the Republic." [9]

After Polverel's departure, the attitude of Sonthonax grew clearer with every day, and the mulattoes now underwent the same painful disillusionment as the white proletariat a few months before. The mulatto caste saw itself thrust into the background, and the *entourage* of Sonthonax grew steadily more and more negro. Lasalle (now appointed Governor-General) saw astonishing changes in his corps of officers. "I found myself," he writes the French Government, "surrounded by epaulettes of all grades worn by slaves of the day before"; and he notes that one of these new citizens had been appointed colonel and inspector-general of San Domingo.[10]

Sonthonax's intentions are still more clearly shown by his letter to the Convention written at the end of July. "The time for shufflings and half-measures," he exclaims, " is past. The slave-drivers and the kings must be put on the same plane. Let them cease their tyranny; let them quit their prey; better still, let them disappear from the surface of the globe." [11]

Obviously, Sonthonax was resolved to wait no longer, and on the 29th of August, 1793, he formally proclaimed the freedom of the slave population throughout the North Province of San Domingo, attempting at the same time to justify his former inconsistencies of conduct. The proclamation opened with a quotation from the "Rights of Man."

"'All men' [it reads] 'are born and remain free and equal.' Behold, citizens, the evangel of France! It is high time that it was proclaimed in all parts of the Republic. Sent by the Nation as Civil Commissioners to San Domingo, our mission there was to enforce the Law of the 4th of April and to prepare gradually, without dissension or convulsion, the enfranchisement of the slaves. . . .

"At that time, citizens, we assert that slavery was necessary, both for the continuance of labor and for the preservation of the inhabitants. For San Domingo was then in the power of a horde of ferocious tyrants, who openly preached that the color of the skin should be the sign both of power and of reprobation. The judges of the unhappy Ogé, the creatures and members of the infamous provost courts who filled the towns with gibbets and torture-wheels to sacrifice the Africans and men of color to their atrocious pretensions;—all these men of blood yet peopled the colony.

"To-day things are changed, indeed. The slave-drivers and cannibals are no more. Some have perished, victims of their own impotent rage; others have sought safety in flight and emigration. Those whites who yet remain are the friends of the law and of French principles. . . .

"The French Republic wishes liberty and equality among all men, regardless of color; the kings are happy only in the midst of slaves. The Republic adopts you among its children; the kings aspire to cover you with chains or to destroy you utterly. The representatives of this same Republic, to aid you, have unbound the hands of the Civil Commissioners. A new order is about to be born, and the ancient servitude shall disappear." [12]

This proclamation, preceded by a "bonnet rouge" at the end of a pike, was ordered solemnly read in every commune of the North, while a delegation was sent to France to implore the ratification of the Convention.

In his report to that body Sonthonax did not attempt to deny that he had acted without orders, but based his defence upon the broad ground of necessity. "The last ships are gone," he writes; "we are without supplies, and all would appear lost to men not resolved to hold out to the last. Under such circumstances the only course was to give a great example of justice. I have attained this end by proclaiming the 'Rights of Man' in the Province of the North." [13] His letter to Polverel was less positive in tone, but stated that the writer was "at least sure of having turned the results of a great disaster to the profit of humanity." [14] Polverel was, indeed, angry and alarmed, but he realized that the step was irrevocable and he presently proclaimed emancipation in the West and South with certain minor qualifications.[15]

If Sonthonax had expected that emancipation would end his troubles, he was soon bitterly undeceived: the proclamation did not rally the negroes to the Republic, but did produce fresh social disorders. Jean-François and Biassou, now formally commissioned in Spanish service and steadily extending their authority over the lesser negro chiefs, replied in no uncertain fashion. "We cannot," reads their letter, "conform to the national will, seeing that since the beginning of the world we have obeyed the will of a king. We have lost the King of France, but we are dear to him of Spain, who constantly shows us reward and assistance. Wherefore, we cannot recognize you as Commissioners until you have enthroned a king." [16]

And not merely was Sonthonax unable to reconcile the negroes in Spanish service; his own ranks suffered daily depletion. At the fall of Le Cap many thousand negroes had taken the tricolor, but as soon as there was nothing more to plunder, these new converts quickly vanished with their booty to take up their careless life among the woods and mountains or to enroll themselves beneath the banner of Spain. Indeed, the one prominent chief whom Sonthonax had converted to the Republic, a certain Macaya, presently changed sides and sent to Sonthonax this astonishing profession of faith: "I am the subject of three kings, — the King of the Congo, lord of all the blacks; the King of France, who represents my father; the King of Spain, who represents my mother. These three kings are descended from those who, led by a star, went to adore the Man-God. If I passed into the Republic's service, I should perhaps be forced to make war on my brothers, the subjects of these three kings to whom I have sworn fidelity." [17]

The social consequences of emancipation were equally disappointing. Up to this time, despite all the disturbances of the last few years, some considerable districts had continued under regular cultivation. But now the negroes everywhere refused to work and broke into complete insubordination. How serious was this state of things may be seen by a letter from the island of Tortuga, hitherto entirely exempt from serious disturbance. "Decidedly," it reads, "all is lost in this colony. Deprived as we now are of our personal property, what becomes of our lands? Nothing. The slaves, become suddenly free, independent, our equals, or rather our superiors (for to-day they give us the law), have been changed into so many scoundrels armed with torch and knife to strike their victims and burn everything at the slightest sign. Like the Janissaries in Turkey, they have become the terror even of those who have freed them and given them arms. Little by little their aversion to work has strengthened. In vain has the attempt been made to keep them on the land they tilled by making them co-owners and giving them a fourth of the product.[18] Unsatisfied, indifferent to this benefit, idleness, indolence, debauchery, theft, and evil-doing are for them the sovereign good, the highest happiness, to which all else is sacrificed. Indeed, they scarcely permit the planters, their former masters, to live in their own houses or to enjoy what little remains to them Such, my dear Armand, are the fatal results of the 29th of August, 1793. The insurrection of 1791 was partial, and was caused by the mulattoes for their own special benefit; to-day this insurrection is general, and 400,000 individuals are being ceaselessly told, 'You are all freemen.' The evil is past cure; the colonies are lost to France; and I doubt whether Frenchmen can here find any more French property." [19]

Our Tortuga planter's description of conditions at Le

Cap was hardly overestimated; the position of Sonthonax had rapidly become such as to endanger his own person. His mulatto troops could, of course, no longer be relied on, while as supplies and money waned so did the subordination of the black soldiery. An attempt to restore discipline ended in riotous mutiny, and the attitude of the thousands of idle and destitute negroes became daily more menacing. Carteau gives a vivid picture of this critical time. "As I was walking to the Commissioner's for my passport," he writes, "I saw a negro raise himself among a group lying under the balcony of a government storehouse and cry loudly to his comrades: That Sonthonax! If some one would give me fifty portugaises I would kill him within the hour.' I marvelled," adds Carteau, "at the negro's audacity in speaking thus so high." [20] When, in early October, this writer at last succeeded in leaving Le Cap, he draws a sad picture of the broad harbor, quite empty now save for a scant half-dozen American vessels scattered along the vast, deserted quays.[21]

Small wonder that Sonthonax had himself departed when, upon these local perils, came the evil tidings that the English had landed in San Domingo, welcomed by both the white and mulatto populations of South and West.

XX

THE ENGLISH INTERVENTION

ENGLISH aid against Revolutionary France had long been the hope of many persons in San Domingo. As far back as the outcry at the Decree of May 15, 1791, the prevalence of such opinions had alarmed Governor Blanchelande,[1] and this sentiment had been still further strengthened by the negro insurrection and its consequences. When in late September, 1791, Edwards arrived at Le Cap with the warships and supplies lent by the Governor of Jamaica, he relates that the assembled inhabitants "directed all their attention toward us, and we landed amidst a crowd of spectators who, with uplifted hands and streaming eyes, gave welcome to their deliverers (for such they considered us), and acclamations of 'Vivent les Anglois' resounded from every quarter."[2] The English officers were splendidly received, and Edwards specifies "a very strong disposition in the white inhabitants of Le Cap to renounce their allegiance to the mother country. The black cockade was universally substituted in place of the tricolored, and very earnest wishes were avowed in all companies, without scruple or restraint, that England would send an armament to conquer the island or rather to secure its voluntary surrender from its inhabitants."[3] And he adds that he was so generally considered an accredited emissary of the British Government that his position became a highly embarrassing one.

This pro-English feeling is well shown by a letter from Le Cap written shortly after the outbreak of the negro insurrection. "I am as good a Frenchman as there is in this world," it reads, "and I am attached to the mother country by ties of blood, affection, and gratitude. But rather than see my fortune, honorably acquired, become the prey of brigands egged on by another set of brigands sitting in Paris, I prefer a thousand times to go over to the English.... And every one else here thinks as I." [4]

If such had been the feeling in the North during the autumn of 1791, the state of the traditionally pro-English South may be imagined two years later after a twelvemonth of Sonthonax's rule in San Domingo. The tragedy of Le Cap had not only loosed the last tie to Jacobin France; it had also shown the South what would follow if the next attempt of the savage mulatto partisan Rigaud should end in victory. Accordingly, on September 3, 1793, the Confederates of the Grande Anse signed a treaty with the Governor of Jamaica which formally transferred their allegiance to the British Crown. "The Inhabitants of San Domingo," runs the first article, "being unable to appeal to their legitimate sovereign for deliverance from the tyranny which oppresses them, invoke the protection of His Brittannic Majesty and bear him their oath of fidelity; begging him to preserve the colony, and to treat them as good and loyal subjects until the general peace, when the French Government and the Allied Powers shall definitely decide the question of the sovereignty of San Domingo." The subsequent articles assured to the French inhabitants the full enjoyment of their old laws and customs.[5]

The Governor of Jamaica acted quickly. On the 19th of September, a small English squadron dropped anchor in the harbor of Jérémie, the stronghold of the Grande Anse, situated at the extreme end of the long peninsula of the South, and nine hundred British soldiers landed amid salvos of artillery and shouts of "Long live King George!" The neighboring parishes at once submitted; only the eastern districts and the city of Les Cayes were still held down by Rigaud and his mulatto soldiery.

And the defection of the South was but the prelude to a still greater disaster. Upon the outermost tip of the northern peninsula stood the great fortress of the Môle-Saint-Nicolas, the key of the Windward Passage, proverbially known as the Gibraltar of the Antilles. Its natural strength had long marked it out as the last refuge in case of supreme disaster, and here were gathered the reserve *matériel* and the only considerable body of white troops, besides Laveaux's shattered battalions at Le Cap, which still adhered to the Republic. This garrison consisted of the Irish battalion "Dillon" and some five hundred French National Guards, but its temper had become increasingly doubtful, and the tactless conduct of Sonthonax was now to bring on irreparable disaster.

On his way to the West after the destruction of Le Cap, Polverel had visited the Môle and had sent an alarming letter to Sonthonax urging decisive measures. "If you do not hasten to change the spirit of this place," he writes, "it will become one more dangerous nest of Royalism, Anglicism, and love of Spain. . . . If the garrison be not changed ... and 'Dillon' replaced by a strong garrison of free companies and new citizens,[6] all is lost in this quarter. It must be totally regenerated." [7]

Sonthonax had immediately begun to take steps in this direction, but he had quickly discovered that the defenders of the Môle absolutely refused to put themselves in his power. At this insubordination Sonthonax had completely lost his temper and had issued a proclamation declaring the whole garrison guilty of "lèse-nation" and "traîtres à la Patrie." The result was inevitable. On the 22d of September a single ship appeared off the Môle with a hundred British grenadiers aboard, but at the mere sight of the English flag Major O'Farrel, of the Irish battalion, came out with proposals of capitulation, and the great fortress, with its two hundred heavy guns, immense *matériel*, and entire garrison of nearly a thousand men, surrendered without striking a blow. The example of the Môle was followed by the German colonists of Bombarde, and the whole peninsula down to the walls of Port-de-Paix had soon thrown off allegiance to the Republic.[8]

These defections of the white districts to north and south were serious enough, but what now began in the West Province reduced the Commissioners to absolute despair. The mulattoes had everywhere greeted Sonthonax's negrophil policy with ill-concealed rage; his emancipation proclamation had roused them to furious mutiny. The mulattoes had always been as bitterly opposed to emancipation as the whites themselves, and at the present moment they were even harder hit, since up to this time they had succeeded in keeping most of

THE ENGLISH INTERVENTION 235

their slaves in some sort of obedience. "These Citizens of the 4th of April," writes Governor-General Lasalle to the French Government, "whom you regard as the true defenders of the colony and whose fortune consisted largely in slaves; how are they now to live? The proclamation of the 29th of August has reduced them to the most frightful misery." [9]

Upon the angry mulattoes of the West the English intervention worked almost as powerfully as upon the whites themselves. It is true that the presence of Polverel and a few mulatto leaders thoroughly committed to the Republic kept Port-au-Prince quiet for the moment, and that the iron hand of Rigaud continued to hold down Les Cayes; but elsewhere all was seething disaffection. When, about mid-October, a thousand more English troops landed in the South, the mulatto stronghold of the Artibonite rose in open revolt and a new Confederation of Saint-Marc called the English into the West. "So long as the Civil Commissioners' proclamations assured our future well-being," announced the mulatto Mayor of Saint-Marc, "I obeyed them to the letter. But from the moment that I realized they were preparing the thunderbolt now shattering everything around us, I took measures to save our fellow citizens and to preserve our properties." [10] The example of Saint-Marc was followed by Léogane, and Port-au-Prince was thus hemmed in on both sides by British territory.

In the North Province the situation was even more hopeless. Laveaux with the wrecks of the European battalions had retired to the stronghold of Port-de-Paix, and behind the walls of this first centre of French colonization he now lay watching the progress of the Spaniards from the east and of the English from the Môle-Saint-Nicolas. His terrible situation is shown by his report to Sonthonax of mid-September. At that moment Laveaux had but seven hundred men fit for duty, and these poor remnants were wasting rapidly under the terrible conditions which prevailed. "I cannot describe to you," he writes, "the horrors of our hospitals. Never cleaned, even the dying are unattended while the dead remain in their beds sometimes two days. . . . Into these dens of pestilence the soldier enters with horror, crying, 'Behold my last abode.'" The food was execrable: a little bread, fish so bad "that men shrink from it," and for drink tafia-grog to which the soldiers laid much of their sickness. "In fine, one sees walking spectres instead of French soldiers." All the supplies having been burned at the destruction of Le Cap, "the troops cannot march for lack of shoes and will soon be absolutely naked." Laveaux closes with a pathetic appeal for Sonthonax's attention.[11]

Laveaux's report on the general military situation at the beginning of October was more hopeless still. Besides the danger from foreign enemies, most of the negro troops were showing a desire to replace him by one of their own number. "We are in a country," he writes, "where by the course of events the white man is detested. The guilty have fled, it is true; but the hatred toward the whites borne by the Africans is not in the least assuaged thereby. Each day the whites are threatened. . . . And who can force these new citizens to do their duty once they have abjured it? Will they respect the handful of

THE ENGLISH INTERVENTION 237

white troops which yet remains?" Laveaux frankly admits that he despairs of keeping order; all he can do is to die at the head of the few soldiers that yet remain. Since the fall of the Môle, he continues, the military situation has become quite untenable. Even a retreat overland into the West is most uncertain, for the attitude of the negro troops is doubtful; if the English once pierce the lines of Port-de-Paix, this attitude will become more doubtful still. "For, after all the examples of their lack of courage or good faith in fighting the brigand negroes, what can you expect of them against the English?" [12]

This crushing series of disasters lashed Sonthonax into a delirium of fury. Weeping with rage, he dashed off incoherent letters to Laveaux and Polverel, urging them to make the whole coast a desert and then retire like maroons into the mountains. But this ferocious counsel Polverel refused to follow, and returned a severe answer stating that such a policy would merely unite all men against them. "Let us," concludes this letter, "indeed, save the colony, liberty, and equality; but let us also understand once for all why we are fighting, whom we are fighting, and what shall be the means." [13]

From insane rage Sonthonax now fell into abject despair, and in late December he wrote to Polverel proposing that one of them should leave San Domingo to carry a report to the Convention; but his colleague administered another severe rebuke, stigmatizing this plan as desertion.[14] Soon after this the demoralized Sonthonax rejoined his colleague at Port-au-Prince.

However, the opening months of 1794 brought no comfort in their train: the North fell more and more into

English and Spanish hands, while in the West the mulattoes continued to abjure the Republic. The extent of this defection is shown by the number of intercepted letters still preserved in the Archives Nationales.[15] In one of these the writer passionately urges his Republican friend to follow his example. He, too, had fought in the earlier mulatto insurrections, but he had since felt "the humiliations which the Civil Commissioners have heaped upon us by making us the servile instruments of their sanguinary passions and their destructive projects." Indeed, he was in complete despair when the coming of the English opened the door of hope.[16] Another letter is still stronger in tone. "Cease; yes, cease, sir," it reads, "to work blindly for the general liberty of the slaves and to further the perfidious and devastating intentions of the Civil Commissioners. Join the party of honest men; preserve your property from destruction and fire. Our rights are safe-guarded by the word of a nation whose established constitution is unmenaced by the fluctuations, crises, and convulsions which cause the present weakness of the French, and which reduce all their colonies to a frightful fluidity." [17]

During these months another blow had been struck at the prestige of the Commissioners. The stream of deported persons flowing constantly into France with alarming tales of outrage and tyranny had excited French public opinion and roused the watchful jealousy of the Convention, which, in July, 1793, passed a decree of accusation against its representatives in San Domingo.[18] "The late disasters at Le Cap," writes a colonist at Nantes to a friend in the island, "have been deeply felt in France.

THE ENGLISH INTERVENTION 239

Polverel and Sonthonax have been denounced to the National Convention as the authors of the ruin of San Domingo, and have been decreed in a state of accusation. Thus we may hope that ere long the colony will be purged of those two monsters." [19] The news had been hailed with delight by the whole English party, which scattered broadcast a violent manifesto summoning the Republican districts to rid themselves of the tyrants whom the Convention had just "broken like a glass of beer." [20] But all regular communication between France and San Domingo had ceased with the outbreak of the English war, and the Commissioners, stigmatizing these reports as libels, showed no signs of obeying the orders of the Convention by a return to France.

The colonists, however, soon realized that the Convention's action toward its Commissioners was a purely personal affair which betokened no change in sentiment regarding the colonies. Indeed, Jacobin France, now full in the throes of the Terror, breathed an ever-increasing hatred of the "Aristocrates de la Peau" and greeted the English intervention with a fresh burst of fury at this new Vendée over-seas. How the returned colonist fared at this moment is revealed by the experiences of Carteau in the month of May, 1794. Scarcely had his ship cast anchor in the harbor of Toulon when the young port officer approached him with a menacing air. "'Well,' he exclaimed loudly, 'at last they are free; those unhappy slaves. After a century of abuse and torture it was high time that they became your equals and enjoyed our precious liberty; for they are as much men as we ourselves.' I was silent," comments Carteau; "it was no time to reply. The guillotines were 'en permanence' upon the public squares." [21]

And Carteau's further experiences show that the port officer's words were but the echo of all those who then dared express an opinion. "From Toulon to my journey's end," he goes on, "in coach or barge, in public house or private home, at cross-road or on city square, — everywhere I found the same prejudice, the same virulence against the colonist. 'Prejudice'! that is too mild a word. It was a furious hatred which prevailed: a hatred of such intensity that our most terrible misfortunes did not excite the slightest commiseration. To those prejudiced minds we appeared more guilty than the most abandoned criminals, to whom are often vouchsafed some dregs of pity. We colonists, . . . just escaped from tempest and prison, destitute, ruined, impoverished, often fated to beg our bread, found only cold hearts and unfeeling souls. Ah! how many there were who, to all this, added signs of detestation and of horror. I could name a great number of persons, men and women, young and old, who to my story of misfortune merely answered, 'You have richly deserved it!' Our detractors had poisoned against us all classes of society: servants, peasants, workmen, — the very day-laborers in the fields. These simple people, impressed only by striking ideas, remembered about us only those reports most sensational in character. In their opinion we colonists were worse than cannibals, and they really believed that we were accustomed to mutilate, flay, and massacre our slaves. I was actually introduced to many persons so touched by the unhappy lot of the slaves that they had long since ceased

THE ENGLISH INTERVENTION 241

to take coffee; thinking that they swallowed only blood and sweat in this sugared drink!'" [22]

Such being the state of French opinion, it is not strange that when Sonthonax's delegates reached France in early 1794, they received a warm welcome and found the Convention disposed to set its seal upon the new order in San Domingo. These three delegates, a white, a mulatto, and a negro, had been sent as deputies to the Convention in pursuance of national legislation which had already assimilated the colonies as ordinary departments of the French Republic. What followed their request for admission to seats in the Convention is well described by the official record in the "Moniteur" [23]: —

"At the session of the 15th Pluviôse, Year II [February 3, 1794], the chairman of the Committee on Decrees rose. 'Citizens, your Committee on Decrees has verified the credentials of the deputies of San Domingo. It finds them in order. I move that they be admitted to seats in the Convention.'

"*Camboulas.* 'Since 1789, the aristocracy of birth and the aristocracy of religion have been destroyed; but the aristocracy of the skin still remains. However, it too is at last doomed: a black man, a yellow man, are about to sit amongst us in the name of the free citizens of San Domingo.' [Applause.]

"The three deputies of San Domingo enter the hall. The black features of Bellay and the yellow face of Mills excite long and repeated applause.

"*Lacroix* (of Eure-et-Loire). 'The Assembly has long desired to have in its midst some of those men of color oppressed for so many years. To-day it possesses two.

I demand that their introduction be marked by the President's fraternal embrace.'

"The motion is carried amid loud applause.

"The three deputies of San Domingo advance and receive the President's fraternal kiss. The hall rings with fresh applause." [24]

Next day the negro deputy Bellay delivered a very violent speech against the Counter-Revolutionary nature of the white colonists, and ended by "imploring the Convention to vouchsafe to the colonies full enjoyment of the blessings of liberty and equality." What followed is strikingly told by the official account in the "Moniteur": —

"*Levasseur* (of Sarthe). 'I demand that the Convention, yielding, not to a moment of enthusiasm, but to the principles of justice, and faithful to the Declaration of the Rights of Man, decree that from this moment slavery is abolished throughout the territory of the Republic. San Domingo is part of this territory; — nevertheless, there are still slaves.'

"*Lacroix* (of Eure-et-Loire). 'When we drew up the Constitution of the French people we did not direct our gaze upon the unhappy negroes. Posterity will severely censure us for that fact. Let us now repair this fault. Let us proclaim the liberty of the negroes. . . . President, do not suffer the Convention to dishonor itself by a discussion.'

"The Assembly rises by acclamation.

"The President pronounces the abolition of slavery amid great applause and repeated cries of 'Vive la République!' 'Vive la Convention!' 'Vive la Montagne!'

"The two deputies of color appear on the tribune;

THE ENGLISH INTERVENTION 243

they embrace. [Applause.] Lacroix conducts them to the President, who gives them the fraternal kiss. [Applause.]

"*Cambon.* 'A citizeness of color, regularly present at the Convention's sittings, has just felt so keen a joy at seeing us grant liberty to all her brethren that she has fainted. [Applause.] I demand that this fact be mentioned in the minutes, and that this citizeness be admitted to the sitting and receive at least this much recognition of her civic virtues.'

"The motion is carried.

"On the front bench of the amphitheatre, at the President's left, is seen this citizeness, drying her tears. [Applause.]

"After some discussion on the wording of the intended decree, Lacroix gets the following resolution carried: 'The National Convention declares slavery abolished in all the colonies. In consequence, it decrees that all men, without distinction of color, domiciled in the said colonies, are French citizens and enjoy all the rights assured under the Constitution.'" [25]

When it is remembered that at this moment San Domingo was the only colony in which any official acts of emancipation had taken place, the spirit of the Convention toward colonial questions in thus abolishing the colonial system by a rising vote without discussion is sufficiently plain.

The effect of all this upon San Domingo may be imagined. More and more the mulattoes of the West renounced their allegiance to the Republic, and the Commissioners' position in Port - au - Prince (now renamed

"Port Républicain") grew worse with every day. Acts of terror availed but little, and the Commissioners, grown suspicious of the whole mulatto caste, leaned increasingly upon the negro population. In early February, 1794, the appearance of an English squadron off Port-au-Prince spurred the Commissioners to fresh exertions, and black battalions were recruited from the half-savage negroes of the Plain and the wild insurgents of the mountains. But this merely precipitated the crisis. Rigaud, the mulatto commandant of Les Cayes, wrote an ominous protest warning the Commissioners that "the soldiers' order and good-will for the service and defence of the country" was waning at sight of the public revenues "entirely given to African laborers who assuredly have not the same needs as themselves." Rigaud asserted that the negroes should serve the Republic without pay, and should also support the mulatto soldiery ".out of gratitude for the debt they owe the former freedmen who now defend them." [26] The mulattoes of Port-au-Prince did not stop at words. On the night of the 17th of March the mulatto battalions suddenly rose, the Commissioners barely escaped from the town, and returned only upon conditions tantamount to an abdication.[27]

Under such conditions the fall of Port-au-Prince was plainly at hand, and toward the end of May the English prepared to strike the decisive blow. The campaign was well planned and skilfully executed. A column of whites from the Grande Anse, about a thousand strong, under the Baron de Montalembert, advanced northwards from Léogane, another column of some twelve hundred white and mulatto Confederates, under Hanus de Jumecourt,

THE ENGLISH INTERVENTION

moved down from Saint-Marc, while on May 30, a strong squadron appeared off Port-au-Prince with fifteen hundred British troops on board. The city made but a feeble resistance. It was soon demoralized by a heavy bombardment from the English fleet, and when the chief land fort had fallen before the assault of De Montalembert's hard-fighting Southerners, the Commissioners and the wreck of their troops sought safety with Rigaud. Despite its misfortunes, Port-au-Prince was a rich prize. The English captured one hundred and thirty pieces of heavy artillery and merchant shipping to the value of four hundred thousand pounds.[28]

But the sands of the Commissioners' rule were now run out. Scarcely had they joined Rigaud when a fast-sailing corvette appeared bearing the Convention's mandate to arrest its refractory delegates and bring them to France for trial under the decree of accusation passed almost a year before. There could be no evading this imperious summons, and on June 12, 1794, Sonthonax and Polverel sailed for France, leaving Rigaud and his half-guerilla soldiery to sustain the struggle against the English and their partisans. In West and South the situation seemed, indeed, hopeless, but in the North a man had appeared in the ranks of the Republic who had already wrested half their conquests from the Spaniards. This man was Toussaint Louverture.

XXI

THE ADVENT OF TOUSSAINT LOUVERTURE

FRANCOIS-DOMINIQUE TOUSSAINT ("LOUVERTURE") was born about the year 1743 on a plantation of the North Plain not far from the city of Le Cap. His father was an African negro from Guinea; his mother, born in the colony, was a negress of uncertain origin. One thing is sure: Toussaint was a full-blooded negro with no trace of white or mulatto blood. The origin of the name "Louverture" is obscure. Toussaint at first served as a stable-boy, but his intelligence was soon remarked by the plantation manager, who made him his coachman, and in the comparative leisure of this occupation Toussaint learned to read and write, albeit very imperfectly.[1] He seems to have gained a certain local reputation among the negroes, and to have already displayed that power over his racial brethren which was to be the keystone of his later authority.[2]

At the outbreak of the negro insurrection of August, 1791, Toussaint was nearly fifty years old. He took no part in the rising until the late autumn, when he attached himself to the bands of Jean-François and Biassou. His ability was, however, recognized from the first, for he was at once made a high officer and appears to have been one of Jean-François's intimate counsellors in the December peace negotiations with the first Civil Commissioners.[3]

Upon the outbreak of war between Spain and the

ADVENT OF TOUSSAINT LOUVERTURE 247

French Republic in the spring of 1793, Toussaint naturally entered Spanish service. His growing importance is shown by the fact that he was already the leader of a band of six hundred well-armed negroes devoted to his orders, and also by the circumstance that he acted no longer as a subordinate of Jean-François, but directly under the Spanish general's orders as a semi-independent commander. During the ensuing year Toussaint's progress was rapid. He induced many of the French regular troops who had deserted to the Spaniards after the destruction of Le Cap [4] to officer his growing bands and train them in the European fashion. Several brilliant military feats increased his prestige to such an extent that by the spring of 1794 he commanded four thousand men, wholly devoted to his person and unquestionably the best armed and disciplined black corps in the Spanish army.[5]

At this moment the cause of the Republic was at its lowest ebb. In the North, Laveaux had retired with the wrecks of the European troops for a last stand behind the walls of Port-de-Paix; in the West, the English were preparing their decisive stroke against distracted Port-au-Prince. Yet this was the moment chosen by Toussaint to enter the Republic's service. Strange as this may at first appear, reflection shows that his decision was determined by motives of sound policy. The progress of the English had greatly alarmed Toussaint, for England had entered San Domingo as the champion of the whites and mulattoes: she was therefor pledged to the maintenance of that slavery which the French Republic had just abolished throughout its colonies.[6] His personal motives also strongly favored a change of side. In Spanish service he could never hope to supplant Jean-François, now become the trusted generalissimo of the black forces entirely devoted to the Spanish cause, and loaded with honors and dignities. On the other hand, the French Republic had failed to gain over any important negro leader, and in its desperate situation was sure to grant Toussaint a position equivalent to that of Jean-François himself.[7]

Accordingly, in April, 1794, Laveaux was overjoyed to receive an intimation that Toussaint was ready to open negotiations, and the details were quickly settled to their mutual satisfaction. In the execution of his project Toussaint now showed to the full that extraordinary duplicity which is the most striking trait in his character. Up to the very hour of his desertion to the Republic he maintained his attitude of complete devotion to the Royalist cause: only a few days previous to his change of side, the Spanish general, after observing the fervor of his religious devotions, wrote, "In this whole world God has never entered a soul more pure." [8] The Marquis of Hermona's feelings may be imagined when on the 6th of May, 1794, Toussaint suddenly massacred the Spanish soldiers under his orders and led his four thousand negro troops into Republican territory. Toussaint's first report to Laveaux contained a fervent Republican profession of faith.[9] This astounding defection completely disorganized the Spanish forces, which rapidly evacuated most of their conquests in the North.[10]

The news of Toussaint's conversion came as a ray of hope to the despairing Civil Commissioners. Their delight is shown by the letter written Toussaint on the eve of their departure for France. "You cannot imagine," it reads, "our joy at such glad tidings. We had long believed those Africans allied with the Spaniards and Royalists as lost to the Republic; but now that the brave Toussaint has come under its banner, now that he is finally disabused of his errors, we hope to see all the Africans of the North imitate his generous repentance and defend their liberty by fighting for France. . . . Bless, citizen, bless the National Assembly, which, by overthrowing the thrones of kings, has founded the happiness of the human race upon equality and liberty. Remember that the distinctions of color are no more: that a negro is as good as a white man; a white as good as a black." [11]

The utter disorganization of the Spanish forces enabled Toussaint to attempt operations against the English in the West. The capture of Port-au-Prince had been the high-water mark of English success. Scarcely had they taken possession of the city when there appeared amongst them the dread scourge which eight years later was to destroy the great army of Napoleon. Yellow fever broke out among the English regiments at Port-au-Prince and within two months swept away nearly seven hundred of the British soldiers.[12] In such circumstances it was madness to expose the troops to active campaigning till the sickness should abate with the autumn; therefore the English failed to push their advantage, and gave time for Rigaud to consolidate his rule in the South and for Toussaint to reorganize the North.

This English inaction was most fortunate for the Republic, since the first attempts of Toussaint and Rigaud showed how strong was the British hold on the West. Toussaint's attack on Saint-Marc in September was a failure, while in December Rigaud's bold attempt on Port-au-Prince ended in a bad disaster, his two thousand mulatto soldiers being terribly cut up. Still, the year 1794 ended well for the Republic. Toussaint had cleared the North of the Spaniards and had driven the English from their footholds on the Cordon de l'Ouest, while Rigaud repaired his defeat before Port-au-Prince by capturing the important town of Léogane. Furthermore, the rapidity with which Toussaint was building up his army presaged fresh successes in the coming year.[13]

The campaign of 1795 was almost exclusively devoted to the struggle with the English. The Spaniards remained strictly on the defensive, and it was quite evident that nothing more was to be feared from them, since peace negotiations had already opened between Spain and the French Republic. The British Government had done little to sustain its cause in San Domingo. Less than two thousand troops arrived during the winter of 1794-95, and when the unhealthy season began in the spring, disease again thinned the ranks of the British soldiery. Still, the English position was very formidable. The whole West Province was dotted with strong forts, and the black and mulatto regiments recruited among the native population fought stubbornly in their defence.

In September, 1795, arrived the momentous news of the signing of the Peace of Bâle, by which Spain ceded her portion of San Domingo to France, though retaining possession till the Republic should be in a position to defend its new territory from attack. But England had

ADVENT OF TOUSSAINT LOUVERTURE 251

at last resolved to make a great effort to conquer San Domingo, and with the healthier days of late October, General Howe and seven thousand troops fresh from home landed at the Môle-Saint-Nicolas. Two years before, this fine army would have absolutely assured the conquest of San Domingo: now it was too late. Rigaud showed his strength by beating off the formidable English attack on Léogane, while Toussaint weathered the storm with slight losses of exposed territory. In a few months the English army had wasted to a shadow, and by early 1796 it was plain that the invaders would make no further efforts of a vital nature.[14]

It was well for the Republican cause that the English peril was thus virtually past, for in these same spring months of 1796 there arose the first storm-clouds of that great convulsion which was to rend San Domingo for the next four years. With the general collapse that followed the destruction of Le Cap in June, 1793, white supremacy was ended, and short of an English conquest or some future supreme effort from France, was ended forever. But what San Domingo was to be had not yet been decided. The South, under the iron rule of Rigaud, was obviously mulatto;[15] the West was for the moment in foreign hands; in the North the policy of Sonthonax had already resulted in black supremacy. Up till now the struggle against the foreigner had obscured the racial issue, but before the year 1795 was out the stage had been set for the coming struggle between the colored castes. On the one side stood the mulattoes both free and slave,[16] joined by the free negroes of the Old Régime and loosely allied to the wild maroon elements; on the other lay the mass of the negro population, — vastly superior in number but only half-conscious of itself and lacking intelligence and organization. Would the mulattoes be able to rivet their domination over the black population as the whites had done before them? That was the question.

Ambitious as were the projects of the mulatto caste, they were already realized in many parishes of the South and West. The sphere of Rigaud's authority now formed a genuine mulatto state in which white and black were alike subject to a domination more severe than that of the Old Régime. The country was systematically exploited by the mulatto caste and the negro population once more reduced to slavery. The character of this mulatto rule is described in the report of an old officer of the *maréchaussée*, sent out by the French Government in early 1794 to investigate conditions in the South. "Ever since the Civil Commissioners got rid of the whites," reports this agent to the Minister of Marine, "the mulattoes have monopolized the public posts. All offices, both civil and military, are now in their power. ... Only the vain appearance of a free government remains. The municipalities are a farce, — all power is lodged with the mulatto commandants. ... The few white troops that remain are perishing of misery and want, while the remnant of the white inhabitants still loyal to the Republic are more wretched than the Africans in slavery days. The Africans themselves are not content, and everywhere complain of their great misery." The worst of the matter was that this mulatto rule was not only despotic but factious and inefficient as well. The commandants were generally ignorant, "and so

ADVENT OF TOUSSAINT LOUVERTURE 253

jealous that they never stop accusing each other. Montbrun says that Beauvais is a traitor, Beauvais says the same of Montbrun, while Rigaud accuses them both." [17]

The great obstacle to mulatto dominion was obviously the rising power of Toussaint Louverture. Hitherto, the black general had been but a distant figure to the mulattoes of the South, since the English occupation of the West Province had completely cut communications. But by late 1795 the English sphere was so shrunken that relations had been resumed. And Toussaint's first act showed the Southern mulattoes both his dangerous intentions and his superiority to their leader Rigaud. The Peace of Bâle had been a great thing for Toussaint Louverture: his one dangerous negro rival, Jean-François, had retired to Spain, while most of the disbanded black soldiery had taken service in Toussaint's army. This powerful accession of strength now led the black leader to venture a further step in the consolidation of his authority over all the negroes of San Domingo. In the Western mountains were certain negro bands which had remained nominally loyal to the Republic. However, while aiding Rigaud in his struggle against the English, the commanders of these negro bands had always refused to admit his authority and had thus drawn down the hatred of the vengeful mulatto. Toussaint realized the situation and resolved to turn it to his own profit. He first gained over the least powerful of these independent commanders, an ambitious negro named Laplume, and then offered Rigaud his assistance in crushing the two chief leaders. Rigaud accepted with joy, and under Toussaint's orders Laplume betrayed his colleagues to the mulatto, who put them to an atrocious death in the dungeons of Les Cayes. But Rigaud's delight was much abated when he learned that Laplume had led the assembled bands over to Toussaint's army, and realized too late that his thirst for vengeance had been satisfied only at the cost of consolidating Toussaint's power over the negroes of the West.[18]

But the enraged Rigaud spied the joint in Toussaint's armor: the journey of the clever mulatto intriguer Pinchinat to Le Cap in early 1796 revealed Rigaud's determination to rouse the mulattoes of the North to decisive action. And Pinchinat found the ground well prepared, for conditions at Le Cap were already so tense that an explosion would have probably occurred even without his incitations.

When Laveaux had withdrawn the European troops to Port-de-Paix in the autumn of 1793, he had left Le Cap in charge of a mulatto officer named Villatte. The wild negroes of the Plain had soon left the ruined town, Villatte had before long established his supremacy, and Le Cap presently became the rallying-point for all the mulattoes of the North. Things had gone well enough for the caste till the close of 1795, when Laveaux took advantage of the improved military situation to return from Port-de-Paix to Le Cap. Completely dependent upon Toussaint and his negro regiments for operations against the English, and already falling under the sway of the black leader's personality, Laveaux was indignant at the nature of Villatte's rule. Tactless attempts to subordinate the mulatto commander to his authority quickly led to trouble. The critical state of affairs at Le Cap is shown by Laveaux's correspondence with the French Government.

"There are here," he writes on January 14, 1796, "many evil persons who work for independence; who cry that the colony has no need of France." And he cites a list of mulatto and free negro agitators with Villatte at their head. "An abominable jealousy exists here among the citizens of color," he continues, "against the whites and negroes. The colored citizens are furious that one of their number does not govern San Domingo. They say to us openly, 'This is our country, not yours. Why do you give us white men to govern our country?' They are abominably jealous of me, and wish Villatte as Governor.

"The citizens of color are in despair at seeing Toussaint Louverture, a negro, become brigadier-general. ... Yes, citizen, I must admit the fact: all the colored citizens and old free negroes are the enemies of emancipation and of equality. They cannot even conceive that a former negro slave can be the equal of a white man, a mulatto, or an old free negro." He concludes with a long account of the predatory rule of Villatte and his followers, "who have ceaselessly crushed the other inhabitants. My efforts have roused the fury of these men, who wish to continue that old life of 1793-94, when the strongest hand seized all"; and he ends by describing a number of partial riots and mutinies.[19]

If such was the state of affairs before Pinchinat's arrival, it is not strange that the presence of this clever intriguer quickly brought on more serious trouble. At the end of January the arrest of one of Villatte's followers for official peculation caused a general riot in which

Laveaux was insulted and his authority openly flouted. His report to the Minister of Marine shows his growing indignation. "Citizen mulatto," he writes, "is resolved to govern this country. He cannot bring himself to be the equal of a black, and he wishes to be more than a white. Crime is nothing to him: when one of his kind is the guilty party, all is excusable. Villatte is quite persuaded that he is going to be Governor, and in this mad idea all his partisans support him." Laveaux attributes the late riots to Pinchinat, the agent of Rigaud, "whose pride and ambition are such that he dreams of becoming Dictator of the colony. The mulatto citizens wish to rule, wish to have every office, wish to embezzle everything: they recognize no laws the moment these hinder their passions and their pride." [20]

Villatte and Pinchinat were, indeed, determined on decisive action. The crisis came with the 30th Ventôse (20th of March). About sunrise the mulattoes of Le Cap rose *en masse*, dragged Laveaux with jeers and insults through the streets, and cast him into prison. But the conspirators now found that by their factious antics they had merely played another's game. From his strongholds on the Cordon de l'Ouest, Toussaint Louverture had watched all that passed at Le Cap. Up to the very moment of the crisis he had made no sign, but that his plans had been carefully laid was soon apparent. The fortified heights above the town were held by the black general, Michel, who now refused obedience to Villatte, curtly ordered the release of Laveaux, and announced that Toussaint was coming with ten thousand men, determined "to sacrifice everything that lived in Le Cap"

ADVENT OF TOUSSAINT LOUVERTURE 257

should any attempt be made on the life of Laveaux.[21] After some bluster the terrified mulattoes released their prisoner: a few days later Toussaint entered Le Cap with a large army, while Villatte and his partisans retreated into the country.[22]

The affair of the 30th Ventôse was a crushing blow to the mulattoes of the North and a great triumph for Toussaint Louverture. The keen-sighted negro had well judged his man, for the impetuous Laveaux was so overwhelmed with enthusiastic gratitude that he virtually surrendered himself into his deliverer's hands. Publicly acclaiming Toussaint as "that black Spartacus prophesied by Raynal, whose destiny is to avenge the outrages upon his race," he made Toussaint Lieutenant-Governor of San Domingo and promised to do nothing without his advice and counsel. Toussaint reciprocated in the same vein. "After God, Laveaux," he cried; and with rather grotesque inconsistency this elderly negro, generally known as "le vieux Toussaint," addressed the youthful French general as "Bon Papa." [23] All this enormously increased Toussaint's prestige among the negroes, and correspondingly weakened white authority. "This," declares Lacroix, "was the death-blow to French authority in San Domingo. It is from this moment that we must date the end of white prestige and the beginning of black rule." [24]

Such was the state of affairs when on May 11, 1796, a third Civil Commission arrived at Le Cap, sent by the new Government of the Directoire to restore French authority over distracted San Domingo.

XXII

THE THIRD CIVIL COMMISSIONERS

IN France the Terror was long past,[1] and the new Government of the Directoire [2] assured a relatively moderate régime. In the general survey which followed its accession to power, the Directoire's attention had been naturally attracted to San Domingo, and in the early spring of 1796 it had resolved to attempt a restoration of French authority. To this end a body of five Commissioners had been despatched to the island with a considerable naval squadron and three thousand troops which succeeded in outwitting the English cruisers.

The personnel of this new expedition was most interesting. The troops were commanded by General Rochambeau, seconded by General Desfourneaux, both of whom had served in the island. And three of the Civil Commissioners were equally familiar with San Domingo politics. The Chairman of the Commission was none other than Sonthonax, acquitted of the charges laid against his previous stewardship after a long and farcical trial. Purged of his extreme Jacobinism, Sonthonax was now a good "Thermidorien" and high in the Directoire's favor. The mulatto Raymond was also upon the board, having thus obtained the post of which he had been baulked in 1792. Another member of the Commission was Roume, though he had been ordered to Spanish Santo Domingo, to prepare that colony for the coming

THE THIRD CIVIL COMMISSIONERS 259

transfer of national authority.³ The other two Commissioners were Leblanc, an ex-Terrorist, and Giraud, a neurotic nonentity of the type of former Commissioner Ailhaud.

The four Commissioners, Sonthonax, Roume, Leblanc, and Giraud, were well received at Le Cap. The return of Sonthonax, the "Liberator of San Domingo," excited the enthusiasm of the negro population; the appointment of the colored leader Raymond pleased the mulatto element: the landing of three thousand white troops overawed the disaffected. The Commissioners' first report describes their triumphal progress between cheering crowds and double ranks of negro soldiery.⁴ They were, however, confronted by a difficult situation. Toussaint Louverture's black regiments held down Le Cap, it is true, but Villatte and his army still lay near by, while the town population was overwhelmingly in his favor. In this delicate situation the Commissioners acted with considerable tact. They induced Villatte to appear before them and then sent him to France for further examination; but they managed the affair without undue violence, and as Villatte was not personally beloved, they succeeded in reconciling the mulatto element to their action.⁵

The Commissioners were evidently uneasy at the complete authority exercised by Toussaint and his lieutenants over the negro population. This feeling shows in their early letters and is strikingly displayed in a long memoir to the Directoire drawn up in the early autumn. "To speak of laws to the negroes," write the Commissioners, "is to burden them with things too metaphysical for their understanding. To these people, the man is everything: at his voice they are quite carried away, and his name is to them what the fatherland is to genuine freemen. The régime which we found established upon our arrival at San Domingo was exactly similar to the feudal system of the eighth century. Law and liberty were but idle names: the cultivators and the soldiers passively obeyed their military chiefs, and fought for them alone while crying, 'Long live the Republic.'" [6]

Given such conditions, it was plain that Toussaint Louverture and his fellows would have to be tactfully handled; but it should have been equally clear that the interests of France required that he should not be allowed to make himself absolute, and that the only possible counterbalance lay in a judicious support of the mulattoes. Unfortunately for France it was not long before the new Commission followed Laveaux's example in favoring the power of Toussaint Louverture. The cause of this fatal policy was Sonthonax's overweening ambition. Time had, indeed, changed the stripe of his political coat, but not his insatiable thirst for power, and he soon conceived the idea of dominating his colleagues through an alliance with Toussaint Louverture. Sonthonax's previous experience with negro chiefs had not increased his respect for their mental ability, and he had no conception of the extraordinary cunning and duplicity of the man whom he proposed to use as his instrument to power. The acclamations of the negroes had intoxicated the "Liberator," while his remembrance of past insults in the West and South prejudiced him against the mulattoes. Accordingly, aided by his fellow Terrorist Leblanc,

THE THIRD CIVIL COMMISSIONERS 261

he soon dominated the weak Raymond and the contemptible Giraud, and quickly showed Toussaint favors of no uncertain character.[7]

However, Sonthonax's policy quickly produced disturbing results. General Rochambeau protested against the new military powers granted the black leader, and Sonthonax promptly used his old methods by formally deporting him to France.[8] The mulattoes of the North showed their feelings in more disagreeable fashion: they incited the negroes to murder the whites by spreading reports that the Commissioners were come to restore slavery. In the district of Port-de-Paix nearly all the remaining whites of that quarter were barbarously massacred in a negro rising of late September. How serious was the situation is shown by a letter from one of the French officials sent out with the Commissioners. "If the Directoire does not promptly send imposing forces," he writes, "the colony is lost forever. The disturbances have become general and the Europeans are everywhere being massacred. The cantons of Port-de-Paix are completely devastated, and outside of the town itself not a white man remains alive. The national authority is flouted; we are at the mercy of the negroes, whom Laveaux has wholly demoralized, . . . and by the time you receive this letter we may have all been massacred."[9]

Equally pessimistic was the report of General Desfourneaux, the commander of the French troops, to the Minister of War. "I have some great truths to tell you, citizen," he writes on the 15th of October, "and as man to man, as a soldier who loves his country, I ought not to leave you ignorant of the greatness of our ills, the deepness of our wounds. . . . San Domingo can be saved to France only by Republican bayonets. Our moral influence here has become absolutely *nil*. Anarchy has brought confusion, pride has engendered schemes of independence: all the colors are mutually to blame. . . . The one remedy is an overwhelming force of at least twenty thousand men who, acting in a body, shall sweep from the surface of this island the enemies of the Republic." [10]

That the Civil Commissioners obtained scant respect from the negro generals is shown by their own correspondence. In their memoir of October 9 they relate a flagrant instance of disobedience on the part of the black general, Michel, adding, "Our position has compelled us to overlook this act of insubordination, as on so many other occasions. These generals leave their posts and disobey our orders. They oppress and plunder the cultivators, who dare not complain. The Commission feels that it would compromise its authority if it tried to make an example of any one." [11]

In the South, the results of Sonthonax's policy were more serious still. Rigaud, furious at the favor shown Toussaint Louverture, absolutely refused obedience to the black leader. And he appeared fully able to sustain his defiant attitude. His virtual reënslavement of the negro population had restored prosperity to the South, and his full warehouses procured him all needed supplies from the numerous American vessels which entered the Southern harbors. His army consisted of several thousand well-armed mulatto troops and a considerable number of black regiments under mulatto officers.[12] Further-

THE THIRD CIVIL COMMISSIONERS 263

more it was impossible to send an expedition against him. The English still occupied most of the intervening West, while their maroon allies of the Eastern mountains made any flank march via Spanish territory impracticable.

What he could not effect by force of arms, however, Sonthonax determined to accomplish by indirection. Accordingly, he sent a sub-commission, headed by his henchman General Kerverseau, to "investigate conditions in the South." [13] No sooner had this commission arrived, however, than it showed its true purpose in no uncertain fashion. Rigaud's report to the French Government details the doings of Sonthonax's pupils. "The delegates had scarcely landed at Tiburon," he writes, "when they began to sow dissension among the troops. 'Why,' they asked the negro subalterns, 'are you not commanders like the mulattoes?' and to the soldiers, 'Why are you not advanced in grade? Join the whites, then, to exterminate these people and have their places.' On their journey to Les Cayes many idle and vagabond negroes came to them, complaining of the punishments inflicted by the inspectors of labor. To these people the delegates replied, 'We are come hither to end the tyranny of the mulattoes. Tell your comrades that they are free and that no one can force them to labor.'" [14] From other accounts of the delegates' conduct this picture appears substantially correct.[15] The Civil Commissioners complain to the Directoire that the Southern troubles were caused by their delegates' efforts "to insure the equal happiness of all citizens; from having wished to destroy a new aristocracy." [16]

It could not be expected that the mulattoes would

long tolerate such efforts to destroy their supremacy. Accordingly, Rigaud soon left Les Cayes, ostensibly to direct some military operations against the English, and in his opportune absence agents rode through the Plain inciting the negroes to rise against the delegates "who had brought chains to reënslave them," and telling the ignorant cultivators "that since the mulattoes and the negroes were the true inhabitants and owners of the colony, everything belonged to them, while the whites should be driven out or exterminated." [17] The ruse worked as successfully with the Southern negroes as with their brethren of Port-de-Paix. On the 10th Fructidor (27th of August), a general rising took place, the few remaining white inhabitants were exterminated, and the delegates were dragged ignominiously to prison. It is true that Rigaud soon reappeared and released the delegates, but they were so obviously under duress that the Civil Commissioners promptly recalled them to Le Cap. Sonthonax was furious but helpless, and Rigaud remained absolute master of the South.[18] Sonthonax frankly confessed his utter failure when eight months later he wrote the Minister of Marine, "The South is quiet, but Rigaud is ever rebellious to authority. Since the massacres he has governed those parts like a Nabob: that is to say, his will is law. The military power is all; the civil authority nothing." [19]

Meanwhile, at Le Cap, Sonthonax had been steadily clearing his path. Giraud was easily bullied into a nervous collapse and left voluntarily for France. Leblanc was of sterner stuff, but he presently died, — not without suspicions of poison. As for the mulatto Raymond, he

THE THIRD CIVIL COMMISSIONERS 265

showed himself too much of a coward to be dangerous, and as he was obviously a useful figurehead for future moves against his caste, both Sonthonax and Toussaint agreed that it was best to let him remain.

Save for the distant Roume at Spanish Santo Domingo, the only prominent European still left in the island was General Laveaux — and him Sonthonax now disposed of by a clever trick. The French Constitution of the Year III had declared San Domingo an integral part of France, and had assigned the island a number of seats in the national legislative bodies. Sonthonax determined to have Laveaux elected deputy for San Domingo and thus remove him from the scene. In this plan Toussaint Louverture heartily agreed. Laveaux was altogether too popular with the negro generals for Toussaint's liking, and his stanch Republican ideals might cause trouble on some future occasion. Accordingly an election was held, and as General Michel threatened to burn Le Cap if the result was unfavorable, it is not surprising that Laveaux was "elected" by an overwhelming majority.[20]

How close were the relations between Sonthonax and Toussaint at this moment is shown by a letter from the black leader to the Directoire. It opens characteristically by a great deal of fulsome flattery, and after the usual invocation of Heaven's blessing upon San Domingo, it expresses the greatest admiration for Sonthonax and Raymond. "The people are attached to the former as the founder of their liberty, and love the latter for the virtues which so honor him." Another phrase of this letter could not have been wholly pleasing to its recipients. "So long as the people are governed by men as wise as those who have thus far guided its destinies," Toussaint informs the Directoire, "France will always find the people obedient"; and adds significantly, "I assure you of the truth of this, Citizen Directors; — I being its chief." [21]

Sonthonax had thus rid himself of the last annoying European presence. Unfortunately, although his own road was clear, he now made the unpleasant discovery that he himself stood in the path of Toussaint Louverture. The black leader had been as willing as Sonthonax to see the principal Europeans removed from the island, but now that this was done, the presence of the ambitious Commissioner was both unnecessary and dangerous. It is therefore not surprising that Sonthonax himself was presently "elected" deputy from San Domingo. Sonthonax did not at all relish this promotion and attempted to gain support among the black generals, but Toussaint's eagle eye was upon him and these plottings merely hastened the dénouement. On August 20, 1797, Toussaint suddenly appeared at Le Cap with several thousand men and urged Sonthonax to take up his legislative duties in France. There was no denying this pressing invitation. The greatest politeness was observed on both sides, but the furious Sonthonax was none the less escorted on shipboard next day. The craven Raymond alone remained as Toussaint's passive instrument.[22]

The last white authority in French San Domingo had thus disappeared, but Toussaint was by no means easy for the future. He well knew that his expulsion of Sonthonax was a virtual act of rebellion which the Directoire would bitterly resent. And this was not all. France was no longer the France of the Terror. Robespierre lay a

THE THIRD CIVIL COMMISSIONERS 267

full four years in his grave, and meanwhile the conservative tide had been sweeping steadily on. Colonists were no longer hunted down as "Aristocrates de la Peau"; instead, they were given a respectful hearing on colonial questions, and in the National Legislature itself voices had been raised for the restoration of the old colonial system.

Toussaint's alarm showed in his measures. A special envoy was sent to the Directoire to explain his recent action, and in a long memoir on the late events Toussaint made the extraordinary assertion that Sonthonax had proposed secession from France and their establishment as joint sovereigns of San Domingo.[23] From Sonthonax this brought forth the following caustic reply: "As to the charge of fomenting independence, I have but two words to say: Toussaint speaks only Creole, hardly understands French, and is perfectly incapable of uttering the language with which he is credited.[24] Up to this time no one has ever accused me of stupidity; nevertheless, this ridiculous conversation makes me a schoolboy under the ferule, stammering absurdities and brought to order by his pedagogue." After asking the Directoire to search his whole career for one word which might support Toussaint's assertions, Sonthonax concludes, "Certes, if any one should be suspected of independence it is he whose whole political life has been one long revolt against France. Toussaint has fooled two kings; he may well end by betraying the Republic." [25]

The attitude of Toussaint Louverture was certainly not one of submission. His letter to the Directoire of September, 1797, opens with the usual flattering phrases, and "takes this occasion to renew the assurance of my inviolable attachment for France"; but goes on in the following strain: "It is to this sentiment, so deeply graven upon my heart, that France owes the preservation of San Domingo. By this time all would have been over if, forgetting the benefits received by the negroes from its immortal decree, I myself had set the example of ingratitude. Independence would have been proclaimed, and instead of submissive and grateful children, France would have found us only rebels." [26]

Still more menacing was Toussaint's warning to the Directoire not to heed the growing demand for the sending of an army to restore San Domingo to French authority. After assuring the Directoire that he knew its wisdom and virtue would never permit it to listen to such projects, Toussaint continues, "You will permit only Republican Frenchmen to come to San Domingo. These we will receive fraternally; but we will ever repel those rash enough to dare tamper with the rights guaranteed us by the Constitution. How would the negroes regard the arrival of a European French army if they knew that their enemies had brought about its arrival in this country for the carrying out of liberticidal projects? ... Citizen Directors, I swear to you that I will die before I will see snatched from my hands that sword, those arms, which France has confided to me for the defence of her rights, for the rights of humanity, and for the triumph of liberty and equality!" [27]

Small wonder that early in 1798 the alarmed Directoire, its hands still tied by the English war, sent the able General Hédouville to repeat his conciliatory triumphs in the Vendée by a diplomatic pacification of San Domingo.

XXIII

THE MISSION OF GENERAL HEDOUVILLE

THE sending of General Hédouville to San Domingo proved the Directoire's fear of Toussaint Louverture. For Hédouville was one of the Directoire's ablest servants. A man of keen insight and strong personality, his considerable military ability was outshone by his remarkable diplomatic talents. His recent exploits in the pacification of the Vendée had marked him out as one of the strong men of the Republic. The Directoire's action thus showed both soundness of judgment and sense of reality. Matters had gone so far in San Domingo that only the Machiavellian dilemma remained. "Crush or conciliate"; — that was the sole alternative: and since Toussaint Louverture could be crushed only by a large army which could not be sent until the close of the English war, conciliation was the one policy which for the present stood any chance of success. Toussaint himself had warned the Directors that half-measures would be fatal.[1] But a man of strong personality and diplomatic ability might dominate the black leader; or, at least, hold the balance between the colored castes till an English peace should give France the choice of other means.

It was toward the end of March, 1798, that Hédouville landed at Spanish Santo Domingo to take counsel of Roume and the other French officials there before beginning his hazardous undertaking. But the tidings which met him in the Spanish capital must have greatly increased his disquietude. Toussaint's apprehensions regarding the possible action of the Directoire had been translating themselves into most vigorous measures. It was perfectly clear that any decisive action against the rival mulatto power in the South must be preceded by the expulsion of the English from the island. Accordingly, no sooner had the departure of Sonthonax freed his hands for the moment than Toussaint began formidable preparations against the foreign enemy. The English were in evil case. The failure of General Howe's great effort in the autumn of 1795 had convinced the British Government that the conquest of San Domingo was impossible, and for the last two years the English had been hanging on by mere inertia and by the preoccupation of their opponents. Even so, they had steadily lost ground, and they now possessed only a strip of the west coast and the two isolated strongholds of the Grande Anse in the South and the Môle-Saint-Nicolas in the North.

As soon as Toussaint began his preparations, therefore, the English commander realized that the days of British rule in San Domingo were numbered; but since this contingency had been long foreseen, he hoped to balance British territorial loss by commercial gains and by political damage to France. For the English fully realized the conflicting aims of the Republic and of Toussaint Louverture. Could they but play upon this fact to obtain Toussaint's friendship, they might hope to deprive the French Republic of that island which they could not hold themselves, and also, by commercial privileges, partially to recoup their enormous losses. Accordingly, when

Toussaint and his army appeared in the West, he was met by courteous envoys who flattered his pride with their attentions and fed his ambition by their hints and proposals. The campaign became one of notes and conferences.[2]

All this convinced Hédouville that no time was to be lost, and on April 21 he arrived at Le Cap. His first acts were well calculated to restore French prestige: his cold reception of Raymond emphasized the Directoire's displeasure at the expulsion of Sonthonax, its agent, while a summons to both Toussaint and Rigaud to appear before him at Le Cap announced the primacy of the Republic's special representative.[3] Both Toussaint and Rigaud obeyed the summons, though the conference which followed was of a purely formal nature. Hédouville realized that the expulsion of the English was as desirable for the Republic as for Toussaint himself, and determined to postpone all questions of internal policy until this end had been attained.

But Hédouville was unable long to maintain this resolution. As representative of the French Republic he was forced to hold a certain supervisory attitude over the English negotiations on penalty of losing all his prestige and appearing as the passive instrument of Toussaint's will. But the course of these negotiations was fast assuming a character which called for the active interference of the Republic's representative. On the 2d of May, the English general signed an agreement with Toussaint for the evacuation of Port-au-Prince and all the other posts in the West. In this same document Toussaint agreed to grant full amnesty to all the English partisans — a clause absolutely contravening the French laws regarding traitors and *émigrés*. And to this first difficulty, the English general soon added another blow at Hédouville's position: he presently offered to surrender the Môle to the French representative, then acceded to Toussaint's protest and delivered the fortress to the black leader. The circumstances of this surrender were striking in the extreme and emphasized yet more strongly the flouting of Hédouville's authority. Toussaint, received with regal honors, again agreed to amnesty the English partisans in defiance of Hédouville's express prohibition, and signed a secret agreement giving the English extensive rights of trade.[4] Lacroix asserts that the English had hoped for much more than this. "I myself and the other staff officers as well," he writes, "saw in the archives captured at Port-au-Prince the secret proposals which were the cause of those public demonstrations.[5] These proposals were to the effect that Toussaint Louverture should declare himself King of Haiti, and Maitland [6] assured him that England would at once recognize him as such if at the moment of assuming the crown he signed a commercial treaty by which England should have the exclusive right of exporting the island's colonial products and of importing manufactured articles. The King of Haiti would then be assured the constant presence of an English squadron to protect him against France." [7]

But Toussaint Louverture took no such action. The mulatto power was still unbroken; his own authority over the black generals was far from secure; lastly, since the Peace of Campo Formio,[8] England was left alone against

France, and for months past had been openly menaced with a French invasion headed by the rising genius of General Bonaparte. Toussaint continued to proclaim his loyalty to the Republic.

Nevertheless, his defiance of the Republic's laws rendered a struggle with its San Domingo representative inevitable. Hédouville had recognized this fact and was already making his preparations. The obvious counterpoise to Toussaint's power was the mulatto caste, and a journey of Rigaud to Le Cap revealed Hédouville's intentions for the future. Of this journey Toussaint was well aware, yet he made no move to prevent the interview. His intentions for this reserved attitude are shown by the following statements made to a white colonist then high in his service. "I have from a Creole worthy of every confidence, now a resident of Paris," writes Lacroix, "that one day he was talking with Toussaint Louverture when some negro officers came in great alarm to inform him that Rigaud had passed through Port-au-Prince *en route* for Le Cap. 'Let Monsieur Rigaud go get his instructions from the agent of the Directoire,' answered Toussaint. 'Do not be alarmed. Go.' The officers obeyed, and my informant started also. 'No,' said Toussaint to him, 'stay. You are never too much with me'; and he continued the following monologue in a far-away voice: 'I might have him stopped; — but God keep me from it. I need Monsieur Rigaud — he is violent — he suits me to make war with — that war which is necessary to me. The mulatto caste is higher than mine; if I did away with Monsieur Rigaud, they might perhaps find a better man. I know Monsieur Rigaud. He is violent. He lets his horse go when he gallops. He shows his arm when he strikes. I gallop, too, but I curb; and when I strike, men feel but do not see. Monsieur Rigaud knows how to make insurrections only by blood and massacre; I also know how to move the people. He trembles, does Monsieur Rigaud, when he sees the people he has excited in fury. I do not suffer fury; when I appear all must be quiet again.'" [9]

The mulattoes' hour had not yet struck, but Hédouville's time was come: the man who had dared measure himself against Toussaint Louverture could not be tolerated in San Domingo. Suddenly the North Plain, the very streets of Le Cap, swarmed with emissaries crying that Hédouville had come to restore slavery. The French general protested loudly, but found his words so much idle wind against the credulity of the negroes, "who, however much they may be maltreated by their chiefs, look upon their word as oracles." [10] Soon the dull roar of insurrection swept across the Plain, the negroes "being quickened by their erotic dances, especially by one around a bull's skull lighted inside." On the night of October 20, a vast horde of negroes appeared before the outskirts of Le Cap, and when the garrison learned that Toussaint was in their midst it refused to offer resistance. Hédouville saw that the game was up. Collecting the few hundred European troops in the town, and followed by about a thousand whites, mulattoes, and free negroes who especially feared Toussaint's vengeance, he set sail for France. His parting shot was a proclamation solemnly warning the inhabitants of the island against Toussaint's plans of independence, and orders to Rigaud not to obey the black leader's commands. The pacifier of the Vendée had lost his laurels in San Domingo.

Hédouville's reflections upon the situation are most interesting. "The facts I have related," he writes the Directoire, "show that all Toussaint's protestations of attachment to the Republic were false; that his sole aim has been to preserve that arbitrary authority usurped before my arrival in the colony; and that even before that time he had been secretly negotiating with Maitland for the evacuation of the English posts on conditions that assured the return of the *émigrés*, free trade with the English and Americans, and his *de facto* Independence [11]; — covering his ingratitude, meanwhile, by oaths of fidelity.

"But, presently, Toussaint Louverture will deceive all those enemies of ours whose tool he may at this time appear, and in the end he will oppress and cover with humiliation those whites whom he fears as much as he hates; yes, even those among them who are especially bound to him and who have encouraged him in his measures.... Toussaint Louverture now receives the *émigrés* with open arms: yet at the same time he never ceases to fill the cultivators with suspicion against all white men, to the end that these may never succeed in destroying his despotism. He is heaping up great wealth by the sale of colonial products to the English and Americans, and to-day San Domingo is practically lost to France. If the Directoire cannot take the very strong necessary measures, the sole hope of checking Toussaint Louverture even for the moment lies in sedulously fostering the hate which exists between the mulattoes and negroes, and by opposing Rigaud to Toussaint Louverture." [12]

XXIV

THE WAR BETWEEN THE CASTES

If Toussaint had feared the anger of the Directoire after Sonthonax's removal, he was still more alarmed at the possible consequences of his expulsion of Hédouville. For Hédouville was one of the strong men of the French Republic and would certainly throw all his influence in favor of vigorous action. Furthermore, the French agent's parting orders had been a heavy blow to Toussaint Louverture. They had legalized the future resistance of Rigaud and had shifted the Republic's moral sanction to the side of the mulattoes. Lastly, there was a distinct possibility that the Directoire would decide to back Rigaud with French troops.

All this made it necessary to strike the decisive blow against the mulattoes. And yet, for the moment, Toussaint still held his hand. The cause of this restraint bears witness to the political sagacity of this extraordinary man. Toussaint was now quite alone in French San Domingo, for by this time Raymond had gone the way of his colleagues. With the approach of the decisive struggle between the negro and the mulatto castes even the subservient Raymond could not be trusted to act against his race; wherefore the usual "election" had called the mulatto Commissioner to a seat in the French Legislature as a deputy for San Domingo. But French authority was still represented by Roume, — for the last two years Civil Commissioner in Spanish Santo Domingo. During these two years, however, Toussaint had carefully studied this man and had by now quite taken his measure. Roume was no Sonthonax to change his opinions with the times. He still remained the humanitarian enthusiast of 1792, and his ideals had been neither shattered by the Terror nor shelved after Thermidor. Toussaint felt certain that by personal contact his own strong personality could win the *doctrinaire* enthusiast to his support and thereby regain that moral sanction of the Republic's name lost since his rupture with Hédouville.

Accordingly he besought Roume to come to French San Domingo as arbiter between himself and Rigaud, and once Roume had accepted this proposal Toussaint quickly gained complete ascendancy over the Frenchman's weaker personality. How complete was Toussaint's triumph is revealed by Roume's letters to the Minister of Marine. "Every opinion that I have held hitherto," he writes from Port-au-Prince on the 11th of February, 1799, "is quite beneath the actual merit of this great man. We understand each other perfectly and do not differ on a single point. . . . Toussaint Louverture and the other black generals are truly the saviors of San Domingo and the benefactors of France." Roume was quite out of sympathy with the mulattoes and with Hédouville's policy of their support. Toussaint, asserted Roume, had the devotion of nine tenths of the population; Rigaud that of only one tenth. Hédouville's idea of supporting this minority seemed to Roume "un-Republican and Machiavellian. I, on the contrary," he contends, "see the guarantee of San Domingo's loyalty in the happiness of its inhabitants and the constitutional organization of the country." He begs the Directoire to grant Toussaint and his partisans a full pardon for all past acts, especially those connected with the expulsion of Hédouville. "If this be done," he continues, "I guarantee that the negro army will be gradually reduced, and that the newly landed European will soon be unable to perceive any difference between the departments of France and of San Domingo." He ends with a warm defence of Toussaint's reception of the *émigrés*. According to Roume an era of universal fraternity was breaking over San Domingo; all the colors had forgotten their former discords and were looking upon one another as brothers.[1] Unfortunately Roume saw with the eye of faith rather than of fact: the unhappy island was about to be convulsed by a death-struggle which for sheer horror would exceed anything that had gone before.[2]

Roume's first act was to call a conference between Toussaint and Rigaud for the settlement of their disputes. The mulatto leader must have attended with great reluctance, since Roume's letter of invitation described his black rival as "a virtuous man," a "philosopher," and "a good citizen devoted to France."[3] Still, nothing was to be gained by refusal, and the meeting soon took place at Port-au-Prince. Here, however, Rigaud found that his surmises were correct. At this time his sphere embraced not merely the South, but also the southern districts of the West Province to the walls of Léogane. Yet in the settlement proposed by Roume the mulatto leader was required to give up nearly all these Western districts to the authority of Toussaint Louver-

THE WAR BETWEEN THE CASTES 279

ture. As this would have meant Rigaud's virtual imprisonment within the remote peninsula of the South, it is not surprising that the mulatto leader left in a rage and broke off the negotiations. This was just what Toussaint had wanted, for the flouted mediator was greatly incensed at Rigaud's conduct and clove yet tighter to the side of Toussaint Louverture.

The decisive struggle was now plainly at hand, and Toussaint began his preparations. Troops assembled at Port-au-Prince while the black leader started on a flying trip to secure the doubtful quarters of the West and North. Before his departure he warned the mulatto population of Port-au-Prince against the consequences of rebellion. Ordering them to assemble in the main church of the town, he denounced from the pulpit a vast mulatto conspiracy against his life and closed with these ominous words: "General Rigaud refuses to obey me because I am black. Mulattoes, I see to the bottom of your souls. You are ready to rise against me. But, in leaving Port-Républicain for Le Cap, I leave my eye and my arm: my eye to watch, my arm to strike." [4]

Toward the end of April, Toussaint formally denounced Rigaud as a traitor, and when the mulatto leader quoted Hédouville's instructions, Roume also proclaimed him guilty of treason and rebellion against France. Nevertheless, although Toussaint soon gathered an army of ten thousand men at Port-au-Prince, the campaign began with a serious reverse. In early June the commandant of Léogane, a free negro of the Old Régime, went over to his caste and betrayed this bulwark of Port-au-Prince to Rigaud. Moreover, this was the signal for further trouble. The mulatto stronghold of the Artibonite rose in arms, while in the North a general mulatto insurrection broke out aided by several black leaders converted by Hédouville's diplomacy to hostility to Toussaint Louverture. Even General Michel, the black commander of Le Cap, was involved in the movement.

If Rigaud had acted promptly, there is no telling what might have happened: unfortunately for the mulatto cause his measures lacked promptness while Toussaint's moves were the springs of an infuriated tiger. Gathering his picked troops and most trusted generals, Toussaint fell like a thunderbolt upon the Artibonite, then dashed straight for Le Cap, while his terrible lieutenant Dessalines raced for the other rebel centre at the Môle-Saint-Nicolas. The punishment of the North was frightful. The mulattoes and free negroes were butchered *en masse;* the survivors were broken by torture and by conscription into black regiments where life was made one long agony. Toussaint characteristically announced the close of the massacres by a sermon to the surviving mulattoes of Le Cap on the Christian duty of pardoning one's enemies.[5]

The way was now clear for the attack on the South. Rigaud's mulatto soldiery opposed a furious resistance and even his black regiments fought stoutly against their brethren of the North, but by the turn of the year, after three months' desperate fighting, Toussaint's superior numbers had driven Rigaud into the peninsula of the South. However, this was only the beginning. The narrow neck connecting Rigaud's territory with the mainland was covered by the fortress of Jacmel, a place of great strength held by the flower of Rigaud's mulatto

THE WAR BETWEEN THE CASTES 281

soldiery under his best lieutenant, Pétion. Until Jacmel had fallen, Toussaint dare not plunge into the mountainous fastnesses of the South, so for three months the terrible Dessalines broke his teeth against the bastions of Jacmel while Toussaint held off the relieving columns of Rigaud. At last, on the night of March 11, 1800, Pétion abandoned the ruined town and cut his way through the black lines. The gate was down at last, and Toussaint's army poured on to the conquest of the South.

Then began a struggle whose horrors have probably never been surpassed. Neither side dreamed of quarter, and the only prisoners taken were those reserved for torture. So ferocious was the racial hatred of the combatants that men often tore one another to pieces with their teeth.[6] But the end was now only a question of time. On July 5, Rigaud's army was crushed at Acquin and the shattered remnants took refuge in Les Cayes. The town was strong and Rigaud still breathed defiance, but the efforts of Roume and a French officer named Vincent finally persuaded him to avoid the further shedding of blood. On the last day of July, Rigaud and his principal officers took ship for the Danish island of Saint Thomas, while his mulatto *corps d'élite*, some seven hundred strong, retired to Cuba rather than obey the orders of a black.[7]

It was on August 1, 1800, that Toussaint Louverture made his triumphal entry into Les Cayes. After a solemn *Te Deum* for his victory, Toussaint mounted the pulpit according to his wont and promised a general pardon. But this was only a ruse. Toussaint knew that the mulattoes were his irreconcilable enemies, and he had no mind to see himself stabbed in the back at the height of some future struggle with France. He therefore appointed the sinister Dessalines Governor of the South with general orders [8] for the "pacification" of the country. And Dessalines did not disappoint his master. Backed by overwhelming masses of negro troops, this ferocious brute born in the wilds of the Congo traversed in turn the districts of the South. Not by sudden massacre, but slowly and methodically, the mulatto population was weeded out. Men, women, and children were systematically done to death, generally after excruciating tortures chief among which was Dessalines's own special invention, — a form of impalement christened "The Bayonet." The number of persons who perished in this atrocious proscription is usually estimated at ten thousand.[9] Toussaint's comment was characteristic. Reproached with Dessalines's cruelty he answered, "I told him to prune the tree, not to uproot it." [10]

Eighteen hundred was, indeed, an evil year for San Domingo: to the depopulation of the South was added the economic ruin of the West. For during those same autumn months which witnessed Dessalines's grim progress through the South, the rains fell upon the island as they had never fallen within the memory of man. The raging mountain torrents soon overwhelmed the great irrigation dams of the Artibonite and Cul-de-Sac, already neglected for the past ten years, and since there was no French capital to repair the loss the prosperity of the semi-arid West [11] vanished forever.[12] The curse of Heaven seemed to have fallen upon the unhappy country.

XXV

THE TRIUMPH OF TOUSSAINT LOUVERTURE

So far back as December, 1799, when his columns had barely appeared before Jacmel, Toussaint Louverture had begun to prepare for the next step in his ambitious career. In that month he had demanded of Roume authorization to occupy Spanish Santo Domingo. We have seen that by the Treaty of Bâle, in 1795, Spain had ceded her portion of the island to the French Republic, but it must also be remembered that by the express desire of France she had agreed to retain possession until an English peace should enable the Republic to occupy the country. The Directoire's intentions were precise on this point, and Roume's instructions had been explicit in their prohibition of any amalgamation with the French portion. Hitherto Roume had appeared the blind instrument of Toussaint's ambition, but as a matter of fact his attitude had come more from the strength of his convictions than from moral cowardice or subservience. Therefore, when Toussaint demanded of Roume something clearly forbidden by the explicit will of France, he was chagrined to receive an uncompromising refusal.[1]

For the moment Toussaint could not afford to break with the French representative. The resistance of Jacmel revealed the power of Rigaud and the slightest reverse might still have been fatal. But as soon as the fall of Jacmel had made his eventual triumph a certainty, Toussaint showed the French agent what it meant to thwart his will. The old tragi-comedy already played upon Sonthonax and Hédouville was now enacted for the benefit of Roume. Toussaint's brutal nephew Moyse, already noted for his hatred of the white race, roused the wild negroes of the hinterland, descended upon Le Cap, and subjected the helpless Roume to insults and menaces. After a fortnight of this maltreatment, Toussaint appeared and rescued the frightened man, but let him know at the same time that further obstinacy might be fatal to the whole white population of the colony. So terrified was Roume by all this that on April 27, 1800, he granted the required authorization.

It was no mere lust of conquest which spurred Toussaint to these extreme measures. In the preceding autumn the 18th Brumaire [2] had made General Bonaparte master of France, and Toussaint's European agents [3] assured him that the young dictator would draw the reins of French authority far tighter than had the weak and discredited Directoire. A struggle with France had become more than ever an ultimate certainty, and in that struggle Toussaint could not afford to leave his whole flank open to attack.

How well Toussaint had judged the necessity for haste was quickly shown. An entire week before Roume's capitulation, a French Commission had landed at Santo Domingo with letters and proclamations from Bonaparte.[4] The proclamation, it is true, was of a reassuring nature, and the letters confirmed Toussaint in his existing rank and dignities, but despite Bonaparte's evident desire to avoid a rupture for the moment there was much

TRIUMPH OF TOUSSAINT LOUVERTURE 285

to rouse the black leader's alarm. The Commissioners were authorized to mediate a truce between Toussaint and Rigaud, and the French Government's determination to maintain the separation of Spanish Santo Domingo was explicitly stated.[5] The personnel of this new Commission was also significant. Its members were Vincent, a white officer with long experience in San Domingo, who, though friendly to Toussaint, had never swerved in loyalty to France; the mulatto Raymond; and one General Michel,[6] an expert well able to discern the true military situation.

Toussaint's action, however, showed that he was resolved on no half-measures. The Commissioners' prestige was promptly destroyed by their rough arrest by Moyse and their appearance as prisoners at Le Cap. Of course, Toussaint at once released them and disavowed his nephew's action, but he expressed great indignation at the proposed truce with Rigaud, neglected to publish Bonaparte's conciliatory proclamation, and shipped the intractable General Michel back to France.

However, Toussaint well knew that it was an ill thing to juggle with the new First Consul. He had received Bonaparte's commands and he had defied them: only decisive action remained. Nevertheless, Toussaint's first attempt on Santo Domingo ended in disaster. Rigaud's still unbroken power in the South made the sending of an army over the Eastern mountains as yet impossible, but early in May Toussaint despatched a white officer with a detachment of black soldiers by sea to take formal possession of the Spanish capital. No sooner had these emissaries landed, however, than the French agent and the Spanish Governor united in refusing to disobey the orders of their respective Governments. And this was not all. The population of Santo Domingo showed greater hostility than the authorities. In the Spanish colony negroes were few,[7] and if the whites abhorred black rule, it is easy to imagine the feelings of the mulatto majority toward the adversary of Rigaud. At sight of Toussaint's black soldiers the population rose in fury, and only an escort of Spanish troops to the border saved them from massacre. Furthermore, the news of this unexpected event had important results in French San Domingo: Roume was encouraged to revoke his authorization, and in July he wrote the Spanish Governor that no occupation would take place.

But these were mere idle words. In August the South lay at Toussaint's feet and by the late autumn Dessalines's proscription had crushed the mulatto caste once for all.[8] As soon as Toussaint's army was thus released for foreign service, the black leader struck quick and hard. Roume (once more left to the brutalities of Moyse) was dragged off to the Western mountains, while the protests of Vincent were answered by veiled imprisonment. The cowardly Raymond, once more Toussaint's passive tool, was contemptuously disregarded. Early in January, 1801, two strong armies crossed the border. The northern column under Moyse overran the back country, while the main body under Toussaint himself struck straight for Santo Domingo. Against these overwhelming forces the slender Spanish garrison could do nothing; the population was too cowed by the recent horrors of the South to offer any resistance; and on the 28th of January,

TRIUMPH OF TOUSSAINT LOUVERTURE 287

1801, Toussaint Louverture made his triumphal entry into the Spanish capital. Within a month he was absolute master of the whole country.

Toussaint's settlement of the conquered territory again showed his political sagacity. The land was strongly held by four thousand black soldiers, it is true, but these were picked troops kept under iron discipline, while their commander was not a negro, but the mulatto Clervaux. The abolition of customs lines was a great economic boon to the Spanish colony, and this material prosperity aided in quieting hostility, albeit San Domingo's welcome to Napoleon's army in 1802 showed that Toussaint had not succeeded in really reconciling the population to his rule.[9]

Toussaint Louverture was at last master of all San Domingo. And yet he faced the future with the gravest disquietude. His success had been gained only at the price of virtual rebellion against France and defiance of the terrible First Consul. The moment an English peace should free Bonaparte's hands, Toussaint knew that he was marked for destruction, while ten years of race war and social dissolution had so worn San Domingo down that only superhuman exertions could make her ready for the blow which lay in store. Up to this moment Toussaint had been absorbed in a series of struggles which had precluded any reconstructive measures, and his power, though no longer threatened by domestic enemies, thus rested on most insecure foundations.

The terrible condition of San Domingo during these years is well shown by the series of secret reports drawn up for the French Government by various trusted agents and officials. How matters stood at the time of Hédouville's expulsion in the autumn of 1798 may be gathered from the report of General Becker, one of the high officers on Hédouville's staff. Becker did not have a high opinion of Toussaint's army and thought it could offer little resistance to a powerful European force, since it was "without regular discipline or instruction. The number of officers is past counting, especially in the higher grades. Naturally vainglorious, these good fellows believe that once they put on epaulettes they are forthwith commanders: in reality the best of them are hardly equal to poor European officers, while the rest are of a stupidity such as I have never seen anywhere else. As to the few white officers, instead of being a useful leaven, they are the corrupters of the colony. They flatter the negro and mulatto chiefs, compare them to the greatest heroes, laud their military talents, hail them as the fathers and saviors of the colony, and assert that the government of San Domingo really belongs to them." He estimates the black army at about twenty thousand men, though the district generals varied their corps at pleasure. "These commandants," he continues, "are in reality so many little monarchs in their respective quarters. They monopolize all the powers of government and obey the higher authorities only when it suits them. In a word, they are so many despots, more or less insupportable as they are more or less evil." The civil administration was in complete anarchy; the generals requisitioned at pleasure, and the officials were mere spoilsmen. The courts were a farce, and justice was always bought and sold. Becker's vital statistics are the most depressing feature of his entire

TRIUMPH OF TOUSSAINT LOUVERTURE

report. He asserts that the whites had diminished by over two thirds, the mulattoes by one fourth, and that of the vast negro population fully a third had perished.[10]

If such had been the state of San Domingo at the close of 1798, its condition could certainly not have been improved by that frightful struggle between the castes which had brought ruin and massacre to every province. Assuredly the picture presented by confidential reports of that later period fully bears out this hypothesis. Only a month before Toussaint's invasion of Santo Domingo, Chanlatte, the French agent, wrote the following lines to Bonaparte: "The Colony of San Domingo is in the most deplorable state.[11] A civil war between North and South has swept away an immense number of cultivators, and although this war is now over, new troubles have arisen which daily sacrifice fresh victims in all parts of the country. Anarchy in every sense of the word is tearing this unfortunate colony." [12]

What these new troubles were of which Chanlatte speaks is described by the reports of persons in the French portion of the island. In the autumn of 1800 the Minister of Marine presented to the Consuls a long report on San Domingo, compiled from interrogations of returned government agents and from the written reports of others still in the island. "According to these," writes the Minister, "the greatest discord reigns between Toussaint Louverture and the different generals under his orders. General Moyse is on very bad terms with his uncle; he has even shown a desire to supplant him. Dessalines apparently enjoys Toussaint Louverture's chief confidence, but may shortly form a new party different from that of Moyse. In such an event, Maurepas, inclined to revolt like the others, would be ready to join Dessalines. Christophe is excessively discontented with Toussaint Louverture, and the white inhabitants would be for him.... The rivalries of Generals Moyse and Dessalines presage new storms for the colony. Toussaint holds them only by hopes of higher command and greater wealth." [13]

Still more alarming was the report of a French official who had left Le Cap in mid-September. He reported that since Roume's arrest Toussaint had set no bounds to his assumptions of sovereignty, the white officials being completely ignored. Toussaint was buying immense quantities of arms and ammunition from the English and Americans, paying for them with the state revenues. He estimated that thirty thousand muskets had been already imported. Before his departure for France the writer had protested to Moyse, whose answer had been a threat to have the Frenchman shot. The white officials were terrorized and dared not write home, since even official correspondence was systematically violated. New officials coming out from France were being thrown into prison. "There is no law left in San Domingo," asserts this writer. "The will of General Toussaint and the other generals' arbitrary whims are the basis for all that is done. The commandants are all negroes and have complete authority, while the civil service and judiciary are only an empty farce." He, too, reports grave dissensions among the negro generals. At the moment of his departure in mid-September, "Toussaint dared not go to Le Cap for fear of General Moyse.... Moyse, more sanguinary but less crafty than Toussaint, has already lifted the mask; he says that he no longer recognizes the laws of France and that the colony ought to legislate for itself. Toussaint, hypocritical, sly, playing the religious devotee, orders crimes and protects the abuses and dilapidations of his creatures, whom he disavows according to circumstances and on whom he throws the odium of his Machiavellian conduct. Dessalines, a ferocious and barbarous Congo, swears he will drink the blood of the whites. . . . In fine, throughout the North I have seen terror and desolation. The towns are deserted and men are fleeing a country in which they can no longer exist." [14]

Such were the difficulties confronting Toussaint Louverture in the autumn of 1800. That only two years later he should have built up the powerful machine which faced Napoleon's army is the greatest triumph of this extraordinary man. For Toussaint held the key to the situation. He knew the natural wealth of San Domingo; he knew how his race could endure forced labor; lastly, he knew that could he but wring sufficient wealth from these two factors, he might hold the loyalty of his greedy generals and buy the products of the civilized world. To this end he now turned the whole power of his ferocious energy — and succeeded in marvellous fashion. Ten years of war's natural selection had already assembled the strong men of the negro race in the ranks of his army, and this army showed no repugnance to execute its leader's will upon the mass of the black population. The whole country was soon scoured by Toussaint's flying columns, and the negroes were herded from their vagabond life in the woods and mountains back to work such as they had never known under the Old Régime. Free men by law, in fact the negro cultivators found themselves once more slaves: slaves of the State, — and of a military State at that. The colony was divided into regular districts, each under its general, with two captain-generals, — Moyse for the North, Dessalines for the South and West. Dessalines showed himself particularly successful in his stewardship. He patrolled his province like a King of Dahomey, surrounded by a corps of executioners, and shirkers and rebels were publicly buried alive or sawn between two planks to encourage the zeal of the *ateliers*. Yet the results of this régime were extraordinary. Ever since the abolition of slavery in 1793, the refusal of the negroes to work had reduced the produce of San Domingo to insignificant proportions. Now, the old prosperity returned with a bound, and despite the tremendous largess bestowed upon the black generals, the treasury and state warehouses were filled to overflowing.[15]

Still more noteworthy was Toussaint's friendly attitude toward the whites. The chief cause of his rupture with Hédouville in 1798 had been his welcome of the *émigrés* in contravention to the laws of the Republic,[16] and ever since then he had shown increasing favor to the returned colonists. Several motives combined to influence Toussaint in favor of this policy. First of all, he realized that he needed the whites' superior intelligence in his plans for reconstructing the shattered edifice of San Domingan society, and he also knew that in this work his white subordinates would be thoroughly trustworthy, both through lack of sympathy for the negroes and from fear of their vengeance should he be overthrown. Again, he realized that nothing would so raise his prestige among the blacks as the sight of their former masters in his service. Lastly, in case of war with France, the whites would be most valuable hostages. For all these reasons, then, the white colonists were invited to return, and all who consented to do homage to the black ruler were assured of his most gracious favor. Their estates were restored and stocked with negroes who were compelled to labor as zealously as their fellows upon the state domains or the private plantations of the black generals. Toussaint himself set up a genuine Court, where amid regal splendors the native force of his compelling personality obtained the respect of all around him.[17]

Most of the black generals were so sated with power and plunder that they asked for nothing better than the continuance of this reign of plenty. But there was a minority whom thirst for power or race hatred alienated from Toussaint and his régime. The leader of this minority was Toussaint's nephew Moyse. We have seen how strained relations between the two had been in the autumn of 1800, and as time passed this tension had increased. Toussaint's iron rule necessarily provoked great discontent among the negro population, and Moyse presently came out as the champion of the exploited masses of his race and the denouncer of Toussaint's pro-white policy. "Whatever my old uncle may do," said Moyse, "I will not be the hangman of my own color. He urges me on in the name of the interests of France, but I notice that these same interests are always those of the whites; — and I shall never love the whites till they have given me back the eye that they put out in battle." [18]

With such sentiments it is not surprising that Moyse's stewardship of the North was not so pleasing to Toussaint as that of Dessalines in the West. Matters were finally brought to a head by an insurrection of the Plain and the massacre of several hundred whites. But Toussaint acted with his usual rapidity. Before his terrible presence the rising died away and Moyse fell helpless into his power. Toussaint never cared to deal a second blow. Moyse was summarily shot, Toussaint's prestige was restored by spectacular executions, and the last overt opposition to his authority was thoroughly stamped out.[19] Only in the inaccessible fastnesses of the Eastern and Southern mountains the savage maroon bands still defied his power. Everywhere else the last murmurs had died away.

The time was now come for the formal consecration of Toussaint's supremacy. In the late summer of 1801 a miniature convention of ten persons met at Port-au-Prince and soon drew up a new constitution for San Domingo. By it Toussaint Louverture was appointed Governor for life with power to name his successor, and the tie with France was reduced to a mere empty acknowledgment of the sovereignty of the Republic. Vincent protested against this virtual declaration of independence, but was sharply bidden to take the document to France for "approval." As, however, Toussaint had at once declared the new constitution in full operation, it was plain that this was only a hollow mockery.[20]

But the sands of Toussaint's rule were running low. Before Vincent had reached France the Preliminaries of Amiens [21] had assured an English peace; and the ban had not been ten weeks lifted from the sea when a great armada sailed for San Domingo bearing twenty thousand veterans from the armies of Italy and the Rhine with Bonaparte's answer to the black who had dared defy his will.

XXVI

THE ADVENT OF BONAPARTE

WHEN the *coup d'état* of the 18th Brumaire [1] gave the sovereignty of France into Napoleon's iron grasp, the French colonial empire had ceased to exist. San Domingo, greatest of them all, was lost to the white race and was at the moment the prey of warring negroes and mulattoes. Guadeloupe had been preserved to the Republic by the brutal energy of the Jacobin Victor Hugues, who from 1794 to 1798 had wrung out of the negro population the necessary sinews of war by a régime of state slavery much like that adopted by Toussaint Louverture; but Hugues's recall in 1798 had been followed by civil broils which were fast reducing Guadeloupe to anarchy. Cayenne, too, still flew the tri-colored flag, but its remote insignificance alone preserved it from attack. Those remote islands of the Indian Ocean, Îsle-de-France and Bourbon, were in open rebellion against the Republic and had maintained the old colonial system in complete defiance of the national will. All the other colonies, Martinique included, had been for years in English hands.[2]

Previous to the 18th Brumaire, Napoleon appears to have been too much absorbed in his plans against Egypt and India to have paid much attention to the West Indian colonies,[3] but no sooner had he grasped the reins of supreme authority than his devouring energy assailed

THE ADVENT OF BONAPARTE 297

a problem which cried so loudly for solution. The first result of his deliberations was a decisive preliminary step that cleared the ground for all subsequent action. The Directoire Constitution of the Year III (1795) had maintained the Jacobin ideal of colonial assimilation. All the French dependencies had been declared integral parts of the Republic, and no difference whatever had been made between the departments of the European mainland and the "departments" over-seas. But all this had remained pure theory. The colonies in English hands and the rebellious islands of the Indian Ocean had simply maintained the old slave régime; the negro and mulatto dictators who ruled San Domingo did as they pleased; lastly, in Guadeloupe and Cayenne, the only colonies where white Republican officials actually ruled, the tricolor had been kept flying only by a crushing exploitation of the new black citizens which violated every principle of "Liberty and Equality."

Bonaparte, however, soon showed that he was resolved to end this empty farce: his Constitution of the Year VIII (1800) abjured the Revolutionary principle of assimilation and declared that the colonies should be henceforth governed by special laws in conformity to their peculiar geographical and social situation. This was a return to the theory of the Old Régime and freed Napoleon's hands for all contingencies.[4]

The basis of future action was thus laid down, but little else could be done for the moment. The iron girdle of the English blockade kept the shattered and disorganized French navy strictly in port, and whatever Napoleon might wring from his weak sea-power must be devoted to his imprisoned Egyptian army. Still, the First Consul determined to be ready for prompt action at the first favorable moment, and to make up his mind what this action should be he now sought to obtain all possible information on the state of the colonies. The opening months of the year 1800 saw a flood of letters and memoirs from all the principal actors in colonial affairs and from many exiled colonists as well. As regards San Domingo these advices were most diverse in character. According to Hédouville, Sonthonax, and most others, Toussaint Louverture was the great obstacle to the restoration of French authority, and Rigaud was the only bulwark against the establishment of San Domingo's *de facto* independence under English protection;[5] yet a minority held that Toussaint should be supported as the one man capable of restoring peace and order to the distracted island.[6] Most of the exiled colonists advised sending new officials to restore French authority; but while some urged their backing by a small army,[7] others maintained that such half-measures would merely drive the negroes to rebellion and open independence. Forfait, the new Minister of Marine, told Napoleon that a strong expedition could restore San Domingo to France, but that until an English peace made such an expedition possible, Toussaint must be most tactfully handled. He advised sending a commission to reassure Toussaint and stop the horrible struggle between the castes, and he warned Napoleon of the dangerous alarm already roused among the negroes of San Domingo, who saw in the reactionary colonial principle proclaimed by the new constitution the first step toward the restoration of slavery.[8]

THE ADVENT OF BONAPARTE 299

It was in consequence of Forfait's representations that Napoleon despatched that Commission which received such cavalier treatment at the hands of Moyse and Toussaint Louverture.⁹

Despite Forfait's advice, however, Napoleon seems to have been sceptical as to the results of these efforts, for at the very moment of the Commissioners' departure he ordered the preparation of a strong squadron at Brest and the concentration of some five thousand soldiers for San Domingo. That even at this early date Napoleon was inclined to vigorous measures is shown both by the choice of its commander and the tone of his instructions. The ideas held by General Sahuguet, the destined leader of this expedition, were certainly not those of conciliation. "Toussaint Louverture and Rigaud, whom an abuse of words makes 'friends of the Republic,'" he writes the First Consul, "are really both of them enemies of France. It is not as the ally of one or the other that I should go to San Domingo. Whichever faction questions the European general's authority should be exterminated. Otherwise all will be lost." ¹⁰ And Sahuguet's instructions were quite in this spirit. He was directed to end the war between the castes, and as soon as possible to banish both Toussaint and Rigaud from the island.¹¹

But Sahuguet's armament was destined never to reach San Domingo. The preparations were slow and faulty, the English blockade was alert and vigilant, and in May Napoleon left Paris for the campaign of Marengo. Not till the beginning of June did a violent storm scatter the English blockading fleet, and no sooner had the San Domingan squadron gained the open sea than it was forced to put back in distress. For ten years of the Revolution had ruined the French navy. The ill-found ships of the San Domingo squadron could scarcely keep the boisterous sea, the supplies were mostly spoiled, and disease was raging among the troops. To attempt the conquest of San Domingo with such an armament was clearly madness, and the expedition collapsed.[12]

Shortly after Napoleon's return from the triumph of Marengo, he began to receive news from the West Indies. This news was of the most contradictory character. His Commissioners reported their bad reception by Moyse, Toussaint's designs on Spanish Santo Domingo, and his refusal to publish Bonaparte's conciliatory proclamation.[13] Nevertheless, Vincent maintained that Toussaint was the one man who could save San Domingo from anarchy, and advised the French Government to send none but persons known for sympathizers of the negroes and of Toussaint's rule. Roume wrote still more strongly. He asserted that the black leader was devoted to France and that his recent conduct had been caused solely by his fear of a new slave régime. To bind him firmly to France all European agents should be recalled and Toussaint left supreme till the peace with England. On the other hand, the French agents in Spanish Santo Domingo gave exactly the opposite advice. They asserted that Toussaint was fast working toward independence, and that Roume and Vincent were writing under duress.[14] "All the bonds of intimacy with the mother country are dissolved," wrote Chanlatte from Spanish Santo Domingo. "Attachment to the French Republic has become a crime or an object of derision.

THE ADVENT OF BONAPARTE

The very name of the national authority is flouted and outraged. . . . I cannot too often repeat that time presses and that the situation is grave: if independence strikes its roots too deep, the means of reëstablishing the love of France will become more and more costly and difficult."[15]

Chanlatte's sentiments were echoed by General Hédouville, then in the United States. "Since the victory over Rigaud," he wrote Napoleon in the late autumn, "the spirit of independence has greatly increased in San Domingo." As one of his proofs Hédouville quoted the following incendiary speech of Dessalines to his troops: "The war which you have just finished is a little war, but you have two bigger ones still to fight: one against the Spaniards, who do not want to give up their land and who have insulted your brave general-in-chief; another against France, who will try to make you slaves again as soon as she is freed from her enemies. And these two wars we will be able to sustain." This speech, adds Hédouville, was no idle boast, for from the port of New York alone twenty-five thousand muskets, sixteen pieces of artillery, and an immense amount of war *matériel* had already started for San Domingo.[16]

From all these reports, however, one fact was certain, — the authority of France was destroyed. Small wonder, therefore, that Napoleon began fresh preparations for an expedition to San Domingo, especially as in August he had opened negotiations with England. But the hopes of peace soon died away, Napoleon was forced to concentrate his attention upon the imprisoned Army of Egypt once more, and all thoughts of a San Domingo squadron had to be again postponed.[17]

Yet just as decisive action had thus become impossible, the news from San Domingo grew worse. In October arrived the tidings of Rigaud's flight and Toussaint's complete triumph over the mulattoes: [18] Napoleon now realized that he would be fortunate if he succeeded in keeping even Spanish Santo Domingo from Toussaint's grasp. In this unpleasant situation the Minister of Marine again urged Napoleon to try conciliation by means of another Commission. "The expedition to San Domingo," writes Forfait, "is at present a diplomatic mission. Your object is to stop bloodshed and to obtain peace without a violent convulsion. The men whom you send thither must act with tact, prudence, and dissimulation toward the negroes. An officer just returned from San Domingo portrays the condition of the whites in the most alarming colors. They are in a state of absolute oppression, ceaselessly threatened with ill-usage which is but too often actually inflicted upon them. The negroes have not disarmed since the submission of the South; on the contrary, they remain on a full war footing and daily increase their military preparations. They make no secret of their intention to conquer the Spanish part of the island and later on to fight France. They look with the gravest suspicion upon the whites, and our unfortunate brothers expect to become the victims of their tyrants at the first intimation that an army is on the way. All this should lead you to flatter Toussaint Louverture, conciliate the other chiefs, and tactfully retain your prestige while awaiting the favor of circumstances." [19]

Sceptical as was Napoleon over the efficacy of fresh conciliation, he agreed to Forfait's proposals; but before

THE ADVENT OF BONAPARTE

the new Commission had sailed there arrived the news of the outrages upon Roume and the conquest of Spanish Santo Domingo.[20] All that the Commission was to have averted had now taken place, and Napoleon countermanded its departure in order not to expose the dignity of France to further humiliations. But the need for Commissions was almost over: already Napoleon had begun those negotiations which were to culminate in the Preliminaries of Amiens. On October 1, 1801, Napoleon's hands were at last free to deal as he saw fit with San Domingo.[21]

What Bonaparte had in mind was perfectly clear, for soon every dockyard from Flushing to Toulon rang with preparations, while twenty thousand veteran troops stood ready to go on board.[22] At the head of this formidable armament was Napoleon's brother-in-law, General Leclerc. His instructions bear impressive testimony to the First Consul's care for San Domingo, while their nature shows how far France had travelled since the 18th Brumaire.

Napoleon divided the conquest of San Domingo into three periods. In the first, lasting from fifteen to twenty days, Leclerc should occupy the coast towns and organize his forces. In the second, a quick converging movement from several points should smash organized resistance. In the third, mobile flying columns should hunt down the scattered negro bands among the woods and mountains. Thereupon the colony should be reconstructed on lines analogous to those of the Old Régime, though chattel slavery was not to be restored. This programme Napoleon tersely sums up in the following words: —

"Never will the French Nation give chains to men whom it has once recognized as free. Therefore all the blacks shall live at San Domingo as those in Guadeloupe to-day."[23]

"Your conduct will vary with the three periods abovementioned.

"In the first period you will disarm only the rebel blacks. In the third you will disarm all.

"In the first period you will not be exacting: you will treat with Toussaint, you will promise him everything he asks, — in order that you may get possession of the principal points and establish yourself in the country.

"As soon as you have done this, you will become more exacting. You will order him to reply categorically to your proclamation and to my letter. You will charge him to come to Le Cap.

"In your interviews with Moyse, Dessalines, and Toussaint's other generals, you will treat them well.

"Gain over Christophe, Clervaux, Maurepas, and all the other black leaders favorable to the whites. In the first period, confirm them in their rank and office. In the last period, send them all to France, with their rank if they have behaved well.

"All Toussaint's principal agents, white or colored, should in the first period be indiscriminately loaded with attentions and confirmed in their posts: in the last period, all sent to France; — with their rank if they have behaved well during the second; prisoners if they have acted ill.

"All blacks in office should during the first period be flattered, well treated, but undermined in authority and

THE ADVENT OF BONAPARTE 305

power. Toussaint, Moyse, and Dessalines should be well treated during the first period; sent to France at the last, in arrest or with their rank according to their conduct.

"Raymond has lost the Government's confidence; at the beginning of the second period you will seize him and send him to France as a criminal.

"If the first period last fifteen days, all is well; if longer, you will have been fooled.

"Toussaint shall not be held to have submitted until he shall have come to Le Cap or Port-au-Prince in the midst of the French army, to swear fidelity to the Republic. On that very day, without scandal or injury but with honor and consideration, he must be put on board a frigate and sent to France. At the same time, if possible, arrest Moyse and Dessalines: if impossible, hunt them down; and then send to France all the white partisans of Toussaint, all the blacks in office suspected of disaffection. Declare Moyse and Dessalines traitors and enemies of the French people. Start the troops and give them no rest till you have their heads and have scattered and disarmed their partisans.

"If after the first fifteen or twenty days it has been impossible to get Toussaint, proclaim that within a specified time he shall be declared a traitor, and after that period begin a war to the death.

"A few thousand negroes wandering in the mountains should not prevent the Captain-General from regarding the second period as ended and from promptly beginning the third. Then has come the moment to assure the colony to France forever. And, on that same day, at every point of the colony, you will arrest all suspects in office whatever their color, and at the same moment embark all the black generals no matter what their conduct, patriotism, or past services; — giving them, however, their rank, and assuring them of good treatment in France.

"All the whites who have served under Toussaint, and covered themselves with crimes in the tragic scenes of San Domingo, shall be sent directly to Guiana.

"All the blacks who have behaved well, but whose rank forbids them to remain longer in the island, shall be sent to Brest.

"All the blacks or mulattoes who have acted badly, whatever their rank, shall be sent to the Mediterranean and landed at Corsica.

"If Toussaint, Dessalines, or Moyse is taken in arms, they shall be passed before a court-martial and shot as rebels within twenty-four hours.

"No matter what happens, we think that during the third period you should disarm all the negroes, whatever their party, and set them to work.

"All those who have signed the Constitution [24] should in the third period be sent to France; some as prisoners, others at liberty as having been constrained.

"White women who have prostituted themselves to negroes,[25] whatever their rank, shall be sent to Europe.

"You will take the regimental flags from the National Guard, give out new ones, and reorganize it. You will reorganize the *gendarmerie*. Suffer no black above the rank of captain to remain in the island. . . .

"The Captain-General shall allow no temporizing with the principles of these instructions; and any person

THE ADVENT OF BONAPARTE

talking about the rights of those blacks who have shed so much white blood shall under some pretext or other be sent to France, whatever his rank or services." [26]

Armed with these instructions, General Leclerc and the main squadron under Admiral Villaret-Joyeuse sailed from Brest on the 14th of December, 1801, for San Domingo.

XXVII

THE COMING OF LECLERC

On the 29th of January, 1802, the Brest fleet under Villaret-Joyeuse and the Rochefort squadron of Admiral Latouche-Tréville lay off Cape Samaná, the eastern extremity of the island of San Domingo. There was no sign of the Toulon-Cadiz division with its forty-five hundred troops, neither had any news arrived of the Havre-Flushing squadron with its twenty-five hundred men General Leclerc thus found himself off San Domingo with barely twelve thousand soldiers. But his troops were veterans, and the lexicon of Napoleonic generals did not contain the word "delay." Leclerc therefore resolved to strike at once. A small squadron was told off to rouse Spanish Santo Domingo, while the bulk of the fleet sailed on west.[1]

During those hours of final preparation, the French fleet had been scrutinized by no less a person than Toussaint Louverture. As the black leader looked down upon the great armada from the high cliffs of Cape Samaná, a moment of discouragement seems to have seized him. "We must perish," he cried to his staff. "All France is coming to San Domingo. She has been deceived; she comes to take vengeance and enslave the blacks."[2] Toussaint seems to have underestimated the magnitude of Napoleon's preparations and to have expected a much smaller armament. His first attitude was therefore

THE COMING OF LECLERC 309

marked by some uncertainty and by a desire to gain time, though it is plain that thoughts of submission were never seriously entertained.

Toussaint's position was, indeed, a strong one. He possessed an army of fully twenty thousand regular troops, the pick of the whole negro population, hardened by years of war, well armed and fairly disciplined. This army was divided into three grand divisions. The North was held by five thousand men under Christophe. The main corps was at Le Cap, while a considerable division, under the able Maurepas, lay at Port-de-Paix to watch the doubtful districts about the Môle-Saint-Nicolas. The West and South were more strongly garrisoned, for the remaining mulattoes were, of course, unreconciled, the maroon tribes were as yet unconquered, and even the ordinary negro population of those provinces had never fallen so completely under Toussaint's influence as had their brethren of the North. All this was well known to Toussaint, who had placed these regions under the terrible Dessalines with eleven thousand soldiers. The third military division — four thousand strong — garrisoned Spanish Santo Domingo. It was commanded by the mulatto Clervaux, seconded by Toussaint's brother, Paul Louverture. It must also be noted that nearly the whole negro population of the French part was armed and could furnish many thousands of guerilla fighters to supplement Toussaint's twenty thousand regular troops. Altogether, the problem facing Leclerc and his twelve thousand French soldiers was by no means an easy one.[3]

However, the French general acted with the greatest boldness. General Rochambeau, with two thousand soldiers, was ordered to capture Fort Dauphin, the most eastern point of French San Domingo; General Boudet and thirty-five hundred men sailed on to seize Port-au-Prince; Leclerc himself with his remaining five thousand troops made for Le Cap.

It was on February 3 that Leclerc appeared off the harbor and demanded the submission of the town. What followed was most significant. At sight of the French fleet the large mulatto and free negro population broke into extravagant rejoicings, while the mayor of Le Cap, himself a free negro of the Old Régime, implored Christophe to offer no resistance. Christophe seems to have been confused by these demonstrations, and it is possible that Leclerc might have been able to enter the harbor by a sudden *coup de main*. Unfortunately a storm now blew up which compelled the French fleet to stand offshore, and this gave Christophe time to regain his resolution and to follow Toussaint's orders. These orders were to burn the town and retreat to the mountains: accordingly, when the French fleet reappeared toward evening of February 5, Le Cap was in flames. Leclerc, however, acted with great promptness, saved part of the city from destruction, and sent out flying columns which preserved the Plain.[4] Furthermore, these troops soon encountered the outposts of Rochambeau, who on February 4 had carried Fort Dauphin by a brilliant *coup de main*. By February 6 the whole of the Plaine du Nord was in French hands.

And on the same day as Lerclerc's capture of Le Cap, Port-au-Prince had fallen almost without a blow. General Boudet had appeared on February 4 and had re-

THE COMING OF LECLERC 311

ceived the same refusal to surrender, but next day he had landed a strong force which advanced boldly on Fort Bizoton, the key to the town. This rash move had been crowned with success. At sight of the advancing French infantry the mulatto commandant of Fort Bizoton cried, "Vive la France," and led his whole battalion over to the invaders. At this defection the garrison of Port-au-Prince had left in such a panic that they neglected to destroy the town, though they dragged away several hundred wretched whites to glut their future vengeance. This striking French success was undoubtedly due to the absence of Dessalines, at that moment enjoying the pleasures of his gorgeous palace at Saint-Marc.[5]

And further triumphs awaited General Boudet. On the very night after the capture of Port-au-Prince a black officer arrived from Laplume, the commander of the South, offering to submit with all his troops. This was the same Laplume who, in 1795, had brought his bands over to Toussaint Louverture, but like most of the Western negroes he showed little personal attachment to the great black of the North Laplume kept his word to Boudet, for on February 7 his soldiers quietly took the oath of allegiance to France. Even his officers showed no signs of discontent.[6]

Moreover, these successes in the French part of the island were surpassed by those in Spanish Santo Domingo. On February 2 the small squadron detailed for this duty appeared off the Spanish capital. The city of Santo Domingo was commanded by Paul Louverture, who refused the French summons to surrender. But at sight of the French squadron the inhabitants showed their hatred of Toussaint's rule by a furious rising. It is true that Paul Louverture's black soldiers finally quieted the town, but the whole back country was ablaze behind him, and when his superior officer, the mulatto Clervaux, submitted at Saint Yago, Paul Louverture himself surrendered. Of the four thousand black troops in Spanish Santo Domingo not a man rejoined Toussaint in the west.[7]

Thus, within a week, Toussaint was reeling under Leclerc's stunning blows, and outside of the North his power had shown scant vitality. So far the results had exceeded Napoleon's expectations. Not even the savage courage of Dessalines had prevented the defection of the West coast. As soon as he learned of the events at Port-au-Prince, Dessalines had rushed from Saint-Marc, picked up the retreating garrison and struck for Léogane to prevent the defection of the South. But Boudet was too quick for him. Hardly had Dessalines arrived at Léogane when a strong French column appeared, and on February 11 the black general was forced to beat a hasty retreat after burning the town. A body of two thousand irregulars left behind in the mountains back of Léogane was quickly smashed by the French, whose communications with Laplume were firmly established.[8]

Meanwhile Leclerc had restored order at Le Cap, and as several days were needed to complete his military preparations, he resolved to try negotiations with Toussaint Louverture. But all his startling reverses had in no way altered Toussaint's determination, and Leclerc soon realized that his adversary was merely seeking to gain time. On the 17th of February, when his prepara-

THE COMING OF LECLERC 313

tions were completed, the French general issued a proclamation putting Toussaint and Christophe beyond the pale of the law and declaring all their armed adherents guilty of rebellion.[9]

Leclerc can certainly not be charged with having wasted time in these negotiations. The armistice was only local, and besides the fighting in the West a fresh blow had been struck in the North. On February 10, General Humbert and twelve hundred men had landed at Port-de-Paix, the strongest point on the North coast. Port-de-Paix was held by the able black general, Maurepas, and two thousand regular troops, but a brilliant action of the French land and naval forces took the town by a *coup de main*. Nevertheless, Maurepas was far from beaten. Port-de-Paix is girt in by rugged hills on which the negroes lay strongly entrenched, while the fanatical hatred of the whites held by the population soon gave Maurepas the backing of many thousand savage irregulars, undisciplined but well armed and full of courage. It is therefore not surprising that when General Humbert attempted to follow up his victory the French troops suffered a bloody check and would have been forced to reëmbark but for the guns of the fleet.[10]

But Leclerc was now ready to strike his decisive blow. On the 14th of February, the Toulon-Cadiz squadron had arrived with its precious reënforcements, and the French commander now had some nine thousand men free for offensive operations, not counting a strong corps of mulattoes and free negroes eager for revenge. Therefore the ink of his proclamation was hardly dry when Leclerc's columns started across the Plain to storm the long mountain wall behind which lay Toussaint Louverture. The French plan was a bold one. Rochambeau was to move from Fort Dauphin and clear the mountains along the Spanish border, while Leclerc and the main body should strike for the Cordon de l'Ouest and roll Toussaint down into the Western plains, where he should be crushed by Boudet's advance from Port-au-Prince.

The week which followed saw a truly Napoleonic campaign. From Fort Dauphin Rochambeau hurled himself like a thunderbolt upon the Eastern mountains, and in three days he lay over the Spanish border with Toussaint's right wing broken to pieces. Leclerc, meanwhile, was mastering the Western mountains, with more labor but with equal success. That old "Cordon de l'Ouest," which had for two years held back the tide of negro insurrection, was no easy prey: its rugged heights and tangled valleys were held by the flower of Toussaint's soldiery, while thousands of wild guerillas swarmed upon every mountain-side. But the veterans of Italy and the Rhine would not be denied, and their tremendous *élan* carried all before them. On the second night Leclerc lay at Plaisance, halfway through the mountains. "Our three divisions," he writes the Minister of Marine, "have everywhere forced back the enemy with the greatest impetuosity. You should see this country to form any idea of the difficulties we encounter at every step. I have seen nothing in the Alps to compare with them." [11]

Torrential rains held up the French columns during the 20th of February, but next day began that final advance which on February 23 culminated in the storming of Toussaint's main position at the Gorge of Couleuvres.

This natural fortress had been greatly strengthened by entrenchments and abattis of felled trees, and was held by three thousand of Toussaint's choicest troops supported by several thousand guerillas. Yet in a few hours all was over: Toussaint had retreated southward leaving a thousand men dead on the field, and the French right slept that night at the Western seaport of Gonaives.[12]

The Cordon de l'Ouest was won — yet the blow was not decisive. Leclerc had expected that Toussaint's retreat would have led him straight into the arms of the French columns from Port-au-Prince; but no such columns appeared, and Toussaint retired safely to his fastnesses in those mountains of the Spanish border overlooking his base of supplies, the inland valley of the Artibonite. The black leader had been saved from the trap by Dessalines's able defence of the West. Although checked at Léogane on the 11th of February, Dessalines had continued to menace Port-au-Prince, and General Boudet had been obliged to take such elaborate precautions to protect his lines that only on February 21 had he dared begin his northward advance. And even then his progress had been slow and difficult. The road from Port-au-Prince to Saint-Marc led through a narrow belt of broken country lying between the sea and the high mountains enclosing the valley of the Artibonite. These natural advantages were skilfully used by Dessalines. His army was of good quality and superior in numbers, and it offered such a stubborn resistance that the French advance had to be continually cleared by artillery. Not until February 25, two days after Toussaint's defeat at the Gorge of Couleuvres, did Boudet enter Saint-Marc.

And the capture of Saint - Marc meant nothing. The town was a heap of ruins, for Dessalines had fired it at the last moment, leaving only the mangled bodies of several hundred white prisoners as his savage greeting to the French; a wide tract of country still lay between Saint-Marc and the Northern mountains: most ominous of all, the black army had disappeared, though its whereabouts were only too well shown by the letter from Toussaint to Dessalines which now fell into Boudet's hands. "Nothing is hopeless, Citizen General," read this despatch, "if you can but deprive the invaders of the resources of Port Républicain.[13] Try to burn that place by every means of force or guile; it is of wood, and a few faithful spies could do the business. Can you not find in your army men devoted enough to undertake this service? Ah, my dear General! what a misfortune that there was a traitor in that town and that our orders were not executed! Watch for the moment when the garrison is weakened by expeditions into the plains, and then try to surprise and capture that town behind them. Do not forget that while we are awaiting that rainy season which should rid us of our enemies, our sole resources are destruction and fire. Remember that the land bathed by our sweat must not furnish the slightest sustenance to our enemies. Ambush the roads, throw dead men and horses into the springs. Destroy all, burn all; so that those who come here to force us back into slavery may have ever before their eyes the image of that hell which they deserve." [14]

This letter, coupled with the ominous disappearance of Dessalines, was quite enough for Boudet, who retreated hastily on Port-au-Prince. The town was defended by only six hundred troops under General Lacroix,[15] and it might have gone hard with this slender garrison but for a diversion of a most unexpected character. We have often noted those formidable maroon tribes of the Spanish border who had so successfully maintained their independence under the Old Régime. Grown still more powerful during the troubled years of the Revolution, these maroons had proved as much of a thorn to Toussaint Louverture as to the former Governors of the French Crown, and though he had succeeded in expelling them from the mountains about the Artibonite he had failed against their chief stronghold in the great woods to the southeast about Lake Henriquillo. No sooner had the French arrived at Port-au-Prince than the maroons prepared to take revenge upon their hated enemy, and at the very moment when Dessalines was doubling back upon Port-au-Prince, two strong maroon bands appeared before the town to offer General Lacroix their services. Informed by these valuable allies of Dessalines's approach, Lacroix put them to skilful use. Weak as was the garrison, he marched boldly upon Dessalines's advance guard of a thousand men, set a maroon ambush, and destroyed it at a blow. When on the night of February 26, Dessalines arrived before Port-au-Prince he dared not attack, and soon retreated before the approach of Boudet's returning columns.[16]

Meanwhile, Leclerc had not been inactive. Although Toussaint and his regulars had been driven into the West, the mountainous regions in French hands still swarmed with guerillas, and much hard work was needed to clear these rugged districts of their presence. Furthermore, the news from Port-de-Paix called for instant action. On the same day that Leclerc had begun his advance against Toussaint Louverture, a strong squadron carrying fifteen hundred men had left Le Cap to reënforce Humbert at Port-de-Paix, while other ships had sailed to raise the Môle-Saint-Nicolas. This latter expedition had been a brilliant success: at sight of the French ships the Môle had welcomed them as deliverers, and the whole region had soon thrown off Toussaint's hated yoke.[17] But what happened at Port-de-Paix was very different. The reënforcements landed on the evening of February 19, and that same night Humbert attacked, hoping to take the negroes by surprise. But Maurepas was on the alert and the French were repulsed with heavier losses than before. A German battalion which headed the assault was completely cut to pieces, and Humbert was forced to resume his defensive attitude.

However, Leclerc's occupation of the Cordon de l'Ouest completely changed the situation. If Toussaint had escaped, Maurepas at least was cut off, and his only refuge vanished with the revolt of the Môle-Saint-Nicolas. Leclerc resolved to crush the black general at once, and on February 25 he despatched a strong column to take Port-de-Paix in rear. But Maurepas cleverly avoided annihilation. The news of Toussaint's defeat at Couleuvres had shown Maurepas his hopeless position, and he had at once approached Humbert with offers of surrender. The defeated French general, ignorant of Leclerc's success, granted Maurepas very favorable terms, and Leclerc was, of course, forced to ratify this capitulation. The black general and his officers retained their rank and were taken into French service, together with the two thousand troops under their orders. The eight thousand irregulars were dismissed to their homes. Leclerc was much chagrined at the moment, but afterwards congratulated himself on this event, for Maurepas served him well, while the black soldiers as usual passively followed their chiefs.[18]

The submission of Maurepas opened the way for the final attack on Toussaint's main position in the mountains about the Artibonite. On March 2, Leclerc ordered a general converging movement, and after a fortnight's confused fighting the French columns met under the walls of the Crête-à-Pierrot. Dessalines had especially distinguished himself in this preliminary campaign, and when at last forced to quit the West he left a ghastly trophy of eight hundred white corpses, largely those of women and children, most barbarously massacred. The Crête-à-Pierrot, a fortress of enormous strength, completely blocked the entrance to the valley of the Artibonite. It had been the chief inland stronghold of the English, and Toussaint had still further fortified it until it was almost impregnable. Held by twelve hundred picked troops, the Crête-à-Pierrot was a most formidable obstacle.

Nevertheless, Leclerc knew that it must be taken — and taken in short order as well. For Toussaint was making desperate efforts to raise the siege. Slipping through the French lines, he burst into the North, and at his presence the negroes rose in furious insurrection. The whole Plaine du Nord was ablaze, Le Cap was closely beset, and Leclerc's communications were completely severed. The French position became most critical. Four desperate assaults broke in vain against the bastions of the Crête-à-Pierrot and merely cost the besiegers fifteen hundred men and some of their best officers. But Leclerc was not to be shaken off. With incredible energy, double lines of circumvallation were drawn about the besieged fortress, and Dessalines's ferocious night attacks from the neighboring mountains were repulsed, the while a terrible three days' bombardment wore the defenders down. At last, on the night of the 24th of March, the garrison threw itself upon the French lines and after losing half its strength cut its way through.[19]

The capture of the Crête-à-Pierrot had cost the French two thousand men, but the moral effect was tremendous. "Now," writes the chief-of-staff to the Minister of War, "we have nothing more to do but to clear the colony of brigand bands which dare not face our soldiers and war only by pillage, massacre, and arson. I hope my next despatch will report their entire annihilation."[20] This letter appears unduly optimistic; nevertheless, everything announced the speedy collapse of organized resistance. Leclerc acted with his usual energy. General Lacroix was ordered to overrun the Artibonite while the Captain-General himself turned back to subdue the rebellious North. This was not accomplished without much hard fighting, for Toussaint again appeared in person to animate resistance, but in a week Leclerc cleared the Plaine du Nord and on April 2, entered Le Cap. The very next day the long-delayed Havre-Flushing squadron arrived, and its twenty-five hundred fresh troops placed

THE COMING OF LECLERC

Leclerc in position to deal the final blows at the insurrection.[21]

But the very arrival of reënforcements made these blows apparently superfluous. The fall of the Crête-à-Pierrot had greatly shaken the negroes, and the coming of these new troops completed their demoralization. In a few days Leclerc received emissaries from Christophe offering to submit on promise of pardon and reception into the French service, and when the Captain-General had agreed to these conditions Christophe carried his twelve hundred regular troops over to the French. To the black cause this defection was a crushing blow. On May 1, Dessalines and Toussaint Louverture capitulated on similar terms, and shortly afterward they made their formal submission at Le Cap. Dessalines followed Christophe's example by entering the French service; Toussaint retired to private life on his estates near Gonaives.[22]

General Lacroix has left an interesting account of these events. "Some days before Dessalines's arrival," he writes, "Toussaint Louverture had come to greet Leclerc. His presence aroused great excitement at Le Cap. The inhabitants of that town, like those of the country through which he passed, showed him every outward sign of the most profound respect. He arrived followed by three or four hundred horse-guards, who during his entire interview with Leclerc remained in the courtyard drawn up in battle array with bared sabres."[23] Toussaint's conduct was certainly not marked by humility: he responded coldly to Leclerc's warm greeting and maintained an attitude of proud sadness, as if already repenting of his resolution.[24]

Lacroix's impressions of Dessalines's submission are most striking. "On arriving at Le Cap," he writes, "I had occasion for most serious reflections. I saw several of our general officers pass by in full uniform; — the inhabitants paid them not the least sign of deference. All at once I heard a murmur, — it was General Dessalines! He was coming to salute Leclerc. The whole population rushed forward and prostrated themselves before him. I was more saddened than angered at the sight. These sombre and painful thoughts followed me to headquarters. In Leclerc's antechamber I found Dessalines. My horror of the man kept me at a distance; but he asked who I was, came over to me, and without looking at me said in a raucous voice, 'I am General Dessalines. In unfortunate times I have heard much of you.' [25] His bearing and his manners were savage; I was surprised at his words, which announced more assurance than remorse. This barbarian must have felt himself strong indeed, to have dared adopt this attitude. I could hardly be polite, for the image of the massacres of Verettes and Petite Rivière rose before my eyes at sight of the man who had ordered those scenes of horror." [26]

This defiant attitude of the black generals is the best proof of the necessity for Leclerc's policy of conciliation. Napoleon, it will be remembered, had ordered him to deport Toussaint and the other negro leaders, and then proceed at once to the disarmament of the whole population; instead of which, Leclerc had allowed the black generals to remain in the island and attempted nothing beyond a slight reduction of the negro regiments. But in this matter the Captain-General had no choice. Or-

THE COMING OF LECLERC   323

ganized resistance was, indeed, at an end, but the effort had cost him half his army. Those terrible drives across mountain and jungle had crushed even the veterans of Italy and the Rhine, and on April 1, Leclerc wrote the First Consul that he had but seven thousand European troops with the colors and five thousand in hospital. As up to that moment fully seventeen thousand men had reached San Domingo, another five thousand French soldiers were dead.[27] By that time Leclerc had seven thousand "colonial troops" in his pay, partly made up of mulatto and free negro corps which could be relied upon with reasonable certainty, but in still greater measure composed of the black regiments brought over by Clervaux, Maurepas, and Laplume. The very ease with which these troops had deserted Toussaint showed their blind devotion to their chiefs and made it almost certain that any violence offered these generals would entail the defection of their men. Leclerc's financial position was also bad, for Napoleon apparently thought that a rich island like San Domingo should pay the costs of campaigning in European fashion, whereas no supplies could be obtained except from the English and Americans, who would take nothing but hard money in payment. Also, the commissary department had broken down and supplies from France were either defective or worthless. Again, the reënforcements announced for San Domingo were no longer choice troops, but raw material, for now that the great blow had been struck, Napoleon was evidently not minded to consume his veterans in policing the island through the dreaded rainy season now at hand. Lastly, Leclerc had learned that the English nego-

324 FRENCH REVOLUTION IN SAN DOMINGO

tiations were going ill. All this made it sheer madness to reject the black generals' proffered terms and force them to a guerilla war to the death.[28]

Leclerc's position is well shown by the following letter to the Minister of Marine, written just before Toussaint's offer of submission. "Toussaint still holds the mountains," writes Leclerc. "He has under his orders some four thousand regular troops and a great number of armed cultivators. I cannot finish this war unless I can both conquer and effectively hold the mountains of North and West, and while I am attacking these regions I must continue to occupy those already held, where the cultivators are beginning to stir again. To finish the conquest of San Domingo I need twenty-five thousand men. At this moment I have eleven thousand European troops and seven thousand colonials,[29] in whom I place far from implicit confidence. While I am successful they will stay by me, but a few reverses might serve to double the strength of my enemies. I cannot take those severe measures which can alone assure San Domingo to France until I have twenty-five thousand Europeans with the colors." [30]

Thus the black generals remained and Toussaint lay in haughty aloofness upon his estates near Gonaives, albeit his captured archives convinced Leclerc of the black leader's treason to France. "Out of the multitude of letters in my hands which show Toussaint Louverture's firm intention of independence," writes the Captain-General to Bonaparte, "I send you these few. They are all anterior to our arrival at Le Cap, and clearly prove that had I allowed myself to be duped by his absurd protestations I should have been an imbecile." [31]

THE COMING OF LECLERC 325

The negroes were thus subdued, not broken. Still, all organized resistance was over, and with no necessity for further active campaigning Leclerc hoped to nurse his army through the unhealthy months and build it up for decisive action in the autumn. Never was hope more cruelly deceived. Within a fortnight after Toussaint's submission the French army became aware that in its midst there stood a foe against which skill and courage were in vain.

XXVIII

THE COMING OF THE YELLOW FEVER

It was about mid-May that yellow fever broke out at Le Cap and Port-au-Prince. During the hot months of summer the disease nearly always appeared at San Domingo, and we have seen how severely it had scourged the English invaders in 1794. Nevertheless, up to this moment it had never been greatly feared. Serious as had been the losses of the French forces in San Domingo during the Revolution, they had been caused mainly by malarial fevers and intestinal disorders aggravated by wretched sanitation. The best proof of how slight a toll yellow fever had hitherto exacted is the fact that until this moment not a single high officer or important civilian had fallen a victim to the disease.[1]

But the horror which now smote the doomed army was unparalleled in the whole history of the West Indies. Before the first week of June was out, three thousand men were dead, while the losses among officers and high civilians were proportionately greater than those of the rank and file. The crowded cantonments of Le Cap and Port-au-Prince became vast charnel-houses, and every night long rows of corpses were laid in the barrack-yards waiting for the death-carts to carry them to the lime-pits without the town. The fleet was as hard hit as the army, and the sailors died by hundreds and by thousands.[2]

These first ravages of the yellow fever are vividly described in the Captain-General's melancholy despatches. "If the First Consul wishes to have an army at San Domingo in October," writes Leclerc to the Minister of Marine on the 11th of June, "he must send it from France, for the ravages of this disease are simply indescribable. Our losses in officers and civil functionaries are out of all proportion to those of the troops. Not a day passes but I lose some whom I bitterly regret. My helpers are dying and leaving me to bear alone a burden already insupportable." [3] This was but too true, for Leclerc himself was a sick man. Almost upon arrival he had been attacked by malarial fever, and only his iron will enabled him to surmount the crises of the disease. In this same letter he asserts that he cannot last long and begs for his recall. This desire must have rapidly increased, for a month later things had grown worse. "This disease continues its ravages over the whole colony," writes Leclerc to the Minister of Marine on the 17th Messidor (6th of July). "Prairial cost me three thousand men; Messidor will probably cost me more still. At present I lose one hundred and sixty men a day." [4]

This terrible visitation had not long continued before a change became apparent in the attitude of Toussaint Louverture. His conduct had been suspicious from the first, for, though ostensibly retired to private life, his two thousand chosen life-guards had all renounced military service and had settled about their general; — technically peaceful cultivators, patently the possible focus of a new insurrection. Toussaint watched the fever's ravages with ill-disguised glee. Soon even generals like Christophe and Dessalines were warning Leclerc of his intentions, and presently intercepted letters transformed suspicion into practical certainty.[5]

What followed is well told by Leclerc. "My position grows worse from day to day," he writes Napoleon on the 6th of June. "Disease takes my men. Toussaint Louverture is playing false—just as I expected. However, I have gained from his submission what I had intended — the winning over of Dessalines and Christophe with their troops. I have just ordered his arrest, and I think I can count on Dessalines (whose spirit I have mastered) to hunt him down if he escapes. At the same time, do not be astonished if I fail. For the last two weeks this man has been very suspicious: not that I have given him cause, but the fact is, he regrets his former power, and these regrets have engendered the idea of re-forming his party."[6]

However, Leclerc's plans had been well laid, and a clever ruse lured Toussaint within the French lines, where he was at once arrested and embarked for France.[7] Leclerc's reflections on the event are contained in the following letter, written on the 11th of June to the Minister of Marine: "In one of my last despatches I told you of the pardon granted General Toussaint. This ambitious man, however, from that very moment never ceased to conspire in secret. He surrendered only because Generals Christophe and Dessalines told him that they saw he had deceived them and that they were resolved no longer to make war upon us. But no sooner had he seen himself thus abandoned than he sought to organize a great insurrection among the cultivators. The reports which came to me even from Dessalines on Toussaint's

THE COMING OF THE YELLOW FEVER   329

conduct since his submission left no doubt on this point. I intercepted letters written to his agent at Le Cap which proved that he was trying to regain his former influence. Under such circumstances I could not allow him time to carry out his criminal projects. I ordered his arrest. The thing was not easy, but it is done. I am now sending to France with all his family this man so dangerous to San Domingo. Citizen Minister, the Government must put him in some fortress in the centre of France, so that by no possibility can he escape and return to San Domingo, where he has the power of a religious leader. For if, three years from now, this man were to reappear at San Domingo, he might well destroy everything that France had done." [8] And on the same day Leclerc wrote Napoleon, "Toussaint Louverture must not be at liberty. Imprison him far within the Republic, that he may never see San Domingo again." [9] The fear of Toussaint's escape seemed to haunt Leclerc, for a month later he wrote the Minister of Marine, "You cannot keep Toussaint at too great a distance from the sea nor in a place too sure. The man has fanaticised this country to such a degree that his appearance would set everything once more aflame." [10]

However, no general outbreak followed Toussaint's deportation. Leclerc's strong precautions worked well; and the few partial risings were at once stamped out. The black generals were not wholly averse to their late master's downfall, and the colonial troops obeyed orders.[11] After Leclerc's vigorous despatches, Toussaint's fate was easy to foresee. Upon his arrival in France he was sent to Fort de Joux, a post in the heart of the Jura near the Swiss frontier. The winter chill of this bleak region was fatal to the aged negro, who presently developed consumption and died on April 7, 1803.[12] Thus the great black vanished from the scene. Judged by white standards Toussaint is in many ways a sinister and repulsive figure; yet he should be measured, not with Europeans, but with the great men of his own race — with the Zulu Chaka and with Macandal.

Toussaint's arrest had caused no overt rebellion, it is true, but Leclerc knew that the negro population was greatly excited and that the slightest shock to his moral prestige might produce a general explosion which would sweep away the poor remnants of his dying army. He also realized that the materials for such an explosion would be always ready to hand while the negro population kept possession of the arms served out by Toussaint Louverture. Hence, although he well knew the desperate risks involved, Leclerc resolved upon the general disarmament of the negroes. This was to be primarily effected by the black generals and their troops, and was to be done by provinces — Laplume in the South, Dessalines in the West, Christophe and Maurepas in the North. Since the North Province was the danger-point, Leclerc ordered it left alone until the disarmament of the other provinces was complete.

The work began about the third week of June. In the South all went smoothly, and Laplume soon reported that within his jurisdiction nothing more was to be feared. In the West there was considerable trouble, but Dessalines showed the same ferocious pleasure in carrying out Leclerc's orders that he had in executing Toussaint's

THE COMING OF THE YELLOW FEVER 331

commands, and broke resistance with barbarous cruelty. Leclerc's report of July 6 is full of confidence. "The black generals," he writes, "now see clearly that I am destroying their influence in this country. Nevertheless, they dare not rebel: (1) because they detest each other and know that I should use them for their mutual destruction; (2) because the negroes are not brave and have been terrified by the war I have waged upon them; (3) because they fear to measure themselves against the man who has broken their chiefs. Under these circumstances I march with rapid strides toward my goal. The South and West are about disarmed; the North will be taken in hand next week. The *gendarmerie* is being organized, and as soon as the *gendarmerie* is in working order and the disarmament is complete I shall strike the final blows. If I succeed, as now seems probable, San Domingo will be truly restored to the Republic." [13]

The North, it is true, proved no easy task. Trouble had begun at the mere news of the disarmament of the South and West, and the first active measures provoked serious risings in several quarters. Leclerc's difficulties in handling the situation are revealed by his correspondence. "Another of these insurrections has broken out at Port-de-Paix," he writes the Minister of Marine on the 22d of July. "It is impossible to send the European troops — they drop on the road. Of colonial troops I have but few; I have been obliged to dismiss many, since I dare not keep them in great number." [14] Still, these risings were only sporadic, Christophe and Maurepas acted loyally, and Leclerc did not doubt his ultimate success.

But at this very moment there arrived news from

France and Guadeloupe which plunged the Captain-General into absolute despair. In Leclerc's instructions Napoleon had expressed his firm resolve not to restore slavery, and had specified the status of Guadeloupe as the future basis for San Domingo.[15] But in the ensuing months the First Consul's attitude had changed. Décrès, the new Minister of Marine, was a strong believer in the restoration of the old colonial system, and his arguments, backed by the appeals of French commerce and the planter exiles, slowly converted Bonaparte. The results of this conversion were soon apparent. On May 20, the French Government announced that no change would take place in the social status of the colonies restored by England; that slavery and the color line should there remain unaltered. And the Home Government soon took a still more serious step. In early June the slave-trade was formally restored for all the French colonies, and it was specifically stated that these new arrivals from Africa were to be genuine chattel slaves even in islands whose present black inhabitants then enjoyed personal freedom. A few weeks later further legislation deprived the mulattoes of their equal rights, restored the color line, and prohibited mixed marriages.[16] About mid-July, just after the disarmament of the North had begun, Leclerc received an authorization to restore slavery in San Domingo whenever he saw fit.

This startling proof of Napoleon's new policy filled Leclerc with terror. Already the negroes were restive under the reports of the pro-slavery agitation in France and the intemperate language of returning planters, while at this very moment the news of the reëstablished

THE COMING OF THE YELLOW FEVER 333

slave-trade sent a wave of sullen fury over the whole colony. To restore slavery while the French army was wasting to a shadow was sheer madness, and Leclerc hastily penned letters beseeching against any such action. "Do not think of establishing slavery here for some time," he wrote the Minister of Marine on the 24th of July; "I believe I can so fix things that my successor will have nothing to do except execute the Government's orders. But after my numberless proclamations assuring the negroes their liberty, I cannot so stultify myself." [17]

Whether Leclerc's tact and prestige would have blinded the negroes to Napoleon's ultimate intentions is impossible to say, for in the last days of July the news from Guadeloupe made further denial impossible. At the beginning of April, Napoleon had sent a certain General Richepanse and four thousand men to reduce that island to obedience. The troubles following the recall of Victor Hugues in 1799 had broken French authority in the island and had ended in mulatto supremacy. This régime Napoleon resolved to destroy, and Richepanse's instructions were even more vigorous than Leclerc's had been. Sweeping as were these directions, however, they had been carried out to the letter. Guadeloupe was so much smaller than San Domingo that the young and vigorous General Richepanse had succeeded in effecting its complete subjection after a few weeks' sharp campaign, and the Napoleonic "third period" had thereafter been put in force at once. The whole population was winnowed like wheat, and three thousand persons were deported. Napoleon's idea proved a sound one, for the loss of all its natural leaders broke the spirit of the colored population, and Guadeloupe gave no further trouble. The entire subjection of the island was so perfectly clear that when Richepanse received Bonaparte's permission to restore slavery he hastened to carry it into effect, and in mid-July the old colonial system was formally restored.[18]

But the reckless and short-sighted Richepanse had given no thought to San Domingo. The news from Guadeloupe quickly reached the greater island — and suspicion became certainty. The effect was terrible. The fanatic North burst into flame, and most of the West followed its example. Even the black soldiers began to desert their generals and go over to the insurgents. The yellow fever continued to rage, and Leclerc's reënforcements vanished almost as quickly as they came. The army of San Domingo entered upon its death-agony.

"My position is in no way bettered," writes Leclerc on August 6 to the Minister of Marine; "the rebellion grows, the disease continues. It will last till the 1st Vendémiaire [23d September]. All the negroes here are convinced by the news from France, by the reëstablishment of the Trade, and by General Richepanse's restoration of slavery at Guadeloupe, that we are about to reduce them to servitude. I can no longer obtain disarmament except after long and obstinate resistance. These men will not surrender. I must confess it: at the very moment of success, those political circumstances above mentioned have almost destroyed my work. You must no longer count upon the moral force I used to have here; it is destroyed. Those measures taken elsewhere have infuriated men's minds. I can reduce the negroes only by force — and for this I must have an army and money." [19]

THE COMING OF THE YELLOW FEVER 335

The most alarming thing about this new insurrection was that it came from below. The black generals had been little affected by the news from Guadeloupe. Leclerc had profited by Toussaint's example, and the negro leaders, sure of their personal safety and loaded with wealth and power, gave no signs of changing sides. Only one black general, Charles Belair, joined the Western insurgents,[20] and his fate merely proved Leclerc's hold upon his fellows, for Dessalines hunted him down, shot him offhand and massacred his soldiers. But if the black generals stood by the French, their lesser officers did not, and it was these hundreds of unknown chiefs who now led over the colonial troops and roused the cultivators to rebellion. "To have been rid of Toussaint is not enough," writes Leclerc on August 25; "there are two thousand more leaders to get rid of as well." [21]

Leclerc's desperate situation is best shown by his report of August 6 to Bonaparte: —

"My position grows trying and may well become worse. Here it is: disease had made such frightful ravages among my troops that when I wished to disarm the negroes an insurrection broke out. . . . Our first attacks drove the insurgents, but they scattered into other cantons. In the present insurrection there is a veritable fanaticism. These men may be killed, but will not surrender. They laugh at death; — and it is the same with the women. I begged you, Citizen Consul, to do nothing to make these people fear for their liberty till the moment when I should be prepared. Suddenly there came the law authorizing the Trade, and on top of that General Richepanse has just decreed the restoration of slavery in

Guadeloupe. With this state of things, Citizen Consul, the moral force I had here acquired is destroyed. I can do nothing more by persuasion; I can only use force, — and force I have none.

"At present, Citizen Consul, now that your colonial plans are perfectly well known, if you wish to preserve San Domingo send a new army, — and especially send money. I declare positively that if you abandon us to ourselves as you have so far done, this colony is lost; — and, once lost, you will never get it back again.

"My letter may surprise you, Citizen Consul, after what I had before written you, but was there ever a general obliged to calculate on the death of four fifths of his army and the uselessness of the rest through lack of money, as I have to do in a country where nothing can be bought save for hard cash and where a little money would have allayed much discontent? Ought I, under these circumstances, to have expected the law on the slave-trade and the decrees of General Richepanse?

"I have explained my position with a soldier's frankness. In bitter sorrow, I see all that I have so far done on the verge of annihilation. Citizen Consul, if you could but have seen the difficulties of all sorts that I had conquered and the results I had obtained, you would tremble with me at sight of my position to-day. Nevertheless, unpleasant as it is, I still hope to succeed. I am making terrible examples; and since terror alone remains, terror I employ.

"But all the planters and merchants arriving from France speak of nothing but slaves. It seems as though

THE COMING OF THE YELLOW FEVER 337

there was a general conspiracy to prevent San Domingo's restoration to the Republic."

Leclerc ends with an appeal for money: "Sacrifice six million francs at this time, Citizen Consul, that you may not have to spend sixty millions in the spring." [22]

August passed, September came; — and the fever still raged on. The colonists all assured Leclerc that with the autumn equinox the disease would rapidly abate and that a fortnight later it would have entirely disappeared. However, on the 13th of September, with the equinox only a week away, there were no signs of a change. The reënforcements which now arrived (mostly North Europeans) stood the climate very badly: these masses of Germans, Dutchmen, Belgians, and Poles, died even faster than the French.

"The moment troops arrive," writes Leclerc, "I have to throw them into the field to repress that general insurrection discussed in my last despatches. For the first few days these troops act with vigor and gain successes; — then the disease smites them, and all my reënforcements are annihilated. People assure me of a certain change of season by the 15th Vendémiaire [7th October], but I greatly fear that by that time I shall have no soldiers.

"I can give you no exact idea of my position: each day it grows worse, and what will most retard the colony's prosperity is the fact that when the disease ceases I shall have no men for aggressive action. If on the 15th Vendémiaire I have four thousand Europeans fit to march, even counting those now on the sea, I shall be glad, indeed. All my corps commanders save two are dead, and I have no fit persons to replace them. To give you an idea of my losses, know that the 7th of the Line came here 1395 strong: to-day there are 83 half-sick men with the colors and 107 in hospital; the rest are dead. The 11th Light Infantry landed here 1900 strong: to-day it has 163 fit for duty and 200 in hospital. The 71st of the Line, originally 1000 strong, has 17 men with the colors and 133 in hospital. And it is the same with the rest of the army. Thus, form your own idea of my position in a country where civil war has raged for ten years and where the rebels are convinced that we intend to reduce them to slavery.

"Citizen Minister, if the French Government wishes to preserve San Domingo it must, on the very day that it receives this letter, order the departure of ten thousand men. They will arrive in Nivôse [January, 1803], and order will be entirely restored before the next hot season: although, if this disease habitually lasts three months on end at San Domingo, we must renounce this colony." [23]

Three days after this despatch a letter to Napoleon announced the abandonment of much of the hinterland and such loss of prestige that one or two of the black generals were beginning to waver, albeit the majority were still loyal.

"My position," writes Leclerc, "is desperate.... The main cause of my present plight is the reëstablishment of slavery in Guadeloupe. As soon as this news arrived, the insurrection, hitherto only partial, became general, and since I was unable to face it everywhere, I have been obliged to abandon many points. The arrival of considerable reënforcements helped me over the first

THE COMING OF THE YELLOW FEVER 339

crisis, but was no lasting benefit, for after twelve days' campaign these corps were annihilated and the insurrection made new progress through the lack of means to crush it. In these last days the force and boldness of the rebels are such that I have been obliged strictly to cover Le Cap. . . . The negro troops are entirely untrustworthy. Recently a whole battalion killed its white officers and deserted — for this struggle is now strictly a war of color.

"Here is the state of my black generals. Maurepas is a dangerous rascal, but I dare not arrest him at this moment, since this would surely entail the defection of all his troops. Christophe has so maltreated the negroes that he is hated by them, and is therefore not to be feared. Dessalines is at present the butcher of the negroes; it is through him that I execute all my odious measures. I shall keep him as long as I need him. He has already begged me not to leave him at San Domingo when I return home. Laplume, Clervaux, and Paul Louverture are three imbeciles whom I shall get rid of at will. Charles Belair has been tried and shot.

"Next month I hope to have eight thousand men — four thousand white troops, two thousand gendarmes, two thousand negro soldiers. But these forces will not suffice to hold the country, and the longer I put off its submission the harder that submission will be.

"Yes, Citizen Consul, such is my position. I have not exaggerated. Each day I have to rack my brains to know how I may repair the ills of the day before. Not one consoling thought to efface or diminish the cruel impressions of the present or the future. The preservation of San

Domingo since the embarkation of Toussaint Louverture is something more extraordinary than my landing and my capture of that general. If I did not know how much you have the success of this expedition at heart, I should believe myself sacrificed. . . .

"Citizen Consul, I must have ten thousand men at once. I must have them to assure you San Domingo. The disease has put us far back, and the longer you delay, the more men you will have to send to remedy the situation."

The fever was raging worse than ever; it was killing from 100 to 120 men per day.[24] The losses to date could be estimated from the following figures: original expedition, 20,000; later reënforcements, 6500; marine artillery, 1500; total, 28,000. Of these Leclerc expected that next month there would be 10,500 alive; but of these only 4500 fit for duty, while 1500 would be convalescent and 4500 in hospital. Also, 5000 sailors had died. "Thus," continues Leclerc, "the occupation of San Domingo has so far cost us 29,000 men, — and as yet we are far from being its masters." He ends by a detailed report on the serious state of his own health and urges Napoleon to send out his successor, for "the situation is such that San Domingo should not be a moment without a head, — and there is no one here to fill my place. Rochambeau, a brave soldier and a good fighter, has not an ounce of tact or policy. Furthermore, he has no moral character and is easily led." [25]

The longed-for 1st Vendémiaire came at last: that Republican New Year's Day or autumn equinox which the colonists had told Leclerc was the date for the abatement of yellow fever. But this particular visitation seemed as unparalleled in its duration as in its virulent intensity, for the fever still raged on. The thin French lines shrunk rapidly toward the coast and the black generals became more doubtful in their attitude.

"My position grows worse from day to day," writes Leclerc to Napoleon on the 4th Vendémiaire, "and the most terrible thing about the situation is that I cannot tell you when or how it will improve. I thought that the ravages of the disease would slacken with Vendémiaire. I was mistaken; it has taken on new virulence. Fructidor [September] has cost me more than four thousand dead, and to-day people tell me that it may last till the end of Brumaire [21st November]. If this be true and its intensity continue, the colony is lost.

"Each day the insurgent forces increase, while mine diminish by loss of whites and desertions of the blacks. Dessalines, who up to this time has not thought of rebellion, thinks so to-day. A month ago he was destroying captured arms; to-day he no longer destroys them, and he no longer maltreats the negroes as he did then. He is a scoundrel. I know him; but I dare not arrest him: I should alarm all the negroes who are still with me. Christophe inspires more confidence. Maurepas is a rascal, but I cannot yet order his arrest.

"Never was general in a more dreadful situation. The troops arrived a month ago no longer exist. Each day the rebels attack, and the firing can be heard in Le Cap. I cannot take the offensive, — it crushes my troops; and even should I attack, I could not follow up the victories I might gain. I repeat what I have said before: San Domingo is lost to France if by the end of Nivôse [January 20, 1803] I do not receive ten thousand men in a body. The partial reënforcements you send me might feed the army in ordinary times, but they can never reconquer San Domingo." [26]

Next day the Captain-General wrote in still more emphatic terms: "You will never subdue San Domingo without an army of twelve thousand acclimated troops besides the *gendarmerie;* — and you will not have this army until you have sent seventy thousand men to San Domingo." [27]

When the 15th Vendémiaire (7th October) had passed with no sign of the usual cessation of the fever, Leclerc wrote the following despairing letter: "Here is my opinion on this country. We must destroy all the mountain negroes, men and women, sparing only children under twelve years of age. We must destroy half the negroes of the plains, and not allow in the colony a single man who has worn an epaulette. Without these measures the colony will never be at peace, and every year, especially deadly ones like this, you will have a civil war on your hands which will jeopardize the future." Leclerc then sketches out what must be done. Let Napoleon send twelve thousand men at once, six hundred men per month through the next hot season, then another fifteen thousand the following autumn, and the thing will be done by the spring of 1804.[28]

This letter was Leclerc's last will and testament. He had written it in the flush of a new malarial crisis which prostrated him for some time, and scarcely had he shown signs of recovery when the first symptoms of yellow fever appeared. For eleven days his iron will battled with the disease, but on the morning of the 2d of November the French army learned that its general was dead.[29] Leclerc has been much blamed for the French failure in San Domingo, but when, in the light of all the attendant circumstances, we picture the Captain-General dragging himself from his bed in the flush of fever or the shiver of ague-chill to pen his luminous despatches, we must agree with Roloff that it is a wonder he did so well.[30]

XXIX

THE LAST PHASE

LECLERC's last days were tortured by new misfortunes. On October 10, the mulatto general, Clervaux, suddenly revolted and carried with him all his troops. This spectacular desertion was another result of the reactionary legislation in France and Richepanse's measures in Guadeloupe. In July, Napoleon had formally reëstablished all the mulatto discriminations of the Old Régime,[1] while at about the same time Richepanse had restored the color line for Guadeloupe and its dependencies. This enraged the mulattoes of San Domingo as much as the restoration of slavery had infuriated the negroes, and since caste feeling was much stronger among the colored people than among the blacks, the mulatto leaders soon initiated decisive action.

Their plans had been so quietly laid that this mulatto defection took the French army by surprise and exposed it to the danger of absolute destruction. Up to this time the colored people had been the negroes' most savage opponents, and Clervaux's mulatto troops had made up the greater part of the garrison of Le Cap itself. For the moment the city was defended by only a few hundred French troops and the white National Guard numbering one thousand infantry and two hundred horse. All this was well known to Clervaux, and two days after his desertion he made a bold attempt to storm Le Cap by a sudden

assault. Backed by fully ten thousand negro rebels his
mulatto troops flung themselves upon the city lines, but
the whites defended themselves with superb courage and
forced the baffled Clervaux to draw off with great loss.[2]

Le Cap was saved, but the mulatto revolt decided the
black generals' attitude. On the following day Christophe
joined Clervaux, the other black commanders in the
North quickly followed his example, and when the news
reached Dessalines he summoned the West to revolt
against white rule.[3] Leclerc's death greatly encouraged
the insurgents, and by mid-November the French held
only Le Cap and the Môle in the North, and the coast
towns of the West. However, the faithful Laplume still
kept the South intact, while Spanish Santo Domingo
vigorously rejected the idea of any coöperation with the
rebel negroes and mulattoes of the French colony.[4]

Indeed, before the month of November was out, the
French cause began to improve. Napoleon had in no way
relaxed his determination for the conquest of San Domingo, but the unprecedented ravages of the yellow fever
had completely upset his plans, while the disorganization of the navy and colonial administration had greatly
hampered his efforts to remedy the situation. Nevertheless, by early autumn these efforts had begun to bear
fruit, and a new system of colonial *dépôts* in the French
ports enabled the First Consul to equip some ten thousand fresh troops for service in San Domingo.[5] Furthermore, in the island itself the convalescents were beginning
to rejoin the colors, and since these men were immune
to yellow fever they formed a growing nucleus of acclimated troops. It is true that the disease continued into

January and swept away many of Napoleon's reënforcements, but the French army steadily gained in strength and soon enabled the new Governor-General, Rochambeau, to take offensive measures. Fort Dauphin was recaptured in December, Port-de-Paix in January, 1803, and much of the hinterland in both North and West was recovered. The chief set-back was in the South. The mulatto element there had been greatly strengthened by the return of all those exiled on the fall of Rigaud, and in mid-January the colored population had made common cause with the disaffected negro element by a revolt against the faithful Laplume. The black general still held many of his people loyal to the French, but he was slowly driven back on Les Cayes. Still, by the beginning of March, Rochambeau had over eleven thousand French troops with the colors, and as only four thousand men lay in hospital it was plain that disease had done its worst by the French army.[6]

Frankly a war of race, the struggle which now ensued acquired a most ferocious character. We have seen that Leclerc's last despatch to Bonaparte had advised a war of extermination,[7] and this opinion was generally shared by both the army and the civilian population. "Almost all the negroes in the *gendarmerie* have deserted bag and baggage to the enemy," writes a white colonist to a lady in France, "and the same thing is true of the black troops. After such examples how can we trust those negroes who appear to desire submission? So long as there remains at San Domingo any considerable body of negroes who for twelve years have made war, the colony will never be reëstablished. The negro who has been a soldier will never again become a cultivator; he prefers death to work. He who has once worn an epaulette holds it dearer than life; he will commit every crime to retain it. If France wishes to regain San Domingo she must send hither twenty-five thousand men in a body, declare the negroes slaves, and destroy at least thirty thousand negroes and negresses — the latter being more cruel than the men. These measures are frightful, but necessary. We must take them or renounce the colony. Whoever says otherwise lies in his throat and deceives France." [8]

Rochambeau fully agreed with these sentiments, and his ruthless energy was eminently suited to the task. Through March and April, 1803, the rebels were steadily rooted out of the open country and forced into the mountains, even man-hunting dogs being imported from Cuba to fill the gaps in the ranks of the French army. The growing peril forced the insubordinate negro bands to yield stricter allegiance to Dessalines, but even so Rochambeau's ultimate triumph grew clearer with every day. Napoleon was equipping fifteen thousand fresh troops to maintain the army during the coming summer, and he had planned another fifteen thousand for the decisive blow in the autumn.[9] But already a shadow lay athwart the path of Rochambeau's success. During these same months Napoleon's negotiations with Great Britain grew more and more hopeless, and on May 12 the short and hollow Peace of Amiens gave place to a new English war.[10]

The English war sounded the death-knell of white San Domingo. A year later the island would probably have been crushed; but as it was, the half-finished work was soon entirely undone. In the last days of June a strict blockade cut off San Domingo from the world and stopped the stream of men and money which fed the French army. The English at once aided the rebels, the flame of insurrection burst forth with new energy, and the hinterland was lost once more. This was a fatal blow. The English blockade stopped all intercommunication by sea, and the scattered garrisons of the coast towns were crushed in turn by Dessalines's overwhelming forces. Early in October the fall of Les Cayes announced the loss of the South; before the end of that month the evacuation of Port - au - Prince heralded the end of French resistance in the West; and on November 10, 1803, Rochambeau sailed out of the harbor of Le Cap to give his sword to the waiting English admiral. On the 28th of November, the evacuation of the Môle-Saint-Nicolas gave the death-stroke to French San Domingo.[11] Napoleon's great effort had ended in complete disaster. Of the fifty thousand soldiers sent thither during those short two years, only a few thousand ever saw France again — and these after years of English captivity; while the ten thousand sailors dead of yellow fever were to be sorely missed on the day of Trafalgar.[12] Only in Spanish Santo Domingo was the French flag still kept flying by a tiny corps of European troops.[13]

And the destruction of French authority was but the prelude to the complete extermination of the white race in "la Partie française de Saint-Domingue." At the moment of the French evacuation Dessalines was the acknowledged war-chief of all the black armies, but with

THE LAST PHASE 349

the removal of external pressure his position became a most critical one. In December, 1803, he formally proclaimed the island's independence, reviving the Indian name of "Haiti" to mark the complete break with its colonial past. The succeeding year saw a fierce struggle with the other black and mulatto chiefs, but in the end Dessalines triumphed over all his enemies, and in October, 1804, he set the seal upon his victory by crowning himself emperor.[14]

The time was now ripe for the final blow. When the French troops had left the country in November, 1803, Dessalines had promised protection to all white civilians who chose to remain, and shortly afterwards a proclamation had invited all white exiles to return. The favorable treatment accorded those who remained after the departure of Rochambeau induced a considerable number of colonial whites to return to San Domingo. But no sooner was the black leader firmly seated on his imperial throne than these unfortunates discovered their mistake in trusting the word of Dessalines. Scarcely had the new year begun when orders went forth to massacre the white population, and on April 25, 1805, a ferocious proclamation set the seal on this awful proscription and laid down that doctrine of white exclusion ever since retained as the cardinal point of Haitian policy.[15]

The nature of these events is well shown by the letter of a French officer secretly in Port-au-Prince at the time, who himself escaped by a miracle to the lesser evil of an English prison in Jamaica. "The murder of the whites in detail," he writes, "began at Port-au-Prince in the first days of January, but on the 17th and 18th March they were finished off *en masse*. All, without exception, have been massacred, down to the very women and children. Madame de Boynes was killed in a peculiarly horrible manner. A young mulatto named Fifi Pariset ranged the town like a madman searching the houses to kill the little children. Many of the men and women were hewn down by sappers, who hacked off their arms and smashed in their chests. Some were poniarded, others mutilated, others 'passed on the bayonet,'[16] others disembowelled with knives or sabres, still others stuck like pigs. At the beginning, a great number were drowned. The same general massacre has taken place all over the colony, and as I write you these lines I believe that there are not twenty whites still alive — and these not for long." [17]

This estimate was, indeed, scarcely exaggerated. The white race had perished utterly out of the land, French San Domingo had vanished forever, and the black State of Haiti had begun its troubled history.

THE END

NOTES

NOTES

CHAPTER I

1. Moreau de Saint-Méry, "Déscription de la Partie Française de l'Isle Saint-Domingue" (2 vols.; Philadelphia, 1797), I, 295.
2. "Morne," the Creole word for "mountain."
3. Moreau de Saint-Méry, I, 295–509. An extraordinarily detailed description.
4. *Ibid.*, I, 103–06.
5. The standard work for the early period is that of the learned Jesuit Charlevoix, "Histoire de l'Isle Espagnole ou de Saint-Domingue." (Amsterdam, 1733, 4 vols.)
6. The standard works on the buccaneers are, besides Charlevoix: Du Tertre (1667–71); Le Pers (MSS., Bibliothèque Nationale, "Fr. 8992"); Labat (1742); Oexmelin (Dutch writer, 1674); Archenholz (1804).
7. Moreau de Saint-Méry, I, 7.
8. From their manner of curing the beef and hides.
9. Vaissière, "Saint-Domingue (1629–1789): La Société et la Vie Créole sous l'Ancien Régime" (Paris, 1909), 13; Levasseur, "Histoire du Commerce de la France" (Paris, 1911), I, 284.
10. Vaissière, 7–11. (He has cleared up this obscure period by his original researches in the English "Calendar of State Papers.")
11. *Ibid.*, 16–17.
12. Anno 1697.
13. The Peace of Utrecht.
14. Vaissière, 25; Levasseur, I, 391–93.
15. Vaissière, 18–24.
16. Levasseur, I, 484–85.
17. Peytraud, "L'Esclavage aux Antilles Françaises avant 1789," 151.
18. Vaissière, 55.
19. *Ibid.*, 56.
20. Speech to the Tiers État by the San Domingo deputy Gouy d'Arcy, at the taking of the Oath of the Tennis-Court, June 20, 1789; "Réquête Présentée aux États Généraux, le 8 Juin, 1789, par les députés de l'Isle de Saint-Domingue" (pamphlet); several other instances to the same effect but with slightly different language.
21. Speech of the San Domingo deputy Cocherel in the National Assembly, November 26, 1789; "Mémoire instructif adressé aux Notables par les Commissaires de Saint-Domingue" (pamphlet,

anno 1787, pp. 5–7); "Opinion de Blin sur la proposition d'un comité coloniale" (pamphlet, November, 1789); other language to the same effect.

CHAPTER II

1. The standard authority on Spanish San Domingo is Moreau de Saint-Méry, "Déscription de la Partie Espagnole de l'Isle Saint-Domingue." (1789.)
2. Roloff, "Die Kolonialpolitik Napoleons I" (Munich, 1899), 37.
3. For description, see *ante*, pp. 1–2.
4. Moreau de Saint-Méry, I, 103–06; Garran-Coulon, "Rapport sur les Troubles de Saint-Domingue, fait au nom de la Commission des Colonies, des Comités de Salut Public, de Législation, et de la Marine, réunis" (official publication; 4 vols.; Paris, Year VI–1798), I, 33–34.
5. Moreau de Saint-Méry, I, 506; II, 6–13; Garran-Coulon, I, 35.
6. Moreau de Saint-Méry, II, 320–406; De Wimpffen, "A Voyage to Saint-Domingo in the Years 1788, 1789 and 1790" (London, 1797; trans.), 206–07.
7. Moreau de Saint-Méry, II, 532–35.
8. Garran-Coulon, I, 36.
9. Vaissière, 153. (MSS. data in the Archives des Colonies.)
10. Sciout, "La Révolution à Saint-Domingue: Les Commissaires Sonthonax et Polverel" (Revue des Questions Historiques, October, 1898), 400.
11. Moreau de Saint-Méry, I, 106; II, 13; II, 533.
12. Girod-Chantrans, "Voyage d'un Suisse dans les différentes Colonies de l'Amérique" (Neufchatel, 1785), 219.
13. Vaissière, 279–80; Du Buisson, "Nouvelles Considérations sur Saint-Domingue" (2 vols.; Paris, 1780), II, 9.
14. Hilliard d'Auberteuil, "Considérations sur l'état présent de la Colonie Française de Saint-Domingue" (2 vols.; Paris, 1776), II, 19–24.
15. See bibliographical note on Hilliard d'Auberteuil.
16. Du Buisson, II, 8–9.
17. Vaissière, 278–79.
18. Mills, "The Early Years of the French Revolution in San Domingo" (Ph.D. thesis, Cornell Univ., 1889), 21.
19. *Ibid.*, 22; Roloff, 6.
20. Hilliard d'Auberteuil, II, 11–13. Raynal, "Essai sur l'Administration de la Colonie de Saint-Domingue" (?: 1785), 145–46; Boissonnade, "Saint-Domingue à la Veille de la Révolution et la Question de la Représentation Coloniale aux États Généraux" (Paris, 1906), 7.

NOTES

21. Vaissière, 131.
22. Boissonnade, 6; Roloff, 6–7; Mills, 22.
23. Mills, 23; also, Roloff, 7.
24. Roloff, 7; Mills, 22–23; Hilliard d'Auberteuil, II, 2–18; Raynal, 145–147.
25. Boissonnade, 6–7.
26. Hilliard d'Auberteuil, II, 17.
27. *Ibid.*, II, 2–18; Raynal, 145–46; Roloff, 7.
28. Vaissière, 108–14.
29. *Ibid.*, 131–52.
30. Déschamps, "Les Colonies pendant la Révolution: la Constituante et la Réforme Coloniale" (Paris, 1898), 11–13.
31. Vaissière, 115.
32. Venault de Charmilly, "Lettre à Bryan Edwards" (London, 1797), pamphlet.
33. Déschamps, 8–10.
34. Raynal, 223.
35. Déschamps, 300 bis. (Appendix.)
36. De Wimpffen, 69–73.
37. Déschamps, 10–11.
38. De Wimpffen, 211–12.
39. Vaissière, 89–92.
40. Boissonnade, 7.
41. Roloff, 9; Mills, 14; Hilliard d'Auberteuil, I, 35–36.
42. Boissonnade, 7.
43. For a full discussion of these proposed reforms, see Daubigny: "Choiseul et la France d'Outremer après 1763." (Paris, 1892.)
44. Mills, 25.
45. Carteau, "Soirées Bermudiennes" (Bordeaux, 1802), 25–26.
46. Vaissière, 85.
47. *Ibid.*, 86–87.
48. Raynal, 177.
49. *Ibid.*, 171–72.
50. *Ibid.*, 177.
51. Vaissière, 112–14.
52. De Wimpffen, 78.
53. Mills, 9.
54. *Ibid.*
55. Leroy-Beaulieu, "De la Colonisation chez les Peuples Modernes" (4th ed.; Paris, 1891), 163–64.
56. Peytraud, 448–50; Leroy-Beaulieu, 164.
57. Moreau de Saint-Méry, I, 100.
58. Déschamps, 4.
59. Moreau de Saint-Méry, I, 100.
60. Déschamps, 5. (Official Report of August, 1791.)

61. The figures for San Domingo are doubtful. Leroy-Beaulieu's 193 millions (p. 167) is far too high. The nearest figure is probably Mills's 176 millions (p. 11), though his authority is doubtful. Even this figure seems slightly high from other evidence; see Treille, 24–25; Boissonnade, 19.
62. Boissonnade, 19; Déschamps, 5–7; Mills, 12.
63. Boissonnade, 20.
64. Déschamps, 19–20; Boissonnade, 21.
65. Déschamps, 7; 19–20; Boissonnade, 21.
66. The best discussion is that of Normand, "Le Pacte Coloniale" (Doctor's thesis, Faculté de Droit, Paris, 1900). See also treatment in Leroy-Beaulieu. Both are based upon the leading economic writers.
67. Normand, 23.
68. Déschamps, 21.
69. Peytraud, 452–53.
70. Normand, 49.
71. Déschamps, 21–22; Roloff, 5.
72. Peytraud, 76; Levasseur, 489.
73. De Wimpffen, 72–77; 85–87; 276–77.
74. Roloff, 5; Mills, 12.
75. Mills, 12.
76. *Ibid.*, 12–13; Roloff, 5; Levasseur, 489.
77. Levasseur, 489.
78. *Ibid.*, 489; Normand, 148.
79. Normand, 148–49; Mills, 13; Roloff, 5–6; Levasseur, 489.
80. Déschamps, 29–37.
81. Boissonnade, 24.
82. *Ibid.*, 17.

CHAPTER III

1. As already seen, not over forty thousand. This figure does not, however, include the garrison troops nor the sailors of the royal or merchant marine in the ports of the colony. These will be considered later.
2. Leroy-Beaulieu, 159.
3. Although loose usage has since obscured its true meaning, the term "Creole" has to do, not with race, but with birthplace. "Creole" means "one born in the colonies." In the eighteenth century, this was perfectly clear. Whites were "Creole" or "European"; negroes were "Creole" or "African."
4. De Wimpffen, 65.
5. Hilliard d'Auberteuil, II, 33–35; 42–43; Moreau de Saint-Méry, I, 9–11.

NOTES 357

6. Hilliard d'Auberteuil, II, 44–45
7. Du Buisson, II, 24.
8. Boissonnade, 31.
9. Raynal, 6.
10. Garran-Coulon, I, 16.
11. Moreau de Saint-Méry, I, 9.
12. Leroy-Beaulieu, 164.
13. This class will be discussed later.
14. Vaissière, 78; De Wimpffen, 81–82.
15. Garran-Coulon, I, 16 (Barbé-Marbois's figures).
16. Vaissière, 279; Moreau de Saint-Méry, I, 13; Raynal, 5.
17. Hilliard d'Auberteuil, II, 42.
18. These social traits will be discussed later.
19. Hilliard d'Auberteuil, II, 45.
20. Ibid., II, 35–36; Roloff, 7.
21. Mills, 14.
22. Leroy-Beaulieu, 155–60; Peytraud, 12.
23. Boissonnade, 31–32.
24. Ibid.
25. The rural gendarmerie.
26. Vaissière, 93–152 (an extremely full treatment of the subject).
27. Ibid., 354–55.
28. Mills, 27.
29. Vaissière, 355–60.
30. For clergy of other islands, see Leroy-Beaulieu, 160; Peytraud, 12–13.
31. Vaissière, 82.
32. Raynal, 236.
33. Ibid., 236–37.
34. De Wimpffen, 280–81.
35. Ibid., 281.
36. Vaissière, 80.
37. Ibid. (Like most of the quotations from this author, the above is drawn from the official correspondence in the Archives des Colonies.)
38. Ibid., 81–82.
39. Boissonnade, 32–33; Peytraud, 13; 270–71; Leroy-Beaulieu, 160–61; Mills, 14–15.
40. Mills, 15; Vaissière, 104–06.
41. Literally "small whites."
42. See ante, p. 15.
43. Peytraud, 4; 13–25; 270; 445–49; 455–57; Leroy-Beaulieu, 161–64; Vaissière, 52; 154.
44. See Peytraud and Leroy-Beaulieu above; also the latter's remarks on Cuba and Porto Rico before development of slavery there, 251–56; 269–70.

45. A large proportion of these were Creoles.
46. Hilliard d'Aubertcuil, II, 40-41; Roloff, 8.
47. See letter of Governor Blanchelande to the German Colony of Bombarde, Archives Nationales, D–xxv, 46; Boissonnade, 31.
48. Schoelcher, 5. (These play a not unimportant part in the Revolutionary disturbances, especially the Maltese demagogue Praloto at Port-au-Prince.)
49. I have noted in lists of prisoners, deported persons, etc., preserved in the Archives Nationales, very many foreign names. Some are even Slav.
50. Vaissière, 338 (Police report of 1780, in Archives Coloniales).
51. *Ibid.*, 229; "Désastres," 130-32; Déschamps, 18.
52. Vaissière, 229; "Désastres," 129-30.
53. The regiments "Le Cap" and "Port-au-Prince."
54. Déschamps, 300 bis. (Appendix.)
55. Moreau de Saint-Méry, I, 8-9.
56. *Ibid.*, I, 12; Vaissière, 301-02; Hilliard d'Aubertcuil, II, 45; Mills, 13.
57. Moreau de Saint-Méry, I, 12; 16-17; Vaissière, 306; De Wimpffen, 65.
58. Vaissière, 302-03; Hilliard d'Aubertcuil, II, 31.
59. Vaissière, 303.
60. *Ibid.*, 305.
61. *Ibid.*, 306.
62. Moreau de Saint-Méry, I, 13.
63. *Ibid.*, I, 12-13.
64. *Ibid.*, I, 13; Vaissière, 305-06.
65. Moreau de Saint-Méry, I, 12 (note); Vaissière, 306-07; and others.
66. Vaissière, 303-06; De Wimpffen, 268.
67. Moreau de Saint-Méry, I, 15-16. Vaissière, 305-06.
68. De Wimpffen, 264.
69. *Ibid.*, 268.
70. Moreau de Saint-Méry, I, 13-15; Vaissière, 308.
71. Moreau de Saint-Méry, I, 17-21; Vaissière, 308-19; Hilliard d'Aubertcuil, II, 31-32.
72. Miss Hassal, "Secret History; or, the Horrors of San Domingo, in a series of Letters, written by a Lady at Cape François to Colonel Burr, Late Vice-President of the United States. Principally during the Command of General Rochambeau" (Philadelphia, 1808), 19-20.
73. Vaissière, 313-18; Moreau de Saint-Méry, I, 20-21.
74. Vaissière, 319-22; Moreau de Saint-Méry, I, 19-20.
75. Vaissière, 61-62; also, see *ante*, p. 4.
76. Moreau de Saint-Méry, I, 7-8.
77. The Peace of Utrecht, in 1714.
78. Vaissière, 63.
79. Déschamps, 4.

NOTES

80. Peytraud, 458.
81. See *ante*, pp. 16-18.
82. Vaissière, 35-36; 68-69; Peytraud, 132-35.
83. Peytraud, 458-59.
84. Moreau de Saint-Méry, I, 11.
85. *Ibid.*
86. Vaissière, 297.
87. *Ibid.*, 296.
88. Moreau de Saint-Méry, I, 11.
89. Vaissière, 295.
90. Du Buisson, II, 2-3; Moreau de Saint-Méry, I, 11; Vaissière, 300.
91. Du Buisson, II, 4.
92. Moreau de Saint-Méry, I, 11.
93. Raynal, 25.
94. *Ibid.*, 7.
95. Vaissière, 64-67.
96. *Ibid.*, 71.
97. *Ibid.*, 72.
98. *Ibid.*, 72-73.
99. *Ibid.*, 73; 327; Moreau de Saint-Méry, I, 10.
100. Vaissière, 334-37; Moreau de Saint-Méry, I, 92-97.
101. Vaissière, 327-50.
102. *Ibid.*, 287-95 (quoting several contemporary descriptions).
103. De Wimpffen, 103.
104. *Ibid.*, 202.
105. Vaissière, 279-80.
106. *Ibid.*, 282-86 (cites instances of various types of plantation life, from contemporary accounts).
107. *Ibid.*, 280-82.
108. *Ibid.*, 323.
109. Du Buisson, II, 4-5; Hilliard d'Auberteuil, I, 107; Vaissière, 319-25.
110. De Wimpffen, 117-18.
111. *Ibid.*, 118-19; Vaissière, 323-24.
112. See the opening pages of Castonnet des Fosses, Dr. Magnac, and articles in various periodicals.
113. See the effect produced by these accounts on Miss Hassal, in 1802 (p. 18); and on Captain Rainsford, at about the same date (p. 104).
114. De Wimpffen, 315-16.

CHAPTER IV

1. "Les Gens de Couleur Libres." This was not a euphemism, but the legal definition.
2. See *ante*, pp. 8-9.
3. That is, of mixed white and negro blood.

4. Moreau de Saint-Méry, I, 90; Hilliard d'Auberteuil, II, 87-88; Roloff, 8.
5. This will be brought out by the course of events.
6. Peytraud, 196-207; Lebeau, 95-100; Vaissière, 214-16.
7. Vaissière, 216.
8. Peytraud, 195-96.
9. *Ibid.*, 205.
10. Mills, 19.
11. Vaissière, 334-37; Moreau de Saint-Méry, I, 19-20; Lebeau, 93-94.
12. Vaissière, 281-82.
13. *Ibid.*, 21.
14. Moreau de Saint-Méry, I, 68-69.
15. Lebeau, 90-93; Vaissière, 217.
16. Vaissière, 76; 216-17; Peytraud, 197.
17. Hilliard d'Auberteuil, II, 79.
18. Vaissière, 221.
19. Moreau de Saint-Méry, I, 89.
20. Vaissière, 219.
21. *Ibid.*, 219-20.
22. *Ibid.*, 220.
23. *Ibid.*, 221.
24. Lebeau, 91-92.
25. Peytraud, 205.
26. In Louisiana and Bourbon: see Lebeau, 92.
27. Lebeau, 92-93.
28. *Ibid.*, 19-21; Peytraud, 424.
29. Hilliard d'Auberteuil, II, 79.
30. Lebeau, 94.
31. Hilliard d'Auberteuil, II, 79. (This in accordance with the Roman maxim, *Partus sequitur ventrem.*)
32. Lebeau, 3-4; Vaissière, 221-22; Peytraud, 425.
33. Moreau de Saint-Méry, I, 71-89.
34. Peytraud, 422-23.
35. Lebeau, 4.
36. Lebeau, 9.
37. That is, with agricultural implements; especially with machetes.
38. Carteau, 60-61.
39. Vaissière, 228.
40. Lebeau, 17-54; 92-94; Peytraud, 425-34; Vaissière, 224-27; Mills, 16-19.
41. Vaissière, 221-24; Peytraud, 423-25; Roloff, 8.
42. Lebeau, 111-15.
43. Déschamps, 18.
44. Gouy d'Arcy, "Idées Sommaires sur la Restoration de Saint-Domingue" (Paris, 1792), 8.

NOTES

45. "Désastres," 130-31.
46. Peytraud, 432-33; Hilliard d'Aubcrteuil, II, 74.
47. "Désastres," 131-32; Schoelcher, 5-6.
48. Peytraud, 206.
49. Vaissière, 229.
50. Ibid., 224.
51. Edwards, 2; Moreau de Saint-Méry, I, 91.
52. Moreau de Saint-Méry, I, 90.
53. Ibid., I, 92-97; Vaissière, 334-37; Peytraud, 429-30.
54. See ante, p. 38.
55. Lebeau, 93-94.
56. Gouy d'Arcy, 8; Moreau de Saint-Méry, I, 17; Ibid., "Considérations," 6-8.
57. Peytraud, 401-21; Lebeau, 58-78; Hilliard d'Aubcrteuil, I, 20-21; De Wimpffen, 14-15.
58. Roloff, 9.
59. See ante, p. 37.
60. Quoted in Peytraud, 434.

CHAPTER V

1. Déschamps, 16 (quoting an economic writer of the later eighteenth century).
2. Peytraud, VII-VIII; 32-34; 143-44; 435-45; Leroy-Beaulieu, 164-65; 189-95; Déschamps, 15-16.
3. See ante, pp. 8-9.
4. Semi-official estimates of 1788-89 give 509,000. See Garran-Coulon, I, 15.
5. Vaissière, 164.
6. Peytraud, 137.
7. See ante, p. 8.
8. Peytraud, 138.
9. Ibid., 139.
10. Moreau de Saint-Méry and Bryan Edwards, both careful contemporary writers, come independently to this conclusion. See Peytraud, 141; Leroy-Beaulieu, 194.
11. Mills, 20; Hilliard d'Aubcrteuil, II, 63.
12. Peytraud, 140.
13. Hilliard d'Aubcrteuil, II, 64; Peytraud, 213-38; Vaissière, 165-69.
14. Hilliard d'Aubcrteuil, II, 64.
15. Du Buisson, II, 43-44.
16. Peytraud, 214-15; 237; 436-37. The fact was noted by colonial writers, but without drawing any conclusions. See Du Buisson, I, 72-73; Ducœurjoly, I, 19.
17. Leroy-Beaulieu, 195.

18. Leroy-Beaulieu, 194.
19. Peytraud, 142 (quoting Wallon).
20. The deficit of eleven thousand persons previously quoted is conservative. Roloff states that fifteen thousand were needed to fill the gaps (pp. 8–9).
21. Peytraud, 135–36.
22. Vaissière, 164.
23. Peytraud, 139.
24. Vaissière, 164. The customs figures are: 1787, 31,000; 1788, 30,000. These are obviously too low. See Peytraud, 139.
25. For a masterly account, see Peytraud, 36–142; also Vaissière, 155–63.
26. Peytraud, 35–76.
27. Déschamps, 19.
28. Boissonnade, 21.
29. Treille, 26–30; Boissonnade, 21; Déschamps, 20.
30. Peytraud, 77–105.
31. *Ibid.*, 106–28; Vaissière, 156–63.
32. Hilliard d'Auberteuil, II, 68.
33. Moreau de Saint-Méry, I, 23.
34. The best account is in Peytraud, 87–90. For more detailed treatment, see observations of Moreau de Saint-Méry, I, 23–25, and of his contemporary Bryan Edwards, on the same types in Jamaica. They tally very closely.
35. Peytraud, 90 (quoting a contemporary account).
36. *Ibid.*, 86.
37. Moreau de Saint-Méry, I, 35.
38. *Ibid.*, I, 40.
39. Ducœurjoly, II, 22.
40. Vaissière, 206.
41. *Ibid.*, 206–08; Garran-Coulon, II, 198–203.
42. Garran-Coulon, II, 23–24.
43. See Moreau de Saint-Méry, I, 43–62; De Wimpffen, 129–32; Ducœurjoly, I, 18–22; Hilliard d'Auberteuil, I, 133–36; Du Buisson, I, 71–75.
44. De Wimpffen, 129–32.
45. Peytraud, 171.
46. Peytraud, 167–81; Moreau de Saint-Méry, I, 35–36; Vaissière, 210–11.
47. Moreau de Saint-Méry, I, 45–51; Vaissière, 178–79; Peytraud, 224.
48. See Sir Spencer St. John, and Hesketh Pritchard's "Where Black rules White."
49. Vaissière, 170–206; Edwards, 5; Hilliard d'Auberteuil, I, 136.
50. Peytraud, 216–18; 226–32.
51. Vaissière, 169–80; 196–205; Peytraud, 216–41; Edwards, 5.

52. Vaissière, 168; Peytraud, 216; 90; Moreau de Saint-Méry, I, 40.
53. Peytraud, 214-16; 290-91; Vaissière, 166-68.
54. Peytraud, 290.
55. Vaissière, 180-81.
56. Peytraud, 193-94.
57. M. Schoelcher (quoted in Peytraud, 291).
58. Peytraud, 291-93; Vaissière, 189-91.
59. Vaissière, 193-94.
60. Peytraud, 144-45; Vaissière, 182-83.
61. The manuscript text of the "Code Noir" in the Colonial Archives is reproduced in full in Peytraud, 158-66.
62. Peytraud, 149-57; Vaissière, 183.
63. Vaissière, 185-86.
64. *Ibid.*, 195-205; Peytraud, 243; Edwards, 14-15.
65. Vaissière, 184-85.
66. *Ibid.*, 181.
67. *Ibid.*
68. Edwards, 13-14.
69. Vaissière, 188.
70. *Ibid.*, 186-88 (entire account of the "Affaire Lejeune").
71. See *ante*, p. 61.
72. Vaissière, 234-35.
73. Du Buisson, I, 77.
74. Vaissière, 235.
75. Peytraud, 344.
76. Garran-Coulon, I, 4.
77. "Lettre au 'Patriote français' par un ancien Officier créol," October 31, 1791.
78. Charlevoix, III, 162. (He is strictly contemporary, for his book appeared only a few years after this event.)
79. *Ibid.*, III, 162-64; Levasseur, 392.
80. At that time the most populous quarter of the colony.
81. Vaissière, 232 (official quotation); also see Charlevoix, IV, 10.
82. Vaissière, 232-33 (official quotation).
83. "Lettre par unancien Officier créol" (*op. cit.*).
84. Vaissière, 236; "Lettre" (*op. cit.*).
85. Vaissière, 237.
86. *Ibid.*, 238-45; 249-53; Peytraud, 317-23; Moreau de Saint-Méry, I, 36.
87. Vaissière, 236-38; 245-49; "Lettre par un ancien Officier créol " (*op. cit.*).
88. In the year 1783.
89. Vaissière, 229-30.
90. De Wimpffen, 336.

CHAPTER VI

1. The Notables had met in February and had been dissolved in May, 1787.
2. See *ante*, pp. 10-15 and 21-22.
3. See *ante*, pp. 16 to 18.
4. Boissonnade, 43-46.
5. *Ibid.*, 46-57.
6. *Ibid.*, 61-67.
7. *Ibid.*, 74-83.
8. *Ibid.*, 90.
9. *Ibid.*, 95.
10. *Ibid.*, 98-113; Mills, 27-28.
11. Boissonnade, 113-125.
12. The meeting of Vizille had been held in July; the Assembly of Romans in September.
13. Boissonnade, 125.
14. *Ibid.*, 7-8.
15. *Ibid.*, 10-11; Garran-Coulon, I, 42; Mills, 40.
16. Boissonnade, 126-27.
17. *Ibid.*, 127-28.
18. *Ibid.*, 69-71.
19. Notably Voltaire, Rousseau, Turgot. (See Zimmermann, 249-50.)
20. Boissonnade, 37-38; Moreau de Saint-Méry, "Considérations," 1-3.
21. A French translation of the name of Clarkson's society.
22. Déschamps, 50-52; Boissonnade, 38-40; Edwards, 19-20.
23. Moreau de Saint-Méry, "Considérations," 16.
24. *Ibid.*, 4.
25. *Ibid.*, 4.
26. Boissonnade, 71; Moreau de Saint-Méry, "Considérations," 3.
27. Boissonnade, 71; Moreau de Saint-Méry, "Considérations," 16.
28. See *ante*, p. 70.
29. Boissonnade, 70-71.
30. Arch. Col., F. 16 (Letter of December 8, 1788).
31. Boissonnade, 138-43.
32. *Ibid.*, 130-48.
33. *Ibid.*, 149.
34. Venault de Charmilly, 48 (himself one of the protestants).
35. Boissonnade, 149-67; Mills, 28-20; Garran-Coulon, I, 46.
36. Boissonnade, 167-70; Mills, 29-30; Garran-Coulon, I, 47-48.
37. Boissonnade, 187-88.
38. *Ibid.*, 192-95; Mills, 39-41.

NOTES 365

39. Boissonnade, 198–202.
40. *Ibid.*, 209–13.
41. *Ibid.*, 202–08.
42. *Ibid.*, 213.
43. Déschamps, 58–59.
44. The 20th of June, 1789.
45. Boissonnade, 214–33; Déschamps, 61–66; Mills, 30–31.
46. Boissonnade, 234–71; Mills, 31.
47. Déschamps, 69.
48. *Ibid.*, 69–70.
49. Boissonnade, 5–6; 273–74; Vaissière, 359–61.
50. Roloff, 22–23.
51. Quoted in Boissonnade, 274; and in Vaissière, 360–61.
52. Vaissière, 361.

CHAPTER VII

1. "Lettre écrite par MM. les Députés de Saint-Domingue à leur Constituans au Cap." (Pamphlet form; also mainly quoted in Garran-Coulon, I, 116.)
2. Mills, 34.
3. Garran-Coulon, I, 57–59; Mills, 35; Déschamps, 90.
4. Mills, 35.
5. This whole topic is exhaustively treated in Brette, "Les Gens de Couleur Libres et leurs Députés en 1789"; in "La Révolution Française," XXIX, 326–45; 385–407 (1895); see also Boissonnade, 172; Edwards, 20.
6. Brette, 329–37; Mills, 35–36; Moreau de Saint-Méry, "Considérations," 8–9.
7. Brette, 385–86; Mills, 35–36; Moreau de Saint-Méry, "Considérations," 8–9.
8. Déschamps, 78–79.
9. De Curt, deputy for Guadeloupe. By this time the other French colonies had been given representation in the National Assembly.
10. Déschamps, 76–77; Garran-Coulon, I, 60–62; Mills, 50.
11. Déschamps, 79–80.
12. Treated in the next chapter.
13. Moreau de Saint-Méry, "Considérations," 17–29; Garran-Coulon, I, 126.
14. Déschamps, 80–81; Garran-Coulon, I, 128.
15. Déschamps, 90–91.
16. The text of the decree may be found in Arch. Parl., XII, 73.
17. For different comments on the decree, see Mills, 54; Déschamps, 93; Edwards, 28–29.

18. Mills, 54; Déschamps, 92.
19. Déschamps, 99-100; Mills, 56.
20. Mills, 56.

CHAPTER VIII

1. See *ante*, pp. 75-76.
2. Mills, 41, 44; Garran-Coulon, I, 71-72.
3. Garran-Coulon, I, 73-74; "Désastres," 139-40; Mills, 41-42.
4. See *ante*, pp. 75-76.
5. See *ante*, pp. 25-26.
6. Mills, 41.
7. Garran-Coulon, I, 80-81; "Désastres," 140; Mills, 44.
8. Mills, 42.
9. Garran-Coulon, I, 75-78; Mills, 43; Schoelcher, 14-15; "Désastres," 141.
10. Mills, 41; 47.
11. "Désastres," 142-43; Garran-Coulon, I, 80-81; Mills, 48-49.
12. Garran-Coulon, I, 80-88; Mills, 45-47; Schoelcher, 14-17; Dalmas, 38-40.
13. Garran-Coulon, I, 88-90; Mills, 45-47.
14. Garran-Coulon, I, 90-95; Mills, 52-53; Edwards, 25-26.
15. Mills, 58.
16. Boissonnade, 172-73; "Désastres," 144.
17. See *ante*, pp. 72-74.
18. *Ibid.*
19. Edwards, 21.
20. Mills, 42.
21. Letter of the local commandant of Maribaroux to the district commandant of Fort Dauphin, October 14, 1789, Arch. Col., F-3, 194.
22. Moreau de Saint-Méry, "Considérations," 17-29.
23. Letter to La Luzerne, February 12, 1790, Arch. Col., C-9, 164.
24. Mills, 47-48; Garran-Coulon, I, 109-14.
25. See *ante*, pp. 46-47.
26. Lacroix, I, 21, 22; "Désastres," 144; Gatereau, 22-28.
27. Lacroix, I, 22-23; "Désastres," 145.
28. "Désastres," 146; Edwards, 23.
29. Lacroix, I, 24; Edwards, 24.
30. See *ante*, p. 46.
31. Lacroix, I, 14-15.
32. *Ibid.*, 24-25.
33. "Désastres," 145; Gatereau, 41-42.
34. Roloff, 22-23.
35. Lacroix, I, 25-28; Edwards, 65.

NOTES 367

CHAPTER IX

1. Garran-Coulon, I, 161–65; Mills, 58.
2. Déschamps, 175.
3. Garran-Coulon, I, 170–75; Mills, 61; Edwards, 32–36.
4. Garran-Coulon, I, 175–98; Dalmas, 45–47; Mills, 77–78; Edwards, 36.
5. See especially *ante*, pp. 2–5.
6. See *ante*, pp. 10–14.
7. See *ante*, p. 83.
8. That is, the *émigrés*.
9. That is, the Clergy and the Vendéens.
10. Garran-Coulon, I, 181–82.
11. Mills, 78.
12. "Désastres," 148–50; Mills, 64–65.
13. See *ante*, pp. 97–98.
14. Mills, 58.
15. "Désastres," 146–48; Mills, 59; Garran-Coulon, I, 159–60.
16. Garran-Coulon, I, 182–87.
17. Mills, 62–65; Edwards, 37; Dalmas, 43–44; "Désastres," 152.
18. "Désastres," 151–52.
19. Letter of June 21, 1790, Arch. Col., C–9, 164.
20. Mills, 66–67; Garran-Coulon, I, 211–13.
21. Garran-Coulon, I, 243–51; "Désastres," 153; Mills, 70.
22. In September, 1789; see *ante*, p. 91.
23. Garran-Coulon, I, 222.
24. *Ibid.*, I, 221–25; Mills, 68; Edwards, 31–32.
25. Edwards, 32.
26. Déschamps, 300 bis. (Appendix.)
27. Garran-Coulon, I, 78, 229.
28. *Ibid.*, I, 225–29; "Désastres," 153.
29. Garran-Coulon, I, 251–55; Mills, 70–71; Edwards, 37–38.
30. That is, "Pompons Blancs."
31. The most detailed account is by Governor Peynier himself, in his report of July 31 to the Minister of Marine, Arch. Col., C–9, 164; Arch. Nat., D–xxv, 46. De Wimpffen, who was in Port-au-Prince at the time, has left some interesting pages (333–40). See also Garran-Coulon, I, 248–51; "Désastres," 154–55; Edwards, 39–40. Both sides later drew up justificatory memorials to the National Assembly; but these, together with other pamphlet literature, have as usual been digested by Garran-Coulon (*supra*).
32. Report of July 31, quoted above.
33. Mills, 71–73; Garran-Coulon, I, 255–61; Edwards, 40.
34. Garran-Coulon, I, 262–69; "Désastres," 154–57; Mills, 72–73.

35. Mills, 73; Garran-Coulon, I, 269–72; "Désastres," 155–56.
36. Garran-Coulon, I, 272–80; Mills, 83; "Désastres," 156–57.
37. Déschamps, 179–80; Garran-Coulon, I, 313–18; Mills, 82–83.
38. Garran-Coulon, I, 272–80; 293–97; Mills, 83.
39. See *ante*, p. 8.
40. The best account of affairs in the North is in the reports of Moreau de Saint-Méry's special correspondent at Le Cap — due allowance being made for party bias, — Arch. Col., F-3, 195, 196. See also Garran-Coulon, I, 300–07; "Désastres," 157–58; Dalmas, 67–68. See also instructive letter of a "Patriot" inhabitant of the North to a friend in Paris (printed as a pamphlet now apparently very rare, Bib. Nat., LK-12, 296).
41. De Wimpffen, 334.
42. Garran-Coulon, II, 42–71; "Désastres," 160–65; Mills, 86–90; Edwards, 44–55.
43. See *ante*, p. 96.
44. For the action of the Government in the West, see official correspondence and Mauduit's report, Arch. Col., C-9, 164. The treatment of this point in the various secondary works is mostly doubtful conjecture.
45. Lacroix, I, 64–65.
46. See next chapter.
47. Garran-Coulon, I, 281–89; Mills, 74–77; Edwards, 56–58.
48. For this period, see official correspondence, Arch. Col., C-9, 164, 165; Arch. Nat., D-xxv, 46; also, the Moreau de Saint-Méry correspondence above, Arch. Col., F-3, 196. This period is not treated in any published work.
49. See Blanchelande's report, March 13, 1791, Arch. Col., C-9, 165; Arch. Nat., D-xxv, 46; other official and semi-official papers summarized in Garran-Coulon, I, 332–43; see also "Désastres," 169–71; Mills, 91–93.
50. Garran-Coulon, I, 348–52; "Désastres," 172–73.
51. For this period, see Blanchelande's correspondence, Arch. Col., C-9, 165; Arch. Nat., D-xxv, 46; Moreau de Saint-Méry correspondence, Arch. Col., F-3, 196; also, Garran-Coulon, I, 348–62; Mills, 93–94 (very summary treatment).

CHAPTER X

1. See *ante*, pp. 87–89.
2. De Wimpffen, 49–51.
3. That is, the General Assembly's "Constitutional Bases"; see *ante*, pp. 101–03.
4. See *ante*, pp. 84–85.
5. "Adresse de l'Assemblée provinciale du Nord de Saint-

NOTES 369

Domingue à l'Assemblée Nationale." (Le Cap, July 13, 1790; official publication.)
6. See *ante*, pp. 105–108.
7. Arch. Parl., xix, 569.
8. Moreau de Saint-Méry, "Considérations," 47–48.
9. Edwards, 65–66; Dalmas, 109–10.
10. For text of this report, see Arch. Parl., xxv, 636 *et seq.*
11. See *ante*, p. 118.
12. The text of these debates, etc., may be found in Arch. Parl., xxv–xxvi, under dates of the 7th, and the 11th to 15th May. For brief accounts, see Déschamps, 219–28; Mills, 97–98.
13. Letter to Minister of Marine, July 16, 1791, Arch. Col., C–9, 165.
14. That is, on May 16.
15. Arch. Parl., xxvi, 122.
16. "Exposé des motifs des Décrets des 13 et 15 Mai sur l'état des Personnes dans les Colonies."
17. See *ante*, pp. 116–18.
18. Letter to the Minister of Marine, July 3, 1791, Arch. Col., C–9, 165.
19. Letter of July 31, Arch. Col., C–9, 165.
20. See especially, letter of the Procureur of the Conseil Supérieure du Cap, and addresses of the North Provincial Assembly to the National Assembly and to the King, Arch. Nat., AD–vii, 16. Others quoted in Garran-Coulon, ii, 111–20.
21. Letter from Le Cap to Havre, July 5, Arch. Nat., D–xxv, 78.
22. Letter to a relative at Bordeaux, July 10, Arch. Nat., D–xxv, 78.
23. Letter to Havre, July 12, Arch. Nat., D–xxv, 78.
24. *Ibid.*
25. Garran-Coulon, ii, 183–93; Edwards, 70–71; "Désastres," 178–79.

CHAPTER XI

1. Letter of Blanchelande to the Minister of Marine, September 2, Arch. Nat., D–xxv, 46; also see good account in Edwards, 72.
2. See *ante*, pp. 94–95.
3. Letter of October 1, 1789, Garran-Coulon, ii, 195.
4. Garran-Coulon, ii, 195–96.
5. Castonnet des Fosses, 81–82.
6. Garran-Coulon, ii, 207–08 (another similar letter quoted).
7. *Ibid.*, ii, 211–12 (quoting the words of one of the prisoners).
8. Garran-Coulon, ii, 210–11; Lacroix, i, 88–89.
9. See *ante*, pp. 62–67.
10. "Désastres," 183; Edwards, 88.
11. Garron-Coulon, ii, 210.
12. Castonnet des Fosses, 82–83; Schoelcher, 30–31.

13. Edwards, 73–75; "Désastres," 183–89; Sciout, 413–14; Castonnet des Fosses, 83–84. History curiously repeats itself. At least one similar outrage occurred during the late negro rising in Cuba (province of Oriente), in the spring of 1912.
14. Edwards, 74–75; Sciout, 413.
15. Garran-Coulon, II, 213–14; Edwards, 78–79.
16. Carteau, 87–88.
17. Edwards, vii.
18. I have here specially in mind the region of Martinique devastated by that great eruption of Mont Pelée on May 8, 1902, which destroyed the city of Saint-Pierre. The contrast between the utter desolation of the lava-scorched fire-zone and the luxuriant vegetation of the surrounding hills was extraordinary in the extreme.
19. Moreau de Saint-Méry, I, 491–92.
20. *Ibid.*
21. Letter of September 2, 1791, Arch. Nat., D–xxv, 46.
22. See *ante*, pp. 25–26.
23. Garran-Coulon, II, 217–18; Edwards, 77–78.
24. Blanchelande to the Minister of Marine, September 13, Arch. Nat., D–xxv, 46.
25. Blanchelande's correspondence through September and October, Arch. Nat., D–xxv, 46; Edwards, 78; Lacroix, I, 105–06; Sciout, 413.
26. Edwards, 82–83.
27. It must be remembered that Edwards was an eye-witness of these early months of the insurrection, and is therefore high authority.
28. Letter of a British officer, dated September 24, 1791, Arch. Nat., D–xxv, 79; see also numerous letters of colonists, merchant captains, etc., preserved in Arch. Nat., D–xxv, 78, 79, 87.
29. Letter of the Colonial Assembly to its commissioners at Paris, November 12, 1791, Arch. Nat., D–xxv, 62.
30. Lacroix, I, 106–07; Sciout, 413–16.
31. Blanchelande's correspondence; especially letter of November 16, Arch. Nat., D–xxv, 46; the best account of these expeditions is found in a series of letters from a militia officer to a friend in Le Cap, Arch. Nat., D–xxv, 87.
32. Private letter from Le Borgne, November 9, 1791, Arch. Nat., D–xxv, 79.
33. "Tableau des Évènemens qui ont eu lieu dans la Paroisse du Trou depuis la Révolte des Nègres," Arch. Nat., D–xxv, 78.
34. See *ante*, p. 130.
35. Garran-Coulon, II, 258–60.
36. "Désastres," 192.
37. Remember the chronic *marronage* and revolts under the Old Régime; see *ante*, pp. 62–67.

NOTES

38. Garran-Coulon, II, 194-96; 209-12; 264-66.
39. Arch. Parl., XXXVII, 222 et seq. (report of January 11, 1792).
40. This is the thesis of Edwards, 87-93; and Governor Blanchelande suspected them at the time: see especially his letter of September 2, 1791, Arch. Nat., D-xxv, 46; see also Moreau de Saint-Méry correspondence, Arch. Col., F-3, 197.
41. Carteau, 75-76.
42. See *ante*, pp. 113-114.
43. Blanchelande to the Minister of Marine, March 13, 1790, Arch. Nat., D-xxv, 46.
44. Garran-Coulon, II, 208.
45. Report of January 11, 1792, quoted *supra*.
46. "Désastres," 190-95; Carteau, 71-85; Lacroix, I, 101-11.
47. Garran-Coulon, II, 209-10; 264-66.
48. *Ibid.*, II, 258; "Désastres," 194-95; Lacroix, I, 108-11.
49. See Blanchelande's correspondence, Arch. Nat., D-xxv, 46; Moreau de Saint-Méry correspondence, Arch. Col., F-3, 197; also very interesting private letter of November 22, 1791, from Le Cap, Arch. Nat., D-xxv, 87; see also Garran-Coulon, II, 237-38; Lacroix, I, 104; Dalmas, 151-53.
50. De Wimpffen, 335-36; to the same effect, see Carteau, 74-75.
51. See next chapter.

CHAPTER XII

1. Garran-Coulon, II, 125-38; "Désastres," 180-81; Edwards, 71-72.
2. Letter of one Labuissonnière to J. Raymond, Arch. Nat., D-xxv, 114.
3. See *ante*, pp. 113-14.
4. Garran-Coulon, I, 348-58.
5. *Ibid.*, II, 139-41.
6. Garran-Coulon, II, 104.
7. *Ibid.*, II, 142-43.
8. *Ibid.*, II, 142-43; Lacroix, I, 116.
9. Garran-Coulon, II, 144-46; Edwards, 84-85; "Désastres," 201-02.
10. Letter of M. de Coigne, September 21, 1791, Arch. Nat., D-xxv, 46.
11. The Colonial Assembly to its commissioners at Paris, October 2, 1791, Arch. Nat., D-xxv, 62; see also sceptical opinion of Civil Commissioner Roume in his comment to the National Assembly on the real value of this and subsequent Concordats: note, dated April 20, 1792, Arch. Nat., D-xxv, 2.
12. Letter of Labadie to J. Raymond, the mulatto leader at Paris, July 9, 1792, Arch. Nat., D-xxv, 114.

13. The popular municipalities were everywhere suppressed, and power restored to the old King's officers, who, of course, were De Jumecourt's followers. See Blanchelande's correspondence, especially letter of October 22, 1791, A'rch. Nat., D–xxv, 46; General Assembly's letter to its commissioners, October 16, 1791, Arch. Nat., D–xxv, 62; also, an interesting letter from their Port-au-Prince business correspondent to Dacosta Frères of Nantes, November 8, 1791, Arch. Nat., D–xxv, 79.
14. It must be remembered that no decree went into effect until after the arrival of the formal document: this the mere news always preceded.
15. See correspondence between Blanchelande and De Jumecourt, Arch. Nat., D–xxv, 46.
16. Letter of a merchant in Port-au-Prince to a merchant in Nantes, Arch. Nat., D–xxv, 87.
17. Garran-Coulon, II, 146–58.
18. See *ante*, pp. 121–22.
19. Garran-Coulon, II, 269–80; for numerous addresses still preserved, see Arch. Nat., AD–vii, 16.
20. For various comments on the decree, see Déschamps, 232–239; Edwards, 95–96; Garran-Coulon, II: 280–81.
21. Edwards, 96–97.
22. See letter of Blanchelande, December 17, D–xxv, 46; very interesting letter from a major of National Guards to a relative in France, December 17, Arch. Nat., D–xxv, 87; another private letter of December 17, Arch. Nat., D–xxv, 79; various pieces of *ex parte* testimony summarized in Garran-Coulon, II, 157–76.
23. Lacroix, I, 194; Schoelcher, 63.
24. Letter of the Colonial Assembly to its commissioners, January 28, 1792, Arch. Nat., D–xxv, 62; Sciout, 420; "Désastres," 212.
25. Letter of January 28, 1792, Arch. Nat., D–xxv, 62. These hideous practices seem to have been frequently perpetrated by the mulattoes in all parts of the colony. For a similar and perhaps even more horrible instance, see the case of the Séjourné family, Edwards, 98; "Désastres," 212; for similar instances in the South, see letter of a merchant of Les Cayes to a relative at Nantes, January 10, 1792, Arch. Nat., D–xxv, 87; deposition of a merchant captain from Les Cayes, Arch. Nat., D–xxv, 79. For similar atrocities of the mulatto leader Candy in the North, see letter of the Colonial Assembly, October 6, Arch. Nat., D–xxv, 62; other atrocities, taken from the Arch. Nat., in Sciout, 415–21.
26. Deposition sent to the Minister of Marine, Arch. Nat., D–xxv, 87.
27. Edwards, 98.

NOTES 373

28. See files of Blanchelande's correspondence, Arch. Nat., D–xxv, 46; of the Colonial Assembly's correspondence with its commissioners, Arch. Nat., D–xxv, 62; also several good private letters, depositions of merchant captains, etc., Arch. Nat., D–xxv, 79, 87.

CHAPTER XIII

1. Garran-Coulon, II, 74–81; also several documents on this point in Arch. Nat., D–xxv, 87.
2. Garran-Coulon, II, 302–03.
3. *Ibid.*, 303–04.
4. The Commissioners to the Minister of Marine, November 29, Arch. Nat., D–xxv, 1.
5. *Ibid.*
6. The Colonial Assembly to its commissioners at Paris, Arch. Nat., D–xxv, 62.
7. The Civil Commissioners to the Minister of Marine, December 23, Arch. Nat., D–xxv, 1.
8. Quite without foundation.
9. Letter of Jean-François and Biassou to the Civil Commissioners, December 9, Arch. Nat., D–xxv, 1. This and subsequent letters from the negro leaders are evidently written by mulattoes or by white priests, the negro leaders being illiterate.
10. That is, from Africa.
11. Letter of Jean-François and Biassou to the Commissioners, December 12, 1791, Arch. Nat., D–xxv, 1.
12. Letter of the Commissioners to the Minister of Marine, Dec. 23, Arch. Nat., D–xxv, 1.
13. Letter of December 29, Arch. Col., F–3, 197. See also similar letter of an Assemblyman to the Commissioners, December 15, Arch. Nat., D–xxv, 1; and similar language in the Colonial Assembly's justificatory memoir to the National Assembly, Arch. Nat., D–xxv, 47.
14. Besides the original documents quoted above, see Garran-Coulon, II, 303–21; Lacroix, I, 147–57. Neither mentions the extraordinary offer made on December 12 by the negro leaders to reduce their followers to slavery in return for personal liberty, although this would seem to be the vital point in the whole affair. Lacroix was undoubtedly ignorant of this letter's existence. Garran-Coulon must have known of it, but suppressed it. This is one of his numerous "sins of omission," against which one must be continually on one's guard.
15. Letter to the Minister of Marine, January 25, 1792, Arch. Nat., D–xxv, 46.
16. Letter of February 20, 1792, Arch. Nat., D–xxv, 1.

17. Memoir quoted above, Arch. Nat., D–xxv, 47.
18. Letter to the Minister of Marine, January 25, 1792, Arch. Nat., D–xxv, 46, for events above narrated, see correspondence of Blanchelande, the Civil Commissioners and the Colonial Assembly; also Garran-Coulon, II, 323–28.
19. Letter to the Minister of Marine, December 23, 1791, Arch. Nat., D–xxv, 1.
20. Mirbeck's report to the National Assembly, May 26, 1792, Arch. Parl., XLIV, 139 *et seq.*; also reflections by Roume, April, 1792, Arch. Nat., D–xxv, 1.
21. Mirbeck's report, *supra.*
22. See *ante*, pp. 151, 152.
23. Letter of January, 1792, Garran-Coulon, II, 427–28.
24. Correspondence of the Commissioners with the Confederates and with Port-au-Prince, in Arch. Nat., D–xxv, 1–2; see also Garran-Coulon, II, 455–70.
25. Saint-Leger's correspondence with his colleagues and with the Minister of Marine, Arch. Nat., D–xxv, 1–2; also, Garran-Coulon, II, 470–72; 487–92.
26. Saint-Leger's correspondence above, Arch. Nat., D–xxv, 1–2; Garran-Coulon, II, 472–506.
27. See *ante*, p. 159.
28. Saint-Leger's correspondence with his colleagues and with the Minister of Marine, Arch. Nat., D–xxv, 2; also, letter of the Colonial Assembly to its commissioners, April 21, Arch. Nat., D–xxv, 62; see also Garran-Coulon, II, 509–15.
29. See *ante*, p. 158.
30. Letter of a private person from Le Cap, spring of 1792, Arch. Col., F–3, 197.
31. Letter dated March 7, Arch. Nat., D–xxv, 83.
32. Mirbeck's report, *supra.*
33. That is, the military mutiny at Port-au-Prince, March 4, 1791; see *ante*, p. 113.
34. Blanchelande's letter to the Minister of Marine, April 1, Arch. Nat., D–xxv, 46; also his letter of April 21, *ibid.*; the Commissioners' report to the Minister of Marine, April 2, Arch. Nat., D–xxv, 2; Mirbeck's report, *supra.*
35. Mirbeck's report, *supra;* Roume to the Minister of Marine, April 2, Arch. Nat., D–xxv, 2.
36. See *ante*, pp. 107–08.
37. That is, the "Législatif."
38. Roume's correspondence with the Minister of Marine, Arch. Nat., D–xxv, 2; Garran-Coulon, II, 406–18.

CHAPTER XIV

1. Déschamps, 239–40.
2. Blanchelande to the Minister of Marine, September 2, Arch. Nat., D-xxv, 46.
3. The Commissioners to the Minister of Marine, November 29, Arch. Nat., D-xxv, 1.
4. The Colonial Assembly to the National Assembly, February 20, 1792, Arch. Nat., D-xxv, 62.
5. The Commissioners to the Minister of Marine, February 20, 1792, Arch. Nat., D-xxv, 1.
6. The "Amis des Noirs" were by that time almost synonymous with the Jacobins; the two societies were being rapidly purged of moderate members in the manner already related of the Jacobins.
7. Speech of December 3, 1791, Arch. Parl., xxxv, 536.
8. See almost any volume of the Arch. Parl. after xxxiii. A large number of petitions, etc., preserved in Arch. Nat., D-xxv, 79.
9. For particularly flagrant instances, see session of December 3, Arch. Parl., xxxv, 535 et seq.; session of February 10, 1792, Arch. Parl., xxxviii, 354 et seq.
10. Blanchelande to the Minister of Marine, January 25, Arch. Nat., D-xxv, 46.
11. See files of correspondence in Arch. Nat., D-xxv, 1, 46 and 62, respectively.
12. The entire correspondence on both sides is preserved in Arch. Nat., D-xxv, 62. As it was strictly confidential in character, it is very valuable. I have already made much use of it in the previous chapters on affairs in San Domingo for late 1791 and early 1792.
13. For this point, see Arch. Parl., xxxv–xxxvi, especially debates of early December.
14. See especially letter of the Colonial Assembly's commissioners, February 26, Arch. Nat., D-xxv, 62.
15. Arch. Parl., xxxvii, 222 et seq.
16. Letter to the Colonial Assembly, February 14, Arch. Nat., D-xxv, 62.
17. See ante, p. 158.
18. Mirbeck's report to the National Assembly, Arch. Parl., xliv, 139 et seq.
19. "La Question politique des Affranchis," Arch. Nat., D-xxv, 113.
20. See also interesting letter by another Assemblyman, January 31, 1792, Arch. Nat., D-xxv, 83.
21. J. Raymond to friends in San Domingo, June 18, 1792, Arch. Nat., D-xxv, 13.

22. For debates, see Arch. Parl., XL, under dates 21st to 28th March, 1792; see also Garran-Coulon's account, he himself being one of the principal advocates of the measure, III, 4–25.
23. Text of the decree in Arch. Parl., XL, 577 *et seq.*
24. These articles will be discussed in the next chapter.
25. That is, Guadeloupe and Martinique.
26. Letter of March 26, Arch. Nat., D–XXV, 62.
27. Letter of one Barillon to a friend in Paris, Arch. Nat., D–XXV, 79.
28. Letter of May 13, Arch. Nat., D–XXV, 62.
29. Letter of June 7, Arch. Nat., D–XXV, 62.
30. Blanchelande to the Minister of Marine, May 18, Arch. Nat., D–XXV, 46.
31. Letter of June 18, Arch. Nat., D–XXV, 13.
32. Letter to J. Raymond at Paris, Aquin, July 18, Arch. Nat., D–XXV, 114.
33. Roume to the Minister of Marine, June 9, Arch. Nat., D–XXV, 2.
34. On this point, see Garran-Coulon, III, 36–44; "Désastres," 228–29.
35. The Assembly to its Paris commissioners, Arch. Nat., D–XXV, 62.
36. Roume to the Minister of Marine, June 9, Arch. Nat., D–XXV, 2.
37. That is, in late March, 1792; see *ante*, pp. 160–61.
38. See correspondence of Blanchelande, Arch. Nat., D–XXV, 46; and of the Colonial Assembly to its commissioners, Arch. Nat., D–XXV, 62 (months of April and May).
39. This document still exists in duplicate in Arch. Nat., D–XXV, 111.
40. Garran-Coulon, III, 71–78.
41. Lacroix, I, 182–83.
42. It must be remembered that news of the new law did not reach Le Cap until the 11th of May.
43. Roume to the Council of Peace and Union, May 9, Arch. Nat., D–XXV, 2. (Note that this was written only two days before the decisive news from France.) See also letter to the Parish of Le Borgne, May 8, Arch. Col., F–3, 197.
44. Roume to the Minister of Marine, July 11, Arch. Nat., D–XXV, 2.
45. See Roume's and Blanchelande's correspondence, Arch. Nat., D–XXV, 2 and 46; also, Garran-Coulon, III, 78–98; Lacroix, I, 181–93.
46. See Blanchelande's correspondence, Arch. Nat., D–XXV, 46; Garran-Coulon, II, 571–609; III, 101–16; Lacroix, I, 193–97; good short account of the military operations in Poyen, 17–19.

CHAPTER XV

1. See text of the law in Arch. Parl., XL, 577 *et seq.*
2. Text in Arch. Parl., XLV, 235 *et seq.*
3. See correspondence with the Colonial Assembly for April, May, and June, Arch. Nat., D–XXV, 62.

NOTES

4. Garran-Coulon, III, 128-29 (himself very prominent in all these events).
5. See *ante*, pp. 173-77.
6. See letter of the Colonial Commissioners, April 24, Arch. Nat., D-xxv, 62.
7. He was born in the Bugey.
8. In Arch. Nat., D-xxv, 11.
9. Garran-Coulon, III, 131.
10. Letter of June 18, Arch. Nat., D-xxv, 13.
11. Letter of Cougnac-Mion to the Colonial Assembly, July 20, Arch. Nat., D-xxv, 11.
12. See especially, Polverel to the Minister of Marine, January, 1793, Arch. Nat., D-xxv, 11.
13. "Mémoire du Roy pour servir d'Instruction aux Sieurs Polverel, Sonthonax et Ailhaud, Commissaires Civils préposés à l'exécution de la Loi du 4 Avril à Saint-Domingue," 17 June, 1792, Arch. Nat., D-xxv, 4.
14. The Civil Commissioners to the Minister of Marine, September 30, Arch. Nat., D-xxv, 4.
15. Letter of September 30, *supra*. For these and subsequent differences between the Civil Commissioners and Desparbés, see Arch. Nat., D-xxv, 4 and 47.
16. The new title given to the head of the civil administration, corresponding to the Intendant of the Old Régime.
17. These documents are all in Arch. Nat., D-xxv, 4.
18. See Arch. Nat., D-xxv, 4. Extracts of all the speeches on this occasion are quoted in Garran-Coulon, III, and in Sciout.
19. See *supra*.
20. *Ibid.*
21. The Commissioners to the Minister of Marine, September 30, Arch. Nat., D-xxv, 4.
22. See *ante*, pp. 162-63.
23. "Les Amis de la Constitution"; later "Les Amis de la Convention."
24. The sarcastic nickname given by the colonial whites to the mulattoes and free negroes decreed equality by the new law.
25. See various papers in Arch. Nat., D-xxv, 4.
26. Papers of trial of Blanchelande in Arch. Nat., D-xxv, 46-47.
27. Garran-Coulon, III, 139-40.
28. At Martinique, it will be remembered, the Old Régime had been restored for the past two years.
29. The name commonly given the negro insurgents.
30. Letter to the Civil Commissioners, Plaisance, October 14, Arch. Nat., D-xxv, 80.
31. Memoir of Adjutant-General Lacombe, Aff. Étr, "F.D.," "Amérique," 14.

NOTES

32. Documents on this affair in Arch. Nat., D–xxv, 4, 47, 56. Sonthonax's report to the Convention, October 25 (Arch. Nat., D–xxv, 4), is an extraordinary garbling of the facts, and is quite worthless. Lacombe's memoir (*supra*) is better, but is couched in the same vein and should be used with great caution. Garran-Coulon's Account (III, 176–94) is partisan and unreliable. This is true of his entire treatment of the second Civil Commissioners, with whom he was closely involved.

CHAPTER XVI

1. The son of the French general so famous in the American War of Independence.
2. Letter of October 25, Arch. Nat., D–xxv, 4.
3. See *ante*, p. 189.
4. All the papers of this case are preserved in Arch. Nat., D–xxv, 4.
5. For Polverel's journey and its consequences, see next chapter.
6. Good summary of these military operations in Poyen, 23.
7. This striking expression is first used by Sonthonax in his letter to the Convention of January 11, 1793, Arch. Nat., D–xxv, 5. Thereafter he uses it constantly to describe the white population of San Domingo.
8. The minutes of the "Commission Intermédiaire" are partly preserved in Arch. Nat., D–xxv, 63, 64.
9. Polverel to Sonthonax, Port-au-Prince, December 14, 1792, Arch. Nat., D–xxv, 12.
10. Sonthonax to Polverel, December 23, Arch. Nat., D–xxv, 12.
11. For these troubles, see Arch. Nat., D–xxv, 5, 11, 14, 50. The number of documents is very large; summary in Sciout, 432–35; Garran-Coulon, III, 227–37.
12. A good picture of conditions is found in "Désastres," 253–54; 269.
13. Sonthonax to the Minister of Marine, December 8, Arch. Col., C–9, 166.
14. Sonthonax to the Convention, December 31, Arch. Nat., D–xxv, 5.
15. *Ibid.*, January 11, 1793, Arch. Nat., D–xxv, 5.
16. See next chapter.
17. Sonthonax to the Convention, February 9, Arch. Nat., D–xxv, 5.
18. France had declared war on England February 1, but of course Sonthonax was not yet aware of the fact.
19. Letter of February 18, Arch. Nat., D–xxv, 5.
20. See *ante*, pp. 188–89.
21. Speech of December 2, 1791, Arch. Nat., D–xxv, 5.
22. Sonthonax to the Convention, February 18, Arch. Nat., D–xxv, 5.

NOTES

CHAPTER XVII

1. Polverel and Ailhaud to the Convention, November 14, Arch. Nat., D–xxv, 11.
2. Besides the official report above quoted, see Garran-Coulon, III, 250–57.
3. Letter of November 14, *supra*.
4. That is, the Plain of Cul-de-Sac, in rear of Port-au-Prince.
5. Polverel and Ailhaud to Sonthonax, November 14, Arch. Nat., D–xxv, 12.
6. See *ante*, pp. 198–200.
7. A port town farther to the south, where similar conditions prevailed.
8. Polverel to Sonthonax, December 14, Arch. Nat., D–xxv, 12; see also detailed memoir of General Lasalle to the Convention, February 16, 1793, Arch. Nat., D–xxv, 50.
9. See *ante*, pp. 160–61.
10. Letter dated November 30, 1792, Arch. Nat., D–xxv, 80.
11. The Convention severely reprimanded Ailhaud and tried him for desertion, but finally contemptuously dismissed him. Documents of trial, Arch. Nat., D–xxv, 12.
12. That is, the plain back of Les Cayes.
13. Polverel to the Minister of Marine, January 22, 1793, Arch. Nat., D–xxv, 11.
14. Garran-Coulon, III, 295–99.
15. See *ante*, p. 63.
16. Composed mainly of mulattoes with white officers.
17. See memoir of Adjutant-General Lacombe, Aff. Étr., "F.D.," "Amérique," 14; Garran-Coulon, III, 299–315.
18. See *ante*, p. 205.
19. Sonthonax to the Minister of Marine, March 10, Arch. Nat., D–xxv, 5.
20. Garran-Coulon, III, 320.
21. Sonthonax to the Convention, June 18, 1793, Arch. Nat., D–xxv, 5.
22. For this whole affair, see the Commissioners' correspondence and other papers, Arch. Nat., D–xxv, 5; also large numbers of documents in Arch. Nat., D–xxv 15; with due precaution, see account in Garran-Coulon, III, 317–59.
23. The mails were by this time so systematically violated that only letters by private hands give real information.
24. Letter from Port-au-Prince dated April 24, 1793, Arch. Nat., D–xxv, 80.
25. Rigaud to the Civil Commissioners, June 24, Arch. Nat., D–xxv, 16.

CHAPTER XVIII

1. Laveaux to Sonthonax, March 7, 1793, Arch. Nat., D–xxv, 19.
2. *Ibid.*, March 9, Arch. Nat., D–xxv, 19.
3. *Ibid.*, March 18, Arch. Nat., D–xxv, 19.
4. *Ibid.*, March 29, Arch. Nat., D–xxv, 19.
5. France had declared war on England February 1, and on Spain March 7, 1793.
6. "Mémoire en forme d'Instructions données par le Conseil Exécutif Provisoire," Arch. Nat., D–xxv, 47.
7. Deposition of Madame Galbaud, July 18, 1794 (30th Messidor, An II). Her evidence is all the more valuable since it was given as a prisoner of the Committee of Public Safety. Galbaud's own official account, together with his correspondence, is preserved in Arch. Nat., D–xxv, 47, 48.
8. The Commissioners to the Commission Intermédiaire, May 29, Arch. Nat., D–xxv, 5.
9. Madame Galbaud's deposition, *supra*.
10. The documentary material on the destruction of Le Cap is enormous. The accounts of Galbaud and other officers are in Arch. Nat., D–xxv, 47, 48; the Commissioners' correspondence is in D–xxv, 5, 6; their official relation (practically worthless) in D–xxv, 6; a large *dossier* of documents in D–xxv, 19. Lastly, an enormous collection of letters, etc., from refugees and other persons is in D–xxv, 79–84. The best printed account is in Sciout, 445–49 (based on the above material); a good short account is in Poyen, 31–33. Garran-Coulon's treatment(III, 423–84) is meretricious special pleading and absolutely unreliable.
11. Lasalle to the Conseil Exécutif (report), Aff. Étr., "F.D.," "Amérique," 14.
12. Carteau, 4–5.

CHAPTER XIX

1. See *ante*, p. 6.
2. Sonthonax to the Convention, July 10, Arch. Nat., D–xxv, 5.
3. *Ibid.*, July 30, Arch. Nat., D–xxv, 5.
4. "Pour la Nouvelle Angleterre." This was a general term applied to the whole coast of the United States.
5. Letter to a friend in France, July 24, Arch. Nat., D–xxv, 80.
6. Carteau, 5.
7. *Ibid.*, 232.
8. This last statement is wholly untrue. Text of this proclamation preserved in Arch. Nat., D–xxv, 5; printed in Sciout, 448, and in Garran-Coulon, IV, 39.

NOTES

9. Text printed in Garran-Coulon, IV, 40.
10. Report to the Conseil Exécutif, Aff. Étr., "F.D.," "Amérique," 14.
11. Sonthonax to the Convention, July 30, Arch. Nat., D-xxv, 5.
12. Most of the text is printed in Garran-Coulon, IV, 59–64.
13. Sonthonax to the Convention, September 9, 1793, Arch. Nat., D-xxv, 5.
14. Sonthonax to Polverel, September 3, Arch. Nat., D-xxv, 5.
15. See Polverel's correspondence with Sonthonax, Arch. Nat., D-xxv, 5; and with his agent Delpech in the South, Arch. Nat., D-xxv, 12. Good summary of this point in Sciout, 453.
16. Lacroix, I, 252.
17. *Ibid.*, I, 253.
18. One of the regulations made by the Civil Commissioners.
19. Letter from Tortuga to a relative in France, early 1794, Arch. Nat., D-xxv, 30. Much information as to the effect of enfranchisement and the working of labor regulations is found in the great collection of documents by parishes in Arch. Nat., D-xxv, 28–30; printed accounts in Carteau, 238–40; Lacroix, I, 251–62.
20. Carteau, 239–40.
21. *Ibid.*, 242.

CHAPTER XX

1. See *ante*, pp. 124–26.
2. Edwards, vii.
3. *Ibid.*, ix-x.
4. Letter to l'Archevesque Thibault at Paris, September 5, 1791; Garran-Coulon, III, 16–17.
5. Text printed in Garran-Coulon, IV, 128–32; also in Edwards: summarized in Sciout, 458–59. The entire history of the English intervention is treated in Edwards with a considerable amount of local detail. It is summarized in Rainsford. The French side, up to 1795, is given in detail by Garran-Coulon, IV, though his account must be read with the usual caution. The main facts are accurately summarized in Poyen, 36 *et seq.*
6. That is, mulatto and negro troops.
7. Polverel to Sonthonax, August 26, Arch. Nat., D-xxv, 5.
8. It must be remembered that these districts contained the largest rural white population of the colony. For details, see Garran-Coulon, IV, 136–48.
9. Lasalle to the Conseil Exécutif, September 5, Aff. Étr., "F.D.," "Amérique," 14.
10. Quoted in Lacroix, I, 278.
11. Laveaux to Sonthonax, "Mémoire sur l'état des troupes europé-

ennes," September 10, Arch. Nat., D-xxv, 19. See similar reports by General Lasalle to the Conseil Exécutif, September 5, Aff. Étr., "F.D.," "Amérique," 14; and to the Minister of War, Arch. Guerre, I, "St. D.," A, Correspondance.
12. Laveaux to Sonthonax, October 4, Arch. Nat., D-xxv, 19.
13. Polverel to Sonthonax, December 1, Arch. Nat., D-xxv, 12. Sonthonax was at this time in the hinterland of the West trying to prevent new defections.
14. Polverel to Sonthonax, January 22, 1794, Arch. Nat., D-xxv, 12.
15. Note that since these are all intercepted letters they form but a fraction of a much more numerous correspondence between the mulattoes of the English and the Republican districts.
16. Letter of the early spring of 1794, Arch. Nat., D-xxv, 38.
17. Letter dated Léogane, March 15, 1794, Arch. Nat., D-xxv, 38.
18. Arch. Parl., LXIX, 39.
19. Letter dated October 24, 1793, Arch. Nat., D-xxv, 38.
20. Text printed in Garran-Coulon, IV, 167-69.
21. Carteau, xxi.
22. Carteau, xxii-xxv.
23. The Archives Parlementaires do not yet go beyond August, 1793. For further proceedings of the National Legislatures, see reports in the "Moniteur Officiel." Most of the important debates, reports, etc., were printed in pamphlet form, and are preserved in the "Collection Camus," Arch. Nat., AD-XVIII C.
24. "Moniteur Officiel," séance du 15 Pluviôse, An II.
25. *Ibid.*, séance du 16 Pluviôse, An II.
26. Rigaud to Polverel, February 26, 1794, Arch. Nat., D-xxv, 28.
27. For these troubles, see Garran-Coulon, IV, 195-235; summary in Castonnet des Fosses, 144-48.
28. For French accounts, see Poyen, 38-39; Castonnet des Fosses, 148-50; for the English side, see Edwards, *supra*.

CHAPTER XXI

1. Toussaint's handwriting remained always crude. The autograph memorials to Napoleon during his captivity are barely legible.
2. Most of what has been written on Toussaint's early life is legend or invention. The analysis and discussion of this material pertains to a biography and is not germane to a general work like this. The essential facts regarding Toussaint's early days are best presented in Castonnet des Fosses, 157; see also Poyen, 41-42.
3. Garran-Coulon, II, 313.
4. See *ante*, p. 222.
5. Poyen, 43-47.
6. February 4, 1794.

NOTES 383

7. Lacroix, I, 299-300; Castonnet des Fosses, 158-59; Poyen, 47.
8. Lacroix, I, 301.
9. Toussaint Louverture to Laveaux, May 18, 1794, Bib. Nat., Dépt. des MSS., "Fonds Fr.," 12102; quoted in full by Schoelcher, 98-100. He has quoted all the essential parts of this correspondence under the heading, "Papiers de Saint-Domingue," and I shall cite him when quoting from this correspondence.
10. Schoelcher, 102-09; Poyen, 48-50; Castonnet des Fosses, 160; Lacroix, I, 302.
11. The Commissioners to Toussaint Louverture, June, 1794, Arch. Nat., D-xxv, 23.
12. Rainsford, 193.
13. Poyen, 50-54; Schoelcher, 107-17; Castonnet des Fosses, 160-62.
14. Poyen, 54-57; Schoelcher, 140-54; Castonnet des Fosses, 163-64.
15. Save the districts of the Grande Anse, in Anglo-colonial hands.
16. See *ante*, pp. 48-49.
17. Cardon's report to the Minister of Marine, Paris, January, 1795 (Nivôse, An III), Arch. Col., F-3, 199.
18. Castonnet des Fosses, 164-65; Schoelcher, 135-39.
19. Laveaux to the Committee of Public Safety, January 14, 1796 (24th Nivôse, An IV), Arch. Nat., D-xxv, 50.
20. Laveaux to the Minister of Marine, February 2, 1796 (13th Pluviôse, An IV), Arch. Nat., D-xxv, 50.
21. *Ibid.*, June 14, 1796 (26th Prairial, An IV), Arch. Nat., D-xxv, 50.
22. For these events, see Laveaux's correspondence with the Minister of Marine, Arch. Nat., D-xxv, 50; also his correspondence with Toussaint Louverture and other documents quoted *in extenso* by Schoelcher, 155-66.
23. Schoelcher, 172; 181-84; Lacroix, I, 309.
24. Lacroix, I, 309.

CHAPTER XXII

1. Robespierre had fallen on the 9th Thermidor, An II (July 27, 1794).
2. Took office November 3, 1795.
3. Spain had ceded her colony of Santo Domingo to France by the Treaty of Bâle, but had agreed to administer the colony until a peace between France and England should enable the Republic to assume effective control. For Roume's instructions, see Aff. Étr., "F.D.," "Espagne," 50.
4. The Commissioners to the Minister of Marine, May 16, 1796 (27th Floréal, An IV), Arch. Nat., D-xxv, 45.
5. See the Commissioners' correspondence, D-xxv, 45; Laveaux's

correspondence, Arch. Nat., D–xxv, 50; also documents quoted in Schoelcher, 167–68.
6. Memoir to the Directoire, October 9, 1796 (18th Vendémiaire, An V), Arch. Nat., D–xxv, 45.
7. The minutes of the Commission unfortunately no longer exist. Our chief source for its internal history is the long memoir of Raymond to the Minister of Marine, of September, 1797. For the later period it is unreliable, being influenced by Toussaint, but for this early period comparative analysis with other correspondence and events shows it to be largely correct. See Arch. Nat., AF–III, 210.
8. For Sonthonax's justification of his conduct herein, see letter to the Minister of Marine, July 23 (5th Thermidor), Arch. Nat., D–xxv, 45.
9. Letter of one Vergniaud to Lesage (of Eure-et-Loire), member of the National legislature, October 18, 1796 (27th Vendémiaire, An V), Arch. Nat., D–xxv, 83.
10. Letter of October 15, 1796 (24th Vendémiaire, An V), Arch. Guerre, I, "St.D.," A, Correspondance.
11. Memoir to the Directoire, October 9, 1796 (18th Vendémiaire, An V), Arch. Nat., D–xxv, 45.
12. Castonnet des Fosses, 175.
13. Sonthonax and Leblanc terrorized Giraud and outvoted Raymond's veto.
14. Rigaud to the Corps Législatif, October 21, 1796 (30th Vendémiaire, An V), Arch. Nat., AF–III, 208.
15. Castonnet des Fosses, 175–78; Lacroix, I, 319–20.
16. Memoir to the Directoire, *supra.*
17. *Ibid.*
18. For these events, see the Civil Commissioners' correspondence, Arch. Nat., D–xxv, 45; also the very full correspondence of Rigaud, both directly with the French Government, Arch. Nat., AF–III, 208–09, and indirectly through the French Minister to the United States via the American ships trading at Les Cayes, Aff. Étr., "F.D.," "Amérique," 14.
19. The Civil Commissioners to the Minister of Marine, May 27, 1797 (8th Prairial, An V), AF–III, 209.
20. See Raymond's report to the Minister of Marine, September 10, 1797; also Castonnet des Fosses, 173–75.
21. Toussaint Louverture to the Directoire, February 1, 1797 (13th Pluviôse, An V), Arch. Nat., AF–III, 209. Two points should be noted regarding Toussaint's correspondence. In the first place, he himself spoke and wrote only Creole French, — a dialect so corrupt as to be often quite unintelligible to a European Frenchman. Therefore all Toussaint's letters are translations by educated

NOTES 385

secretaries. The style of his letters is also very peculiar. The language is so verbose as to be hard to quote briefly. There is always much fulsome flattery and obscure language. Only occasionally does some significant phrase like the one just quoted reveal the iron hand in the velvet glove.
22. Besides Raymond's account, see Lacroix, I, 320–27; Poyen, 63–64.
23. Report to the Directoire, September 4, 1797 (18th Fructidor, An V), Arch. Nat., AF–III, 210.
24. Toussaint's report (*supra*) is in the form of long dialogues, written as if word for word with the supposed conversations reported.
25. Sonthonax to the Directoire, January 27, 1798 (8th Pluviôse, An VI), Arch. Nat., AF–III, 210.
26. Toussaint Louverture to the Directoire, September, 1797, Arch. Nat., AF–III, 210.
27. Toussaint Louverture to the Directoire, October 5, 1797 (14th Brumaire, An VI), Arch. Nat., AF–III, 210.

CHAPTER XXIII

1. See *ante*, pp. 267–68.
2. Lacroix, I, 337–38.
3. For this and subsequent events, see Hédouville's correspondence with the Directoire, Arch. Nat., AF–III, 210. The main facts are fairly well treated in Lacroix, I, 338 *et seq.*
4. This document, together with the preliminaries extending over several months previous to the event, are preserved in Arch. Guerre, I, "St.D.," A, Correspondance (first carton). They were found among Toussaint's archives after the capture of Port-au-Prince by Napoleon's invading army in 1802.
5. That is, the striking honors shown Toussaint by the English. For good account of this, see Lacroix, I, 344–45.
6. The English commander.
7. Lacroix, I, 346.
8. October, 1797.
9. Lacroix, I, 353–54. Lacroix is so careful in his quotations, and the words themselves are so completely in accord with all Toussaint's acts, that the interview above quoted must be considered as of the highest authority and substantially correct.
10. Hédouville's report to the Directoire upon his return to France, December, 1798 (Frimaire, An VII), Arch. Nat., AF–III, 210.
11. All this was quite true, as shown by the secret documents afterward discovered in Toussaint's archives and now preserved in the Arch. Guerre.
12. Report to the Directoire, *supra*.

CHAPTER XXIV

1. Roume to the Minister of Marine, "Port Républicain," February 11, 1799 (23d Pluviôse, An VII), Arch. Nat., AF-III, 210.
2. For accounts of this struggle see Lacroix, I, 373–94; Castonnet des Fosses, 194–214; Poyen, 70–74; Schoelcher, 245–70 (for reproduced documents).
3. Castonnet des Fosses, 196.
4. *Ibid.*, 199.
5. Lacroix, I, 379–80; Castonnet des Fosses, 205.
6. Lacroix, I, 381.
7. Besides the longer accounts quoted in note 2, a good short summary is found in Roloff, 17–18.
8. This was Toussaint's customary method. He could thus always disavow particular acts as having exceeded his instructions.
9. Lacroix, I, 393–94; Castonnet des Fosses, 212–14; Poyen, 73–74.
10. Castonnet des Fosses, 214.
11. See *ante*, p. 7.
12. Castonnet des Fosses, 215.

CHAPTER XXV

1. Roloff, 37–39. Henceforth Roloff is one of the main sources. His work is based upon elaborate research in the French archives and is in every way fundamental. See also Lacroix, opening pages of vol. II; Castonnet des Fosses, 216–17.
2. November 9, 1799.
3. Toussaint was always well informed of European events and their meaning.
4. Bonaparte's policy will be treated in the next chapter.
5. Roloff, 30–31.
6. Of course not to be confused with the negro general, Michel, formerly commander of Le Cap.
7. See *ante*, p. 6.
8. See *ante*, pp. 281–82.
9. For this whole topic, see Roloff, 37–44; Lacroix, II, 1–21; Castonnet des Fosses, 216–28; Poyen, 74–76.
10. Becker, "Observations sur l'état de Saint-Domingue" (apparently for the use of the Minister of War), Arch. Guerre, IV, Mémoires historiques, A, Période de la Révolution, "Colonies" (1789–1804).
11. "La Colonie de Saint-Domingue"; i.e., the French part of the island.
12. Chanlatte to the First Consul, Santo Domingo, December 15, 1800 (24th Frimaire, An IX), Arch. Nat., AF-IV, 1212.

13. Report to the Consuls on San Domingo by the Minister of Marine, September 29, 1800 (7th Vendémiaire, An IX), Arch. Nat., AF–IV, 1187.
14. "Notes sur l'état politique de Saint-Domingue"; addressed to the Minister of Marine, Paris, December 30, 1800 (9th Nivôse, An IX), Arch. Nat., AF–IV, 1212. This memoir is apparently annotated by the hand of Napoleon.
15. Roloff, 44–46; Lacroix, II, 46–47; Castonnet des Fosses, 233–38.
16. See *ante*, pp. 271–72.
17. Lacroix, I, 394–410; Castonnet des Fosses, 237–46; Poyen, 79–83.
18. Lacroix, II, 49.
19. *Ibid.*, II, 48–51.
20. Lacroix, II, 21–34; Roloff, 47–48; Castonnet des Fosses, 246–59.
21. Signed October 1, 1801.

CHAPTER XXVI

1. November 9, 1799.
2. Roloff, 18–24. This splendid work, based on the fullest archival research, is the main source of this chapter.
3. Roloff, 24–28.
4. *Ibid.*, 28–29.
5. At this moment (early 1800), people in France knew only of the outbreak of the war between Rigaud and Toussaint Louverture.
6. For able memoirs not mentioned in Roloff, see the anonymous "Mémoire sur les Colonies," drawn up by an expert for the Minister of Foreign Affairs, Aff. Étr., "F.D.," "Amérique," 20, asserting the necessity of subduing Toussaint; Admiral Truguet's secret memoir to Napoleon, Arch. Nat., AF–IV, 1187, strongly asserting the contrary.
7. All realized that the sending of a large army was impossible during the English war. No great fleet of slow-moving troop-ships could possibly escape the English cruisers.
8. Roloff, 29–30.
9. See *ante*, pp. 284–85.
10. Sahuguet to the First Consul, Arch. Nat., AF–IV, 1187.
11. Roloff, 32–33.
12. *Ibid.*, 32–34.
13. See *ante*, pp. 284–85.
14. Roloff, 49–51.
15. Chanlatte to the First Consul, Arch. Nat., AF–IV, 1212.
16. Hédouville to the First Consul, Philadelphia, November 15, 1800, Arch. Nat., AF–IV, 1212.
17. Roloff, 51–52. For draft instructions to the leader of this proposed expedition, see Arch. Guerre, I, "St.D.," A, Correspondance.

18. See *ante*, pp. 281–82.
19. Forfait to the First Consul, February 14, 1801, Arch. Nat., AF–IV, 1188.
20. See *ante*, pp. 286–87.
21. Roloff, 52–56.
22. For details of these preparations, see Poyen, 87–94; also, Roloff, 65–67.
23. That is, legally free, but compelled to work.
24. That is, Toussaint's Constitution. See *ante*, p. 294.
25. The negro generals had greatly abused their power in this respect. For Toussaint's gross misconduct in this regard, see Lacroix, II, 104–05.
26. "Notes pour servir aux instructions à donner au Capitaine-Générale Leclerc," October 31, 1801 (9th Brumaire, An X), Arch. Nat., AF–IV, 863: quoted in full by Roloff, 244–54.

CHAPTER XXVII

1. For details, see Poyen, 95–97; Roloff, 79–80. These two works, both based on most extensive archival research and summarizing the pith of contemporary secondary material, are my main authorities for this and subsequent chapters.
2. Poyen, 98.
3. Poyen, 99–102; Roloff, 80.
4. Poyen, 104–11; Roloff, 80–81.
5. Poyen, 111–15; Roloff, 81.
6. Poyen, 117–18.
7. *Ibid.*, 118–19.
8. *Ibid.*, 115–17.
9. Poyen, 120–36; Roloff, 82–83.
10. Poyen, 130–31.
11. Quoted in Poyen, 138.
12. Poyen, 137–44; Roloff, 83–85.
13. The Revolutionary name of Port-au-Prince.
14. Quoted in Poyen, 148.
15. The author of the valuable work so often quoted. Poyen has, however, incorporated the essential parts of Lacroix in his military treatise, so I have forborne to quote Lacroix for the military operations.
16. Poyen, 147–51; Roloff, 85.
17. Poyen, 141.
18. Poyen, 139–41; 144–46; Roloff, 85–86.
19. Poyen, 152–88; Roloff, 86–87.
20. General Dugua to the Minister of War, Arch. Guerre, I, "St.D.," A, Correspondance.

NOTES

21. Poyen, 189-95; Roloff, 87-88.
22. Poyen, 195-202; Roloff, 88-89.
23. Lacroix, II, 192-93.
24. Poyen, 200.
25. It was Lacroix who had so roughly handled Dessalines before Port-au-Prince.
26. Lacroix, II, 191-92.
27. Leclerc to the First Consul, April 1, 1802 (11th Germinal, An X), Arch. Nat., AF-IV, 1213.
28. See Leclerc's correspondence with the First Consûl, Arch. Nat., AF-IV, 1213; and with the Minister of Marine, Arch. Guerre, I, B, Régistre 4-A, 94, 8; also Roloff, 89-91.
29. That is, negro and mulatto soldiers.
30. Leclerc to the Minister of Marine, April 21 (1st Floréal, An X), Arch. Guerre, I, B, Rég. 4-A, 94, 8.
31. Leclerc to the First Consul, March 5 (14th Ventôse, An X), Arch. Nat., AF-IV, 1213.

CHAPTER XXVIII

1. Poyen, 239-40.
2. Poyen, 240-54; Roloff, 93-94.
3. Leclerc to the Minister of Marine, June 11 (22d Prairial, An X), Arch. Guerre, I, B, Rég. 4-A, 94, 8.
4. Leclerc to the Minister of Marine, July 6 (17th Messidor, An X), Arch. Guerre, I, B, Rég. 4-A, 94, 8.
5. Poyen, 210-12; Roloff, 94-95.
6. Leclerc to the First Consul, June 6 (17th Prairial), Arch. Nat., AF-IV, 1213.
7. Poyen, 212-15; Roloff, 95-96.
8. Leclerc to the Minister of Marine, June 11 (22d Prairial, An X), Arch. Guerre, I, B, Rég. 4-A, 94, 8.
9. Leclerc to the First Consul, June 11 (22d Prairial, An X), Arch. Nat., AF-IV, 1213.
10. Leclerc to the Minister of Marine, July 6 (17th Messidor, An X), Arch. Guerre, I, B, Rég. 4-A, 94, 8.
11. See Leclerc's correspondence, *supra;* also several reports of district commanders preserved in Arch. Guerre, I, "St.D.," A, Correspondance.
12. Toussaint's last letters and memorials are still preserved in Arch. Nat., AF-IV, 1213. His appeals to Napoleon's clemency show a rather surprising lack of fortitude. One of them has been published under the title, "Mémoires du Général Toussaint Louverture, écrits par lui-même" (Paris, 1853). Poyen quotes some interesting reports of officials at Fort de Joux, preserved in the Arch. Col.

(Poyen, 220-33); also, see journal of Caffarelli, Governor of Fort de Joux, published under the title, "Toussaint Louverture au Fort de Joux," "Nouvelle Revue Rétrospective," vol. XVIII, no. 94 (1902).
13. Leclerc to the Minister of Marine, July 6 (17th Messidor, An X), Arch. Guerre, I, B, Rég. 4–A, 94, 8.
14. Quoted in Poyen, 257.
15. See *ante*, pp. 303-304.
16. Roloff, 70-74.
17. Leclerc to the Minister of Marine, July 24 (5th Thermidor, An X), Arch. Guerre, I, B, Rég. 4–A, 94, 8.
18. Roloff, 117-24.
19. Leclerc to the Minister of Marine, August 6 (18th Thermidor, An X), Arch. Guerre, I, B, Rég. 4–A, 94, 8.
20. Charles Belair had been Toussaint's favorite, and was the only high general sincerely attached to Toussaint by personal affection. Revenge for Toussaint's arrest played the leading rôle in his defection.
21. Leclerc to the Minister of Marine, August 25 (7th Fructidor, An X), Arch. Guerre, I, B, Rég. 4–A, 94, 8.
22. Leclerc to the First Consul, August 6 (18th Thermidor, An X), Arch. Guerre, I, B, Rég. 4–A, 94, 8.
23. Leclerc to the Minister of Marine, September 13 (26th Fructidor, An X), Arch. Guerre, I, B, Rég. 4–A, 94, 8.
24. A much higher death-rate than at first, considering the small numbers of the French army.
25. Leclerc to the First Consul, September 16 (29th Fructidor, An X), Arch. Nat., AF–IV, 1213.
26. Leclerc to the First Consul, September 26 (4th Vendémiaire, An XI), Arch. Nat., AF–IV, 1213.
27. *Ibid.*, September 27 (5th Vendémiaire, An XI), Arch. Nat., AF–IV, 1213.
28. Leclerc to the First Consul, October 7 (15th Vendémiaire, An XI), Arch. Nat., AF–IV, 1213.
29. Poyen, 298-302.
30. Roloff, 112-13.

CHAPTER XXIX

1. Roloff, 74.
2. Poyen, 270-72.
3. *Ibid.*, 273-74.
4. *Ibid.*, 289-97; 303-20.
5. Roloff, 130-32; 142-43.
6. Poyen, 321-85; Roloff, 114-16.

7. See *ante*, p. 342.
8. Letter from Le Cap, October 6 (14th Vendémiaire, An XI), Arch. Nat., AF-IV, 1213.
9. Roloff, 143-44.
10. For a very able discussion of these events, see Roloff, 134-50.
11. Poyen, 401-59.
12. Roloff, 157; Poyen, 459-66.
13. Poyen, 477-546. After Napoleon's seizure of Spain in 1808 this French force was expelled by an uprising of the Spanish inhabitants.
14. In imitation of Napoleon's recent action.
15. Poyen, 467-75; Castonnet des Fosses, 350-52.
16. That is, impaled in Dessalines's own special fashion.
17. Private letter from Kingston, Jamaica, to a friend in France, June 1, 1805, Arch. Nat., AF-IV, 1213.

BIBLIOGRAPHY

BIBLIOGRAPHY

(This is a select bibliography. It mentions only the sources used, and, except in the section devoted to works on Toussaint Louverture, it makes no mention of material only remotely pertinent.)

CONTENTS

A. ARCHIVAL MATERIAL.
  1. Archives du Ministère des Colonies.
  2. Archives Nationales.
  3. Archives du Ministère des Affaires Étrangères.
  4. Archives du Ministère de la Guerre.
  5. Bibliothèque Nationale (Département des Manuscrits).
B. PUBLISHED DOCUMENTS.
C. CONTEMPORARY BOOKS AND PAMPHLETS.
  1. Books.
  2. Pamphlets.
D. MODERN WORKS.
  1. Books.
  2. Articles.
E. WORKS ON TOUSSAINT LOUVERTURE.

A. ARCHIVAL MATERIAL

1. ARCHIVES DU MINISTÈRE DES COLONIES.

These archives contain the best material. Unfortunately I was able to obtain access to only a small portion of all that is here preserved. The contents of these archives are still imperfectly known; no complete inventory exists; and access is granted to only a part of even that which is known and inventoried.

The most important collection of documents for my subject is Series "C." The sub-series "C-9" contains the official correspondence from San Domingo to the Minister of Marine. Series "C" is the chief source used by modern writers on the Old Régime in the Antilles (Vaissière, Peytraud, Lebeau), and is one of the main sources of the modern writers on Napoleon's expedition to San Domingo (Poyen, Roloff). Unfortunately that portion of the series dealing with the years 1792–1804 is now completely closed to investigation, and I was permitted to see only nos. C–9, 164, 165, 166, covering the years 1790–92. This was extremely unfortunate. I was able to turn the difficulty somewhat as regards the official despatches of the highest functionaries, since many of these were copied for the use of the Committees on Colonies in the various National Assemblies, which copies are still preserved in the Archives Nationales. But "C–9" also contains numerous reports and letters from minor officials and private individuals, and this loss was of course irreparable, especially as the period from 1789 to 1802 has never been worked up from archival material.

The other chief source that I was permitted to see was the "Collection Moreau de Saint-Méry," Series "F–3." This contains many copies of official correspondence, otherwise inaccessible, for the early years of the Revolution, and, still more important, the files of Moreau de Saint-Méry's private correspondence from his friends in San Domingo for the years 1789–92; also a few scattering letters, etc., of later date. The important numbers of this series are F–3, 150, 194, 195, 196, 197, 198, 199, 200, 201, 202.

2. ARCHIVES NATIONALES.

This is the main field of my accessible archival source material. The most important series is "D–xxv," an extensive series of 114 large cartons exclusively devoted to the Revolutionary troubles in San Domingo. Nos. 1–45 deal with the first three Civil Commissions. The subsequent numbers contain a great variety of material; copies of official correspondence, collections of private letters and memoirs, minutes of colonial assemblies, etc.; the whole forming a collection of the greatest value.

Series "AF–III," nos. 202–10 and 244–51, contain official correspondence, etc., for the period of the Directoire (1796–99).

Series "AF–IV," nos. 1187–94, 1212–16, contain the same material for the period of the Consulate (1799–1804).

3. ARCHIVES DU MINISTÈRE DES AFFAIRES ÉTRANGÈRES.

The section "Fonds Divers," Series "Amérique," nos. 14, 15, 17, 20, contains a large number of official letters and many

BIBLIOGRAPHY

valuable memoirs drawn up for government information. In series "Espagne," nos. 50 and 210, there are a few documents of some value.

4. ARCHIVES DU MINISTÈRE DE LA GUERRE.

A vast amount of material on my field is here preserved. Most of it is technical military matter, but there is a certain amount possessing distinct value for the subject as herein treated. In "I Partie," the section "A, Correspondance, Expédition puis Armée de Saint-Domingue (1792–Mars, 1802)" (2 cartons), contains many important documents, especially the originals of Toussaint Louverture's correspondence with the English; also a number of special reports of Government agents and army officers upon political and social conditions. The series "Armée de Saint-Domingue (7 Mars, 1802–12)" (9 cartons) contains a number of important letters and reports. The same is true of the section "Armée de Saint-Domingue (affaires politiques, commerciales, etc.) (1791–1812)" (2 cartons). The most important material preserved in these archives for my purposes, however, is found in "B, Régistre 4-A, 94, 8," a valuable collection of copies of Leclerc's correspondence with the Minister of Marine and of much of his correspondence with the First Consul. Some of these letters are quoted by Poyen and a few are found in Henry Adams's article (*infra*). In "IV Partie," the series "Mémoires historiques, A, Période de la Révolution (1789–1804)," nos. 1–16, contains a number of valuable reports and memoirs by army officers.

5. BIBLIOTHÈQUE NATIONALE (Département des Manuscrits).

In "Fonds Français," nos. 12102, 12103, 12104, contain the correspondence between Toussaint Louverture and General Laveaux (1794–98). Also, "Nouv. Acquisitions Françaises," no. 9326, a manuscript history of San Domingo by Beauval-Ségur (eighteenth century).

B. PUBLISHED DOCUMENTS

The great collection of published documents for this subject is the "Archives Parlementaires," a work unfortunately not yet completed. It gives not only the minutes of the various National Assemblies, but also many reports, letters, etc. For the period subsequent to that reached by the Archives Parlementaires, see the official minutes of the National Assemblies published in the "Moniteur Officiel." Also, most of the important speeches and reports were published in pamphlet form, and this series is preserved complete in the "Collection Camus" of the Archives Nationales, — Series "AD-xviii-c." Most of the official proclamations, etc., published in San Domingo, are preserved in the "Collection Rondonneau" of the Archives Nationales, — "AD-vii."

C. CONTEMPORARY BOOKS AND PAMPHLETS

1. Books.

Abeille (J.): "Essai sur nos Colonies et sur la Rétablissement de Saint-Domingue" (Paris, 1805). A panegyric of Bonaparte. Extremely anti-negro in tone. Written by a former planter. Of little value.

Anonymous: "Détails sur quelques-uns des Évènemens qui ont eu lieu en Amérique pendant les Années xi et xii" (Paris, 1804). The comments of an army officer on the last phase of Leclerc's expedition.

Anonymous: "Histoire des Désastres de Saint-Domingue; précédée d'un Tableau du Régime et des Progrès de cette Colonie depuis sa Fondation jusqu'à l'Époque de la Révolution française" (Paris, 1795). A very detailed account of events down to the destruction of Le Cap (June, 1793). Viewpoint that of a moderate Liberal. Well informed. Generally attributed to Barbé-Marbois, though from internal evidence I believe that he is not the author.

Anonymous: "Réflexions sur la Colonie de Saint-Domingue" (2 vols., Paris, 1796). A series of general observations of no special importance in this connection. Attributed to Barbé-Marbois.

Barré Saint-Venant: "Des Colonies Modernes sous la Zone torride, et particulièrement celle de Saint-Domingue" (Paris, 1802). Exceedingly thin.

Carteau (F.): "Soirées Bermudiennes: ou Entretiens sur les Évènemens qui ont opéré la Ruine de la Partie française de Saint-Domingue" (Bordeaux, 1802). An account of events in San Domingo down to October, 1793, by an upper-class colonial

BIBLIOGRAPHY 399

planter, an eye-witness of events in the North Province. Interesting and valuable.

Chalmers (C.): "Remarks on the late war in San Domingo" (London, 1803). On the English intervention. Unreliable and of no special value.

Charlevoix (Père P. F. X. de): "Histoire de l'Isle Espagnole ou de Saint-Domingue. Écrite particulièrement sur des Mémoires manuscrits du Père Jean-Baptiste le Pons, Jésuite, Missionaire à Saint-Domingue, et sur les pièces originales qui se conservent au Dépôt de la Marine" (4 vols., Amsterdam, 1733). The standard work on early San Domingo.

Cullion (C. F. V. de): "Examen de l'Esclavage en générale, et particulièrement des Negres dans les Colonies françaises de l'Amérique" (2 vols., Paris, 1802). Written from a strong pro-slavery standpoint.

Dalmas (M.): "Histoire de la Révolution de Saint-Domingue: depuis le Commencement des Troubles jusqu' au Prise de Jérémie et du Môle-Saint-Nicolas par les Anglais" (2 vols., Paris, 1814). Written in exile in the United States during the winter of 1793–94. Gives events in San Domingo down to the autumn of 1793. The viewpoint is strongly Royalist, the author being the apologist of the "Government" party.

Delacroix (J. V.): "Mémoires d'un Américain" (Lausanne, 1771). Shows anti-slavery feeling in radical circles thus early.

Déscourtilz: "Voyage d'un Naturaliste" (3 vols., Paris, 1809). The author, a botanist, was for some time a prisoner of the blacks. Fairly good.

De Wimpffen (Baron F. A. S.): "A Voyage to Saint-Domingo. In the Years 1788, 1789 and 1790" (translated by J. Wright, London, 1797). A keen observer and trenchant critic. Of great value both for conditions on the eve of the Revolution and for the early events in 1789–90.

Dorvo-Soulastre: "Voyage par terre de Santo-Domingo au Cap Français" (Paris, 1809). Mainly descriptive of the Spanish portion of the island.

Du Buisson (P. U.): "Nouvelles Considérations sur Saint-Domingue, en réponse à celles de Monsieur H. D'A" (2 vols., Paris, 1780). A criticism of Hilliard d'Auberteuil (*infra*). Valuable both as a check on d'Auberteuil and as showing the colonial viewpoint at that date.

Ducœurjoly (S. J.): "Manuel des Habitants de Saint-Domingue" (2 vols., Paris, 1803). The work of a former planter. Some interesting comments on social and racial problems.

Edwards (Bryan): "An Historical Survey of the French Colony of San Domingo: comprehending an Account of the Revolt of the Negroes in the Year 1791, and a Detail of the Military Transactions of the British Army in that Island in the Years 1793 and 1794" (first edition, London, 1796). The edition here used contains a postscript of events down to the British evacuation in 1798 (Philadelphia, 1806). The best account in English of events in San Domingo, especially down to the fall of Le Cap in June, 1793. An eye-witness of the negro insurrection of 1791. Valuable for the English viewpoint as well as a record of events.

Ésmangart (C.): "Des Colonies Françaises, et en particulière de l'Isle de Saint-Domingue" (Paris, 1802). Of little value.

Fedon (B.): "Réclamations contre un Ouvrage intitulé: 'Campagnes des Français à Saint-Domingue'" (1805). A criticism of Rochambeau's governership.

Gala (I.): "Memorias de la Colonia francesa de Santo Domingo; por un viagero español" (Madrid, 1787). Superficial.

Garran-Coulon (J.): "Rapport sur les Troubles de Saint-Domingue, fait au Nom de la Commission des Colonies, des Comités de Salut Public, de Législation, et de la Marine, Réunis" (official publication, 4 vols., Paris, An VI, 1798). The main official report for the troubles in San Domingo down to 1794. An immense amount of official and private correspondence, memoirs, and pamphlet literature summarized and discussed. The last two volumes, dealing with the second Civil Commissioners (Sonthonax, Polverel, and Ailhaud), are of much less value than the first two volumes, which deal with earlier events of the Revolution. These later volumes are a whitewash of the Commissioners and are so prejudiced that they must be used with the greatest caution.

Girod-Chantrans (J.): "Voyage d'un Suisse dans différentes Colonies d'Amérique pendant la dernière Guerre" (Neufchatel, 1785). A good observer. The book contains reflections of some value.

Guillermin (G.): "Précis historique des derniers Évènemens de la Partie de l'Est de Saint-Domingue" (Paris, 1811). Confined to a relation of events in the Spanish portion after the death of Leclerc.

Hassal (Miss): "Secret History; or the horrors of St. Domingo, in a series of letters, written by a lady at Cape François to Colonel Burr, Late Vice-President of the United States. Principally during the Command of General Rochambeau" (Philadelphia, 1808). Miss Hassal arrived at Le Cap in May, 1802, and remained until shortly before Rochambeau's evacuation in November, 1803. Interesting viewpoint, though so gossipy and personal in tone as to be generally unavailable for exact quotation in this connection.

Hilliard d'Auberteuil (M. R.): "Considérations sur l'État Présent de la Colonie française de Saint-Domingue. Ouvrage Politique et Législatif, Présenté au Ministre de la Marine" (Paris, 1776). A detailed discussion of conditions in San Domingo toward the close of the Old Régime. Should be read in connection with the critical work of Du Buisson (*supra*), to understand mutual prejudices.

Howard (Lieutenant): Manuscript journal of occurrences during service in the British army of occupation in San Domingo (3 blankbooks). In Boston Public Library. Interesting details, especially of the sufferings of the British.

Joinville-Gauban: "Voyage d'Outre-mer et Infortunes de M. Joinville-Gauban" (Bordeaux, 180–). The reminiscences of a former overseer. Extremely anti-negro. Some instructive features, but generally unreliable.

Laborie (P. J.): "The Coffee-Planter of San Domingo; containing a view of the Constitution, Government, Laws, and State of the Colony previous to 1789" (London, 1798). Extremely thin.

Lacroix (General P. A. de): "Mémories pour Servir a l'Histoire de la Révolution de Saint-Domingue" (2 vols., Paris, 1819). The standard general work on the entire subject. Good throughout. Lacroix was an eye-witness of events during Leclerc's expedition and a prominent actor therein as well.

Lattre (P. A. de): "Campagne des Français à Saint-Domingue, et réfutation des Réproches faits au Capitaine-Général Rochambeau" (Paris, 1805). A spirited defense of Rochambeau's governorship subsequent to Leclerc's death. Note that the author was a former planter.

Lemonnier-Delafosse: "Seconde Campagne de Saint-Domingue, précédée de Souvenirs historiques de la première Campagne" (Havre, 1846). The memoirs of an army officer; an eyewitness, though one of minor importance. Good local color.

Maclean (H.): "An Enquiry into the Nature and Causes of the Great Mortality among the Troops at San Domingo" (London, 1797). The author was three years with the British army of occupation. Some interesting points.

Malenfant: "Des Colonies, et particulièrement de celle de Saint-Domingue" (Paris, 1819). Of little value.

Malouet (V. P.): "Collection des Mémoires et Correspondances officielles sur l'Administration des Colonies" (4 vols., Paris, 1802). Contain much valuable information concerning the old colonial system.

Mantegazza (C.): "Viaggio à Santo Domingo" (Milan, 1803). A series of letters during the period of Leclerc's expedition. Superficial.

Mazères (F.): "De l'Utilité des Colonies, des Causes de la Perte de Saint-Domingue, et des Moyens d'en recouvrir la Possession" (Paris, 1814). Extremely thin and visionary.

Moreau de Saint-Méry (M. L. E.): "Déscription Topographique, Physique, Civile, Politique et Historique de la Partie Française de Saint-Domingue. Avec des Observations générales sur la Population, sur la Caractère et les Mœurs de ses divers Habitans; sur son Climat, sa Culture, ses Productions, son Administration, etc. Accompagnées des Détails les plus propres à faire connaître l'état de cette Colonie à l'Époque du 18 Octobre, 1789" (2 vols., Philadelphia, 1797). An invaluable compendium of information of every kind about San Domingo. The fruit of many years' researches. It stops strictly at 1789. This, indeed, is one of its best features, for the author sticks to his material and does not allow later events to color his work in the least. After much general information of the highest value, the bulk of the work is a description of the colony parish by parish; the most remote and unimportant being included.

Moreau de Saint-Méry (M. L. E.): "Déscription . . . de la Partie Espagnole de l'Isle Saint-Domingue" (Philadelphia, 1799). Similar to the former work. Briefer but excellent.

Napoleon Bonaparte: "Mémoires" (Montholon). Four notes on the book of General Lacroix (*supra*). In vol. I, pp. 194–218.

BIBLIOGRAPHY 403

These remarks are an attempt to throw the blame of the failure in San Domingo on to the shoulders of Leclerc. Extremely unfair. Characteristic Napoleonic special pleading.

Nicolson (Père): "Essai sur l'Histoire Naturelle de Saint-Domingue" (Paris, 1776). The author was Apostolic Prefect of the Dominican Mission. Mostly concerned with natural history, the book contains a few remarks on the state of the colony.

Page: "Traité d'Économie politique et de Commerce des Colonies" (Paris, 1802). The work of a former colonist. Of little value.

Pradt: "Les Trois Ages des Colonies" (2 vols., Paris, 1802). Fantastic and unreliable.

Rainsford (Marcus): "An Historical Account of the Black Empire of Hayti, comprehending a view of the Principal Transactions in the Revolution of Saint Domingo, with its Antient and Modern State" (London, 1805). Pompous, and devoid of merit or accuracy.

Raynal (the Abbé): "Essai sur l'Administration de la Colonie de Saint-Domingue" (?, 1785). A detailed discussion of conditions in San Domingo on the eve of the Revolution.

Saintard: "Essai sur les Colonies françaises; ou Discours politique sur la Nature du Gouvernement, de la Population, et Commerce de Saint-Domingue" (Paris, 1754). An arraignment of the arbitrary nature of the colonial government of the Old Régime. Interesting as belonging to such an early date.

Sanchez Valverde (A.): "Idea del Valor de la Isla Española" (Madrid, 1785). French translation in manuscript in the Bibliothèque Nationale, Departement des Manuscrits, "Nouv. Acquisitions françaises," no. 1371. Mostly on the Spanish part of the island. Interesting as being one of Moreau de Saint-Méry's chief sources for his work on the Spanish part of San Domingo (*supra*).

Venault de Charmilly: "Lettre à Bryan Edwards" (London, 1797). Despite its title, a good-sized volume, criticizing Edwards's book (*supra*). The writer, an actor in the early troubles of the Revolution in San Domingo, furnishes material of considerable value. He convicts Edwards of many minor errors, but fails to shake the Englishman's work as a whole.

Wante: "Importance de nos Colonies Occidentales" (Paris, 1805). Of little value.

2. PAMPHLETS.

The pamphlet literature is extensive, but its value is much less than its size would lead one to expect. The most valuable portion is that appearing before the year 1793, although even here the authors are concerned more with France than San Domingo. After 1792 the Terror prevents any free discussion of the general subject, and the pamphlets of the next few years are mere personal recrimination. The Consulate was also a period unfavorable to free discussion, and the pamphlets and brochures of this epoch are generally apologetics for the policy of Bonaparte.

The valuable part of this literature has been analyzed and discussed by modern writers or in Garran-Coulon's voluminous official report published in 1798 (*supra*). A nearly complete collection is preserved in the Bibliothèque Nationale, Series LK–9 and LK–12. The next best collection in existence is probably that bequeathed to Cornell University by Andrew D. White. The Harvard University Library possesses a collection of considerable importance, and a number of pamphlets relating to San Domingo are also to be found in the British Museum.

References to all pamphlets directly utilized in this work will be found in the Notes. The great body of official and private correspondence preserved in the French archives has yielded such superior historical material that I have generally preferred it for exact quotation.

D. MODERN WORKS

1. BOOKS.

Boissonnade (*P.*): "Saint-Domingue à la Veille de la Révolution et la Question de la Représentation aux États-Généraux (Janvier, 1788–Juillet, 1789)" (Paris, 1906). A very able monograph based on archival material, published documents, and all important contemporary books and pamphlets. Impartial, it exhausts the subject.

Daubigny (*E.*): "Choiseul et la France d'Outre-Mer après la Traité de Paris (1763)" (Paris, 1892). An able general account of the attempts made to remedy the abuses of the colonial régime after 1763.

Castonnet des Fosses (*H.*): "La Révolution de Saint-Domingue" (Paris, 1893). Popular in form (no footnotes), and contains many minor errors; yet good on the whole. Contains some things not well treated elsewhere.

Déschamps (L.): "Les Colonies pendant la Révolution: la Constituante et la Réforme Coloniale" (Paris, 1898). A detailed discussion of the colonial question in the Constituent Assembly (i.e., to October, 1791). Based mainly on the Archives Parlementaires. Prejudiced in favor of the Revolutionary ideas. Devoted to events in France, it is of little value for events in San Domingo.

Gaffarel (P.): "La Politique Coloniale en France, de 1789 à 1830" (Paris, 1908). Good summary, though of course very general.

Lebeau (A.): "De la Condition des Gens de Couleur Libres sous l'Ancien Régime (Thèse pour le doctorat en droit, — Université de Poitiers," Poitiers, 1903). A very able, unprejudiced, and scientific discussion of the color line under the Old Régime. Based on archival material, juristic works, etc. Of the highest value.

Leroy-Beaulieu (Paul): "De la Colonisation chez les Peuples Modernes" (4th edition). An authoritative general economic work.

Levasseur (E.): "Histoire du Commerce de la France" (vol. I, avant 1789, Paris, 1911). Another economic work, more detailed and a good complement to Leroy-Beaulieu (*supra*).

Magnac (Dr.): "La Perte de Saint-Domingue: 1789–1809" (Paris, 1909). A brief popular work. Inaccurate and with no new features.

Mills (H. E.): "The Early Years of the French Revolution in San Domingo." (Doctor's thesis, Cornell University, Cornell, N.Y., 1889.) A scholarly discussion of events down to May, 1791. No unpublished archival material has been used, but nearly all the published documents and pamphlets are examined and discussed. Of great value.

Pauliat (L.): "La Politique Coloniale sous l'Ancien Régime" (Paris, 1887). An attempt to prove the superlative excellence of the Old Régime. Curious distortions of fact. Of little value.

Parsons (R.): "Montesquieu et l'Esclavage. Études sur les Origines de l'Opinion anti-esclavagiste en France au XVIIIe Siècle" (Paris, 1911). An interesting study of the anti-slavery movement preceding the French Revolution.

Poyen (Lieutenant-Colonel H. de): "Histoire militaire de la Révolution de Saint-Domingue" (Paris, 1899). A technical military history by a French army officer. For the period of Leclerc's expedition (the bulk of the work), it is based on a wealth of archival material and on all the important publications of the time. From its special viewpoint it exhausts the subject.

Poyen (Lieutenant-Colonel H. de): "Les Guerres des Antilles, de 1793 à 1815" (Paris, 1896). Valuable for checking up events in the other islands.

Pritchard (Hesketh): "Where Black Rules White" (London, 1900). An Englishman's travels through the Black Republic. Interesting description of present conditions, which appear to have changed but little since the early years of negro independence.

Roloff (G.): "Die Kolonialpolitik Napoleons I" (Munich, 1899). A very able, authoritative, and unprejudiced exposition of this subject; based on archival material, published documents, and all the important works. From the standpoint of international politics it exhausts the subject and is an excellent complement to Poyen's military work (*supra*).

St. John (Sir Spenser): "Haiti, or the Black Republic" (London, 1884). The author was for many years British Minister at Port-au-Prince. He traces the historical continuity of present conditions from the early period in most instructive fashion. An extremely useful book.

Schoelcher (V.): "Vie de Toussaint Louverture" (Paris, 1889). The work of a French anti-slavery writer of the mid-nineteenth century, it is so prejudiced as to be of little value as a book, but since it contains many documents and letters quoted *in extenso*, its serves occasionally as a handy collection of printed documents.

Treille (M.): "Le Commerce de Nantes et la Révolution" (Paris, 1908). This work, based upon the local archival material of the Nantes Chambre de Commerce, throws much light on the old colonial system, especially since Nantes was the chief centre of San Domingo commerce and of the slave-trade. Thoroughly scientific and reliable in character.

Vaissière (P. de): "Saint-Domingue: La Société et la vie Créoles sous l'Ancien Régime" (Paris, 1909). An exceedingly able and valuable exposition of colonial conditions under the Old Régime, based on archival material, both French and English, and on a wealth of publications, many of them very rare. This book, together with those of Lebeau and Peytraud (*supra*), forms a trilogy invaluable for an understanding of conditions in San Domingo before the Revolution.

Zimmermann: "Die Franzoesische Kolonien" (Berlin, 1901). The best general work on the history of the French colonies.

2. ARTICLES.

Adams (Henry): "Napoleon I and San Domingo." In "Historical Essays" (New York, 1891). A scholarly discussion of Napoleon's colonial policy, with special reference to its bearing upon the United States.

Brette (A.): "Les Gens de Couleur Libres et Leurs Députés en 1789." Published in "La Révolution Française," vol. XXIX (1895), pp. 326–45; 385–407. A minute analysis of speeches in the Constituent Assembly and of pamphlets on the point. Rather partial to the mulattoes.

Déschamps (L.): "La Représentation Coloniale au Constituante." In "La Révolution Française," vol. XXXVII (1899), pp. 130 *et seq*. An expansion of one or two points in his book (*supra*).

Du Hautais (Vicomte Odon): "Une Famille bretonne à Saint-Domingue au XVIIIe Siècle." In "Revue de Bretagne," vol. pp. 237–64 (1899). Some local color.

Girault (A.): "La Politique Coloniale de la Révolution Française." In "Revue Politique et Parlementaire" (1899), pp. 358–64. Comment and critique of Déschamps' book (*supra*).

Hardy (J.): "Correspondance intime du Général Hardy de 1797 à 1802 (Expéditions d'Irlande et de Saint-Domingue)." In "Revue des Deux Mondes," IVe période, vol. CLXI, pp. 92–134 (1900). Some interesting letters of one of Leclerc's most vigorous division commanders. Good local color.

Hennet: "Rentrée en France de la Dépouille mortelle du Général Leclerc." In "Carnet de la Sabretache," November, 1908. Explained by title.

Lallemand: "Saint-Domingue sous le Consulat. Fragment des Souvenirs du Général Lallemand." In "La Nouvelle Revue Rétrospective," vol. XVII, pp. 361–73; vol. XVIII, pp. 37–41 (1903). Recollections of some interest.

Le Maire (D.): "Un Dunkerquois Colon à Saint-Domingue. Lettres inédites de Doménique le Maire." In "Bulletin de l'Union Fauconnier. Société Historique de Dunquerque," vol. IV, pp. 461–529 (1901). Certain instructive points.

Mopinot (J.): "Ma Campagne à Saint-Domingue (1802–04)." In "Revue de Champagne et de Brie," IIe série, vol. XII, pp. 1–36 (1900). The reminiscences of an officer in Leclerc's expedition. Some good points.

Mosbach (A.): "Der Franzoesische Feldzug auf Sanct Domingo (1802–03). Nach den Berichten vier polnischer Offiziere" (Breslau, 1882).

Moulin (H.): "Le 'Courrier' et le 'Hazard'; dernier Épisode de l'Insurrection de Saint-Domingue." In "La Révolution Française," vol. VI, p. 683.

Sciout (L.): "La Révolution à Saint-Domingue: les Commissaires Sonthonax et Polverel." In "Revue des Questions Historiques," no. CXXVIII (October 1, 1898), pp. 399–470. Based on archival material, it is a most useful monograph, though with a certain Royalist-Clerical bias.

Trémaudan (J. de): "Le Commerce de Nantes (XVIIe et XVIIIe Siècles)." In "Revue de Bretagne," vol. XXX, pp. 16–22 (1903). Another sidelight on the colonial trade under the Old Régime.

E. WORKS ON TOUSSAINT LOUVERTURE

Because of the special interest in Toussaint Louverture I have thought it advisable to devote to him a special section of this bibliography. The poverty of the appended list will be disappointing to those interested in the personality and carrer of the black leader, but it will show the difficulty in the way of any scientific biography.

Cousin d'Avallon (C. Y.): "Histoire de Toussaint Louverture, chef des Noirs Insurgés de Saint-Domingue" (Paris, 1802). Stolen from Dubroca (*infra*).

Dubroca (J. F.): "La Vie de Toussaint Louverture" (Paris, 1802). Short and thin. Apparently a bookseller's job, written to support Bonaparte's policy in sending out Leclerc's expedition. Wholly unreliable.

Gragnon-Lacoste: "Toussaint Louverture" (Paris, 1877). A

panegyric of the black leader. Full of apocryphal and legendary matter.

"Letters of Toussaint Louverture and Edward Stevens, 1798–1800." Collection of documents published in the "American Historical Review" (October, 1910), vol. XVI, pp. 64–101. Concerned with trade relations between San Domingo and the United States during the period of Toussaint's rule.

"Mémoires du Général Toussaint Louverture, écrits par lui-même," with appendix by Saint-Remy (Paris, 1853). Despite its pretentious title, these so-called "Mémoires" of Toussaint Louverture are merely one of several justificatory memorials written during his French captivity to obtain Bonaparte's clemency. Concerned only with certain of his public acts during the last years of his career, it is extreme special pleading. The original manuscript is preserved in Archives Nationales, AF–IV, 1213.

Métral (A.): "Histoire de l'Expédition des Français à Saint-Domingue sous le Consulat de Napoléon Bonaparte; *suivie* des Mémoires et Notes d'Isaac Louverture sur la même Expédition et sur la Vie de Son Père" (Paris, 1825). Métral's account is brief and unimportant. The appended account of Isaac Louverture, son of the black leader, contains certain interesting features, though inexact and romantic in character.

Périn (R.): "L'Incendie du Cap, ou le Règne de Toussaint Louverture" (Paris, 1802). A diatribe against the black leader. Of little value.

Rainsford (Marcus): "St. Domingo, or an Historical, Political, and Military Sketch of the projected Black Republic, with a view of Toussaint Louverture" (London, 1802). A pretentious bit of "fine writing"; most inaccurate and of practically no value.

"Recueil de lettres et pièces originales sur Saint-Domingue." Three manuscript volumes in the Bibliothèque Nationale, Département des Manuscrits, "Fonds Français," nos. 12102, 12103, 12104. Contains many of Toussaint's proclamations and numerous letters to General Laveaux between the years 1794 and 1798. This material, quoted largely *in extenso*, forms the bulk of Schoelcher's book (*supra*). The letters were intended for public consumption; their tone is extremely inflated and artificial.

Saint-Remy: "Vie de Toussaint Louverture" (Paris, 1850). Written at second-hand on rather slender material, it is of little value. The author, a mulatto, is not over-fond of the black leader.

Stephen (J.): "Buonaparte in the West Indies; or, the Story of Toussaint Louverture, the African Hero" (London, 1803). A panegyric of the black leader and a diatribe against the French in general and the First Consul in particular. Absurdly prejudiced and very thin.

Stephen (J.): "The History of Toussaint Louverture" (London, 1814). A variation of the earlier work (*supra*), and equally devoid of value.

"The Life and Military Achievements of Toussaint Louverture, from 1792 until the arrival of General Leclerc. Also his Successor's till 1803" (London, 1805). A pamphlet, similar in character to Stephen's productions.

"Toussaint Louverture au Fort de Joux" (1802). Article in "Nouvelle Revue Rétrospective," XVIIIe année, no. 94, 10 Avril, 1902. The journal of Caffarelli, Governor of Fort de Joux, the place of Toussaint's French captivity. An eye-witness's account of the black leader's last days. Of the highest value. In this connection, note also some interesting reports of officials at Fort de Joux, preserved in the French colonial archives and never previously published, quoted in Poyen, pp. 220–33.

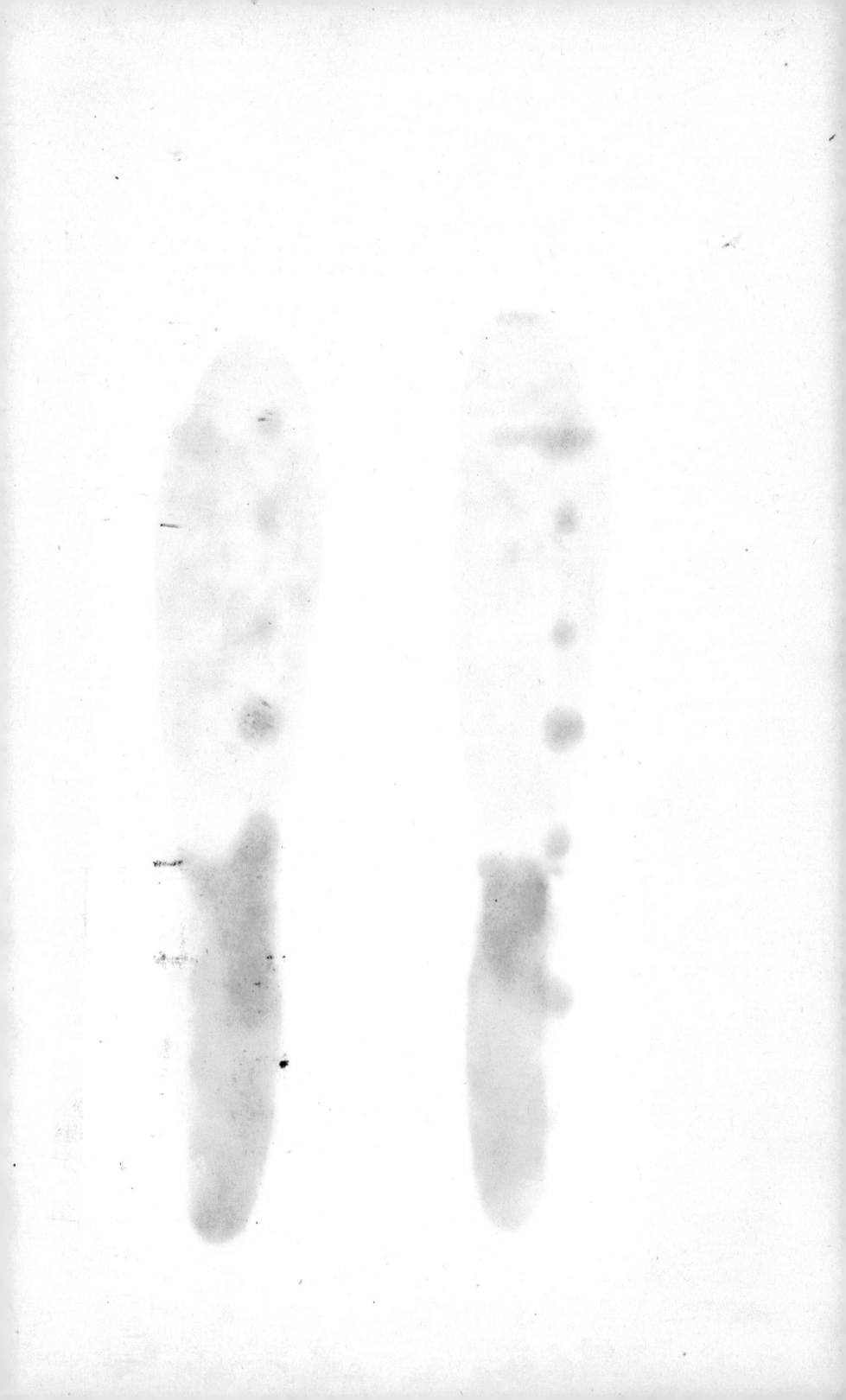

F
1923
.S87
1970